Why Why Why are lions lazy?

MC
PUBLISHERS

First published as hardback in 2006 by
Miles Kelly Publishing Ltd, Bardfield Centre,
Great Bardfield, Essex, CM7 4SLCopyright
© Miles Kelly Publishing Ltd 2006

This 2009 edition published and distributed
by:

Mason Crest Publishers Inc.
370 Reed Road, Broomall, Pennsylvania
19008
(866) MCP-BOOK (toll free)
www.masoncrest.com

Why Why Why—
Are Lions Lazy?
ISBN 978-1-4222-1569-2
Library of Congress Cataloging-in-
Publication data is available

Why Why Why—?
Complete 23 Title Series
ISBN 978-1-4222-1568-5

Printed in the United States of America

Contents

What is the biggest cat?	4
Where do tigers live?	5
Why do lion cubs have to leave home?	5
What is a caracal?	6
Why do tiger cubs have to hide?	7
Are jaguars good swimmers?	7

Do big cats live in groups?	8
Which cats can scream?	9
Why are lions lazy?	9
Why are tigers stripy?	10
Which cat is in danger?	11
What do ocelots eat?	11

What is the bounciest cat? 12

Do cats change their coats? 13

Why does a lion roar? 13

Why do leopards climb trees? 14

How can humans help big cats? 15

What is a puma's favourite food? 15

How fast can a cheetah run? 16

Why do people hunt big cats? 16

What time do tigers go hunting? 17

Which big cats live in grasslands? 18

Why do cats wash their faces? 19

How often do tigers eat? 19

What is a group of cubs called? 20

Why do leopards fight each other? 21

Which cat lives in the treetops? 21

Do big cats live in rainforests? 22

What animals do jaguars hunt? 23

How do cubs learn to hunt? 23

How do snow leopards keep warm? 24

Which cat goes fishing? 25

How do tigers stay cool? 25

What is the most mysterious cat? 26

Why do cats always land on
their feet? 27

How many babies do tigers have? 27

Why are cats the perfect hunters? 28

How do cats see in the dark? 29

Do big cats have enemies? 29

Quiz time 30

Index 32

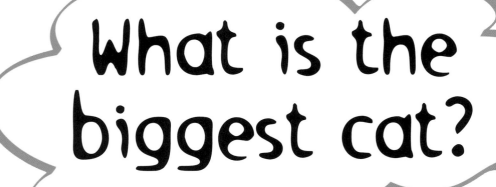

What is the biggest cat?

The Siberian tiger is the biggest cat, and one of the largest meat-eating animals in the world. The heaviest Siberian tiger was recorded at weighing 1,023 pounds — that's the same weight as 23 of you! It also has thick fur to help it survive in freezing conditions.

Where do tigers live?

Tigers only live in southern and eastern Asia, in forests, woodlands and swamps. They used to live in much larger areas, but humans have now built houses and farms on much of the land. Siberian tigers live in snow-covered forests where temperatures can be -58°F.

Siberian tiger

Hair-head!

Male lion cubs begin to grow thick fur around their head and neck at about three years old. This fur is called a mane.

Why do lion cubs have to leave home?

Male lion cubs don't get to stay with their family group or pride, they get pushed out at about three years old. By then they are old enough to look after themselves. Soon they will take over new prides and have their own cubs.

Discover

Tigers are only found in certain parts of the world. Look on a map and see if you can find them.

What is a caracal?

A caracal is a smaller type of wild cat that lives in hot, dry desert-like places. It hunts small animals, such as rats and hares, and can leap up to 10 feet high to catch a passing bird.

Caracal

Think

Jaguars are good swimmers. Can you think of some other animals that can swim?

Why do tiger cubs have to hide?

Tiger cubs hide behind their mothers for safety. Adult male tigers will kill any cubs that aren't their own. Less than half of the tiger cubs born in the wild live to the age of two years old.

Jaguar

Are jaguars good swimmers?

Jaguars are very good swimmers. Of all cats, they are the most water-loving. They like to live in swampy areas or places that flood during the rainy season, and they enjoy cooling off in rivers. Jaguars are mainly found in Central and South America.

Tiny kitty!

The black-footed cat of southern Africa is one of the smallest cats in the world. It's half the size of many pet cats.

Do big cats live in groups?

Lions are the only big cats that live in large family groups, called 'prides'. A pride is normally made up of four to six female lions, one or two males and their cubs. Some prides may have up to 30 animals if there is plenty of food nearby.

Pride of lions

Pretend

Imagine you are a prowling lion creeping up on your prey. See how slowly and quietly you can move.

Which cats can scream?

Small cats such as pumas make an ear-piercing scream instead of a roar. The cat family can be divided into two groups — big cats that can roar, and small cats that can't. A screaming cat can still be just as frightening!

Lady-lion hunt!

Female lions, called lionesses, do nearly all of the hunting for the pride. Male lions will only help with the hunt if it's a big animal such as a buffalo or a giraffe.

Why are lions lazy?

Lions seem very lazy, but they have to rest to keep cool in the hot African sun. Usually, lions rest for around 20 hours a day. Hunting normally happens in the morning or at night when it's coolest, and once a lion has had a meal it doesn't need to eat again for several days.

Why are tigers stripy?

Tigers are stripy to help them blend into their shadowy, leafy surroundings. Stripes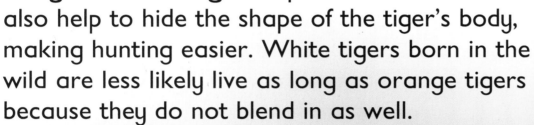
also help to hide the shape of the tiger's body, making hunting easier. White tigers born in the wild are less likely live as long as orange tigers because they do not blend in as well.

Tiger cubs

Going, gone!

It's too late for some big cats. The Taiwan clouded leopard, and the Caspian, Bali and Javan tigers are extinct (have died out).

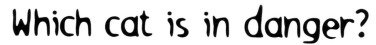

Which cat is in danger?

The Iberian lynx, found in Spain and Portugal, is the most endangered cat. This is because humans have cut down many forests where they live. Lynx numbers are also falling because of the drop in the number of rabbits, which are their main food.

Iberian lynx

What do ocelots eat?

Ocelots, also called 'painted leopards', are small wild cats found mainly in South and Central America. They eat lots of different foods including rats, birds, frogs, monkeys, fish, tortoises and deer.

Think

How many types of food do you eat in a day? Is it as many as an ocelot?

What is the bounciest cat?

The bounciest cat is the African serval. It can leap 3 feet high and travel 13 feet as it jumps. Unusually, it hunts in the day, for frogs, locusts and voles. Servals are like cheetahs, with slim, graceful, spotty bodies.

Serval

Do cats change their coats?

The lynx changes its coat with the weather. It lives in forests in northern Europe and Asia. In summer, the lynx's coat is short and light-brown, but in winter its coat is much thicker, and light gray. This helps it to hide throughout the year.

Why does a lion roar?

Lions roar to scare off other lions that stray onto their patch of land or territory. They also roar to let other members of their pride know where they are. A lion's roar is so loud it can be heard up to 6 miles away!

Roaring lion

Wear

Cats are kept warm by their thick coat of fur. Put on some furry clothes. Do they keep you warm?

Why do leopards climb trees?

Leopards climb trees to rest or to eat their food in safety. These big cats often kill prey that is larger than themselves. They are excellent climbers and are strong enough to drag their prey up into a tree, away from other hungry animals.

Leopard

Paint

Using face paints, ask an adult to make your face spotty like a leopard's.

How can humans help big cats?

Humans can help big cats by protecting areas of rainforest and grassland where they live. These areas are called 'reserves'. In a reserve, trees are not allowed to be cut down and the animals can live in safety.

Puma

No boat? Float!

In ancient times, Chinese soldiers used blown-up animal skins to cross deep rivers. They had to coat them with grease to keep the air in, and blow them up by mouth.

What is a puma's favorite food?

Rabbits, hares and rats are favorite foods for a puma. They will attack bigger animals too. In places where humans have built their homes near the puma's natural surroundings, people have been attacked by these cats.

How fast can a cheetah run?

Cheetahs are the world's fastest land animals. In a few seconds of starting a chase, a cheetah can reach its top speed of 65 miles per hour – as fast as a car! Cheetahs have 30 seconds to catch their prey before they run out of energy.

Why do people hunt big cats?

Mainly for their beautiful fur. For many years, cats have been killed in their hundreds of thousands so that people can wear their skins. Tigers especially were hunted for their body parts, which were used in Chinese medicines.

Make

With a paper plate and some straws for whiskers, make a tiger mask. Cut out eyeholes and paint it stripy!

Can't catch me!

Even though cheetahs are super-fast runners, only half of their chases end with a catch. Sometimes they scare their prey off before they get close enough to pounce.

Cheetah

Tiger

What time do tigers go hunting?

Almost all cats, including tigers, hunt at night. It is easier for a tiger to creep up on its prey when there is less light. A tiger may travel many miles each night while hunting. Tigers hunt deer, wild pigs, cattle and monkeys.

Which big cats live in grasslands?

Many big cats, including cheetahs, lions and leopards, live in grasslands called 'savannahs'. The savannah is dry, flat and open land, and is home to many other animals including gazelles, wildebeest and zebra. One of the best-known savannahs is the Serengeti in Africa.

Cheetahs hunting on the savannah

Cheetah cub

Play

With a friend, collect some pebbles and sticks and use them to mark out your own territories in your garden.

Why do cats wash their faces?

Cats wash their faces to spread their scent over their body. Cats have scent-producing body parts called glands on their chin. They use their paws to wipe the scent from their glands and when the cat walks, it can mark its area, or territory.

Slow down!

In the wild, cheetahs have a short lifespan. Their running speed gets a lot slower as they get older so they are less successful when they hunt.

How often do tigers eat?

Sometimes, tigers don't even eat once a week. When tigers catch an animal they can eat 88 pounds of meat. They don't need to eat again for eight or nine days.

What is a group of cubs called?

A group of cubs is called a litter. There are usually between two and four cubs in every litter. Cubs need their mother's milk for the first few months, but gradually they start to eat meat. The young of some cats, such as the puma, are called kittens.

Mother puma and kittens

Sharpen your claws!

Unlike other cats, a cheetah's claws don't go back into its paws. This is why they don't often climb trees — they find it hard to get back down.

Leopards fighting

Why do leopards fight each other?

Leopards fight each other to defend their territory. Each leopard has its own patch of land, which it lives in. Leopards use scent-marking and make scratches on certain trees to warn other cats away, too. Sometimes, a fight will end in death.

Draw

Lots of other animals live in trees? Draw some pictures of animals that live in trees near you.

Which cat lives in the treetops?

Clouded leopards are excellent climbers and spend much of their time in the treetops of their forest home. These animals have been seen hanging upside-down from branches only by their back legs. Clouded leopards are fantastic swimmers, too.

Do big cats live in rainforests?

Jaguar

Yes, they do. Tigers and leopards live in rainforests in India, and jaguars live in South American rainforests. Here, the weather stays hot all year, although there is often lots of rain.

What animals do jaguars hunt?

Young jaguars climb trees to hunt for birds and small animals. As they grow bigger they get too heavy for the branches. Adult jaguars hunt on the ground for deer and small mammals, and sometimes cattle and horses.

How do cubs learn to hunt?

Cubs learn to hunt by playing. Even a tortoise is a fun toy and by playing like this, cubs learn hunting skills. Many mothers bring their cubs a small, live animal so they can practice catching it.

Think

Are you as playful as the lion cubs? Invent some new games of your own to play with your friends.

Lion cubs

It's a wrap!

The ancient Egyptians are well known for their 'mummies'. They even mummified animals including cats, birds and crocodiles.

How do snow leopards keep warm?

Snow leopards live on snowy mountains in Central Asia. To keep warm in winter they grow a thick coat of fur and store extra layers of fat under their skin. They also wrap their long tails around their bodies when they sleep to keep in heat.

Snow leopard →

Make

Paint a picture of your favourite big cat. Make it as colorful as you like and give your big cat a name.

Which cat goes fishing?

The jaguar is an expert at fishing. Sometimes it waves its tail over the water to trick hungry fish before it strikes. Jaguars also fish for turtles and tortoises. Their jaws are so powerful that they can easily crack open a turtle shell.

Jaguar

Snowshoes!

Siberian tigers have large padded paws. They act as snowshoes and stop the tiger from sinking into the snow as it walks.

How do tigers stay cool?

Tigers such as the Bengal tiger live in places where it gets extremely hot in the summer. They can often be seen laying in pools of water to cool off, or resting in a shady area out of the hot sun.

What is the most mysterious cat?

The clouded leopard is the most mysterious cat. It is so shy and rare that it is unusual to spot one. Clouded leopards grow to over 6 feet in length, half of which is its tail. It uses its tail to balance as it leaps through the trees.

Clouded leopard

Why do cats always land on their feet?

Cats have bendy bodies and strong muscles. If a cat, such as a caracal, falls from a tree it can twist its body round so that it can land on its feet. Its muscles and joints take in the shock of the ground for a soft landing.

A caracal lands on its feet

Big teeth!

The sabre-toothed cat really did exist, about 10,000 years ago. It was the size of a small lion and its teeth were 10 inches long!

How many babies do tigers have?

Tigers normally have between two and four babies called cubs. The mother tiger is pregnant for three months, and the cubs are born blind. Most births happen at night, probably because it is quieter and safer.

Measure

Using a measuring tape, see if you can measure how long a clouded leopard is.

27

Why are cats the perfect hunters?

Because they have excellent eyesight and hearing, strong bodies and sharp teeth and claws. Many cats, such as lions, have fur that blends into their surroundings, which means they can hunt while staying hidden.

Lion hunting

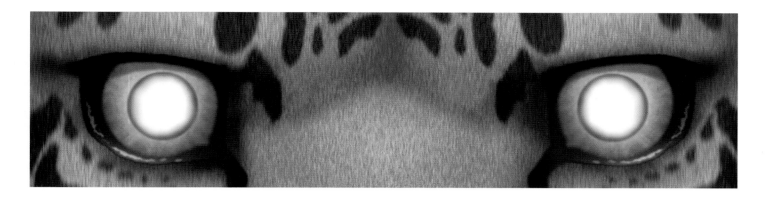

How do cats see in the dark?

Cats have special cells at the back of their eyes that reflect light. They are able to see objects clearly even in dim light, which is why many cats hunt at night. Cats can see four times better in the dark than humans can.

Try

How well can you see in the dark? Turn off the light and wait for your eyes to adjust. Can you see anything?

Do big cats have enemies?

Big cats don't have many natural enemies. However, they watch out for animals, such as hyenas, that will gang up to steal their meal. A group of hyenas will attack and kill a big cat if it is weak or injured.

'Eye' can see you!

Cats have very good eyesight, in daylight and at night. For cats that live in grasslands, this helps them to spot distant prey on the open land.

Quiz time

page 11

Do you remember what you have read about big cats? These questions will test your memory. The pictures will help you. If you get stuck, read the pages again.

3. Which cat is in danger?

page 11

4. What do ocelots eat?

page 4

1. What is the biggest cat?

5. What is the bounciest cat?

page 12

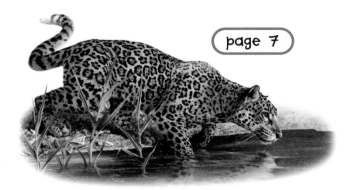

page 7

2. Are jaguars good swimmers?

page 15

6. How can humans help big cats?

30

7. Why do people hunt big cats?

page 16

page 26

11. What is the most mysterious cat?

8. What time do tigers go hunting?

page 17

12. How many babies do tigers have?

page 27

9. Why do cats wash their faces?

page 19

13. Do big cats have enemies?

page 29

10. Why do leopards fight each other?

page 21

31

Index

A
African serval 12

B
babies *see* cubs
Bali tiger 11
Bengal tiger 25
birds, catching 6, 11, 23
birth 27
black-footed cat 7
buffalo 9

C
caracal 6–7, 27
Caspian tiger 11
cattle 17, 23
cheetahs 12
  claws 21
  in grasslands 18
  lifespan 19
  speed 16–17, 19
claws 21, 28
climbing trees 14, 21, 23
clouded leopard 21, 26
coats *see* fur
crocodiles 23
cubs
  lions 5
  litters 20
  play 23
  tigers 7, 10, 27

D
deer 11, 17, 23

E
ears 28
extinction 11
eyesight 28, 29

F
faces, washing 19
feet, landing on 27
fighting 21
fishing 25
frogs 11, 12
fur
  hunting big cats for 16
  lions 5, 28
  lynx 13
  snow leopards 24
  tigers 4

G
grasslands 15, 18, 29

H
hearing 28
hunting 28
  learning skills 23
  at night 17, 29
hyenas 29

I
Iberian lynx 11

J
jaguars
  climbing trees 23
  fishing 25
  in rainforests 22
  swimming 7
Javan tiger 11

K
kittens 20

L
leaping 6, 12
leopards
  climbing trees 14, 21
  extinction 11
  fighting 21
  fur 24
  in grasslands 18
  in rainforests 22
  rarest 26
lifespan, cheetahs 19
lions 18
  cubs 5
  fur 28
  hunting 9, 28
  laziness 9
  manes 5
  prides 5, 8
  roaring 13
litters 20
lynx 11, 13

M
manes 5
milk 20

N, O
night, hunting at 17, 29
ocelot 11

P
'painted leopards' 11
play 23
prides 5, 8
puma 9, 15, 20

R
rainforests 15, 22
reserves 15
rivers, crossing 15
roaring 9, 13
running 16–17, 19

S
sabre-toothed cat 27
savannah 18

scent glands 19, 21
Serengeti 18
serval 12
Siberian tiger 4, 5, 25
sight 28, 29
snow leopard 24
snowshoes 25
sounds 9, 13
speed 16–17, 19
stripes 10, 13
swimming 7, 21

T
tails 24, 26
Taiwan clouded leopard 11
teeth 27, 28
territory 19, 21
tigers
  cubs 7, 10, 27
  extinction 11
  hunting 16, 17
  in rainforests 22
  Siberian tiger 4, 5, 25
  snowshoes 25
  staying cool 25
  stripes 10, 13
  trees
    climbing 14, 21, 23
    living in 21
    scent-marking 21

W
washing 19
weight, tigers 4
white tigers 10
wildebeest 18

Z
zebras 18

Home Repair *That* PAY$ OFF

150 Simple Ways to Add Value *Without* Breaking Your Budget

HECTOR SEDA,
America's Home Improvement Coach

Aadamsmedia

Avon, Massachusetts

Published by
Adams Media, a division of F+W Media, Inc.
57 Littlefield Street, Avon, MA 02322. U.S.A.
www.adamsmedia.com

ISBN 10: 1-59869-802-8
ISBN 13: 978-1-59869-802-2

Printed in the United States of America.

J I H G F E D C B A

Library of Congress Cataloging-in-Publication Data
is available from the publisher.

This publication is designed to provide accurate and authoritative information
ith regard to the subject matter covered. It is sold with the understanding that
 publisher is not engaged in rendering legal, accounting, or other professional
ce. If legal advice or other expert assistance is required, the services of a com-
t professional person should be sought.
        —From a *Declaration of Principles* jointly adopted by a Committee of the
 American Bar Association and a Committee of Publishers and Associations

he designations used by manufacturers and sellers to distinguish their
 claimed as trademarks. Where those designations appear in this book
 Media was aware of a trademark claim, the designations have been
 itial capital letters.

 ok is available at quantity discounts for bulk purchases.
 For information, please call 1-800-289-0963.

To my parents, Hector and Dolores Seda, and my sister, Yvonne Jones.

Acknowledgments

Nothing in life is really ever done alone and for this reason I would like to thank the following people for their friendship, support, and advice:

To my good friends, Emery and Sheila Wilson and August and Tammy Cardella

To my family, James and Annette Seda, Dinah Curkin, and Elisa Seda

Special thanks to my agent and friend, John Willig of Literary Services, Inc.

And to everyone involved at Adams Media, especially Paula Munier, Director of Acquisitions and Innovation; Brendan O'Neill, Associate Editor; and Elisabeth Lariviere, Layout Artist and Designer.

Contents

Acknowledgments **v**

Introduction / xv

PART I

Your Home's Exterior / 1

01 **Exterior Upkeep / 3**
Structural Maintenance **5**
Surface Maintenance **7**
Railing Maintenance **8**
Stair Repair **10**
Lay or Replace an Area of Pavers **14**
Replace or Reset Individual Paver Stones **15**
Replace a Concrete Walkway **17**
Keep a Clean, Fresh Pool **19**
Open the Pool **20**

02 **Proper Landscaping / 23**

Get a Visual **28**

Mulch for Effect **30**

Add a Classic Touch to Your Yard **31**

Construct a Gravel Pathway **32**

Clear It Up **34**

Edge Your Lawn **34**

Trim Your Lawn **35**

Do the Job **38**

03 **Your Driveway and Garage / 41**

Repair Cracks in Asphalt **43**

Repair Holes in Your Driveway **44**

Garage Door Maintenance **46**

Keep the Seal Tight **48**

The Messy Garage: Find a Path Through Yours **48**

04 **Keeping a Roof Over Your Head / 51**

Clean a Dirty, Stained Roof **53**

Locate a Roof Leak **54**

Replace Damaged Shingles **57**

Repair Worn Shingles **59**

Patch Corroded Roof Flashing **60**

05 **Proper Cleaning and Drainage / 63**

Prepare Your Home for an Exterior Cleaning **65**

The Cleaning Process **66**

Select an Area for Suitable Drainage **68**

Perfect the Pitch **69**

Clear Your Gutters **73**

Repair Gutter Seams **74**

Repair a Hole in the Gutter **74**

Re-nail a Standard Gutter **75**

06 **Proper Masonry and Foundation Maintenance / 77**

Mix Mortar **79**

Tuck-Pointing **80**

Seal Your Stone, Brick, or Block Foundation **83**

Seal a Concrete Foundation Crack **84**

Check Your Concrete Slab **86**

PART II

Your Home's Interior / 89

07 **Doors, Locks, and Hinges / 91**

Unstick Sticky Doors **94**

Remedy a Problem Bi-fold Door **95**

Are Pocket Doors Rubbing You the Wrong Way? **95**

Adjust a Storm Door **97**

Replace an Old Storm Door Closer **98**

Lubricate the Locks in Your Home *99*

Adjust the Lockset **100**

Lubricate Key Cylinders **100**

So, the Strike Won't Latch . . . **101**

Silence Door Hinges **103**

Keep the Doorknobs Uniform **103**

Clean a Gummed Lockset **105**

08 **Windows / 107**

Replace a Broken Screen **109**

Clean Your Screens **110**

Preventive Window Maintenance **115**

Unsticking Your Window **116**

Out with the Old Caulk and In with the New **116**

Insulating Windows in Older Homes **118**

Eliminating the Draft Around Your Windows **119**

09 Floors / 121

Erase Minor Scuffs and Stains **124**

Buff Your Hardwood Floor **125**

A Quick Wood-Floor Transformation **126**

Fix the Squeak from Underneath **127**

Fix the Squeak from Above **129**

Get Rid of a Noisy Stair **130**

Replace the Padding **132**

Install a Carpet Patch **133**

Fix a Squeaky Carpet **135**

10 Walls / 137

Clear, Patch, and Clean **139**

Prime and Paint **141**

Patch Nail Pops **144**

Repair Cracked Seams **144**

Fix a Gouge in a Wall **145**

Mend Drywall Cracks **145**

Fix Small Drywall Holes **146**

Repair Large Drywall Holes **146**

Restore Damaged Wall Corners **148**

Repair a Crack in Plaster **149**

Remove the Wall to Get at the Problem **150**

11   The Kitchen / 151

Remove an Existing Countertop **156**

Get the Countertop Right **157**

Install a New Laminate Countertop **158**

Repair a Stripped Cabinet Hinge and Door **160**

Change the Look by Painting Your Kitchen Cabinets **160**

Install an Under-Cabinet Light **161**

Change the Washer in That Faucet **164**

12   The Bathroom / 167

Remove an Old Vanity **169**

Install a New Vanity Base **170**

Replace an Old Vanity with a Pedestal Sink **172**

Install a Crescent-Shaped Shower Curtain Rod **173**

Change Out an Old Water Closet **175**

Maintain, Remove, and Replace Ceramic Tiles **176**

Replace a Ceramic Soap Dish or Toothbrush Holder **180**

Add Charm with a Few Accents **181**

Fix a Leaky Shower Door **181**

Remove Corrosion from a Shower Door Frame **182**

Clear Your Bathtub Drain **184**

Unclog Your Toilet Bowl **185**

Clear Your Tub's Waste Line **185**

Unclog a Toilet Bowl with an Auger **186**

Fix a Leaking Showerhead **186**

Replace a Worn Tub Diverter **186**

Inspect the Caulking and Grouting Around Your Home **187**

Stop That Constantly Running Toilet **189**

Hot Tub and Whirlpool Maintenance **192**

13   **Heating and Cooling / 193**

Air Conditioner Maintenance **195**

Central Air Conditioning Maintenance **196**

What to Do If Your Furnace Is Not Running **199**

Replace a Forced-Air System's Filter **202**

What to Do When Your Thermostat Fails **204**

Clean Your Thermostat **205**

Replace a Low-Voltage Thermostat **206**

Check the Accuracy of Your Thermostat **207**

Clean the Inside of Your Hot Water Heater Tank **208**

Clean, Organize, and Get Your Mechanicals Together **209**

Are You Still Waiting for Water? **210**

Clear the Aerators **211**

14   **Fireplaces and Chimneys / 213**

Maintain Your Fireplace **216**

Between You and Your Fireplace—Fireplace Doors **218**

Flues and Chimneys **220**

15   **Electrical Issues / 223**

Label the Circuit Breaker or Fuse Panel **226**

Change a Receptacle **226**

Replace a Bad Light Switch **228**

Match Your Outlet and Switch Cover Plates **231**

Troubleshoot Doorbell Problems **233**

Troubleshoot Smoke Detector Issues **235**

Replace a Lighting Fixture **236**

Fix an Unbalanced Ceiling Fan **237**

16   **Keep It Safe and Clean / 239**

Keep a Handle on Things: Handrails and Safety **241**

Is There a Mouse in the House? **243**

Dust Control **246**

Quick Leak Fix **253**

17   **Go Green / 255**

Twenty Simple Ways to Go Green **259**

Don't Let Water Be a Drain on Your Wallet **263**

Save Water Outside Your Home **265**

Appendix A: How to Choose a Contractor / 269

Appendix B: Kicking Up Curb Appeal / 273

Resources / 277

Index / 279

Introduction

Regular maintenance preserves a home's value. Not only does it keep it functioning efficiently, but proper care helps to increase the equity you have in your home as well as keeping hard-earned cash in your pocket. Homes, for the most part, appreciate in value on their own. One way to maintain appreciation is by proactively and systematically doing minor routine maintenance tasks, and making simple improvements. These simple tasks help to keep a home safe and keep it operating at peak performance throughout the year. Changing rotted lumber, adding a decorative path, and keeping your furnace clean are all little things that make a big difference in terms of property equity. Completing such simple home repair tasks is easy and smart.

Automobile owners know it's important to take the time to change the oil in their car in order to keep it running properly. This preserves the lifespan of the investment. Considering the cost of a house, shouldn't homeowners take care of their home just as much? Scheduling regular maintenance is key to keeping your home in optimal shape.

Major home catastrophes can easily be avoided if homeowners take just a few minutes to do some simple routine tasks. Losing the air conditioning, heat, or hot water can be very unpleasant in the midst of a party. Don't think it can't happen? Remember Murphy's law. In addition to avoiding unpleasantness, being proactive can save you loads of money. Purchasing a replacement item is usually much more costly than paying for simple maintenance. Don't get caught in a bind; set a schedule for routine household maintenance.

Think of preventative maintenance as a powerful tool that can save you hundreds, thousands, and even tens of thousands of dollars. The object is to have the components that make up your home reach full life expectancy without costing you unnecessarily and depleting the equity in your home.

Not only will proper home maintenance save you money, it can also earn you money. The better you maintain your home, the greater its value will be. By devoting a few hours to completing these tasks, your equity will grow. Proactive home maintenance is a no-brainer.

Home Repair That Pays Off teaches you what to do and how to do it. I will show you some simple home preventative maintenance tasks and projects that you can do to keep your home running like a fine-tuned instrument. (We'll keep it simple, brief, and as painless as possible.) Each chapter is made up of individual tasks for certain areas of your home. At the start of each individual task, you'll find easily recognizable icons that will denote the skill level and estimated time needed to perform each one. And at the end of each chapter, dollar-sign icons will summarize the equity you save by completing the chapter's tasks.

DIFFICULTY

Each project requires a different level of experience. Therefore, each task has been rated on the following skill level scale. If you are new to home improvement projects, it's best to start with Skill Level 1-rated tasks to develop experience.

Skill Level 1: Novice—No prior home repair or maintenance experience

Skill Level 2: Intermediate—Some prior repair and maintenance know-how; semi-skillful with their hands

Skill Level 3: Experienced—A seasoned do-it-yourselfer

TIME

Time per project can vary due to a number of factors. Therefore, each project has an estimated time of completion, ranging from one hour for smaller projects to up to ten hours for daylong projects.

MONETARY RETURN

Each chapter comes with an estimated monetary return that falls within one of the following ranges:

$500–$750

$750–$1,000

$1,000–$1,500

$1,500–$2,500

Having been a homebuilder, home improvement consultant, and homeowner, I can't stress enough how important it is to keep your home in good physical shape. Taking just a few minutes a day to implement the tasks found in this book can help you from unnecessarily throwing buckets of hard earned cash out the window and saving you from pulling out your hair from the stress of a needless emergency. From simple do-it-yourself tasks to contracted improvements, you will know what to look for, what is needed, and how it should look when complete. We've got work to do. So, put on that tool belt and let's get going!

PART I

Your Home's Exterior

CHapter

V

Exterior Upkeep

The combination of hot and cold temperatures with wind and water over time can cause exterior finishes and surfaces to become dull, worn, and unstable. The purpose of this chapter is to give you simple solutions to a variety of issues that arise in the areas outside your home. Whether they're maintenance suggestions to avoid costly repairs or installations to increase your home's worth, the tasks in this chapter will have you outside enjoying the fresh air and adding value to your home.

Project Worksheet

MONETARY RETURN: $750–$1,000

PROJECT START DATE: _____

TASKS COMPLETED: _____

_____

_____

_____

TOOLS NEEDED:

- ❏ 1" diameter straight pipe (cut to the required length)
- ❏ 1" x 4" lumber (several pieces)
- ❏ 2" x 4" (approximately 7' long)
- ❏ Adjustable wrench
- ❏ Circular saw
- ❏ Cold chisel
- ❏ Edger
- ❏ Flat shovel
- ❏ Gas-powered or hand tamper (depending on area size)
- ❏ Ground-fault protected extension cord
- ❏ Hammer
- ❏ Hard rake
- ❏ Hatchet
- ❏ Hose and water
- ❏ Level (3' level for small areas, an 8' level for large areas)
- ❏ Margin
- ❏ Mitre saw
- ❏ Pick
- ❏ Pointer trowel
- ❏ Pressure washer
- ❏ Protective goggles
- ❏ Pry bar
- ❏ Push broom
- ❏ Rubber mallet
- ❏ Sandpaper, electric sander, or sand block
- ❏ Shovel
- ❏ Sledgehammer
- ❏ Tape measure
- ❏ Trowel
- ❏ Wet-saw
- ❏ Wheelbarrow
- ❏ Work gloves

Your Deck

A deck is a great place to retreat to read a book, enjoy a barbecue, entertain, or just sit and savor a cup of coffee on a sunny morning. Decks can be found on homes anywhere from countryside backyards to rooftops in the city. While decks in the country allow homeowners to enjoy the sprawling landscape, city decks become mini-get-away locations for urbanites. The sound of a waterfall, smell of lush plant life, or sight of a colorful collage of flowers help city dwellers get away from the hustle and bustle of everyday city life, creating a garden of relaxation and bliss after a hard day's work.

The components of a deck can be broken down into four different maintenance tasks:

1. Structural Maintenance
2. Surface Maintenance
3. Railing Maintenance
4. Stair Repair

Let's get started on keeping your deck in great shape, so that it will continue to be your oasis.

Structural Maintenance

SKILL LEVEL

2

TIME

4–5 h

The time can vary depending on the number and condition of the structural members.

Concrete piers, posts, ledger board, joists, bridging, and cross bracing are required to help stop a deck from shifting side to side and to sustain load movements. These pieces are not usually visible when standing on the deck, but can be seen from underneath.

Joists, girders, and posts usually support the structural members under the decking. These wood members need to be checked periodically for any deterioration.

1. Look for defects in areas that are not easily visible. These areas can go for long periods without an inspection and are usually prone to long-term dirt and moisture accumulation, making them susceptible to rot or rust. Check suspicious areas for rotting wood by poking

them with a screwdriver. If the screwdriver easily penetrates the lumber there may be cause for concern. This can mean that the wood has rot or termite infestation. If the screwdriver easily penetrates the wood, it will either crumble or have a spongy feel to it and brownish or yellowish discoloration may also be apparent. In some cases, you may need to use a flashlight under the decking if it is low to the ground, making it dark and difficult to see.

2. Although exterior fasteners are galvanized, after time nails and joist hangers can rust and corrode. When replacing defective nails, screws, bolts, or hangers, remove them one at a time. Removing them all at once can make the project very unsafe.

3. Look under the deck at the ledger board that keeps the deck connected to your home. Ledger boards are bolted every two feet. Bolts hold much better than nails. At times, you may find that a ledger board has been nailed instead of bolted. Nails can become loose over time and permit movement or shifting of the ledger board. This may cause the board to pull away from the main structure and could result in a collapse. If you find loose nails remove them and replace them with a slightly wider diameter lag bolt. Make sure that the bolts are tight and secure.

4. Look on top of the deck where the ledger board, decking, and house meet. Inspect along the length of the board and check to see if there is flashing and, if there is, its condition. (Flashing is a strip of aluminum that runs horizontally along the length of the ledger board preventing water and debris from getting between the ledger board and the home.)

5. Flashing should be attached under the siding at a 90-degree angle overlapping the ledger board. If flashing is absent, it must be installed; if the flashing is defective or corroded, it must be replaced.

INSTALLING NEW FLASHING

1. In order to replace or install flashing, the closest deck board to the home will need to be removed. Aluminum flashing can be purchased at your local home improvement center or hardware store.

2. Cut a sufficient amount to run the length of the ledger board.

3. Slide the flashing under the siding, allowing enough flashing to wrap over the top of ledger board.
4. Secure the flashing by nailing it to the house, right below the siding.
5. Bend the flashing at a 90-degree angle over the ledger board, slightly pitching it downward beyond the ledger board allowing water to flow off and away from the house.

6. Inspect the deck posts. They should be in galvanized cradles that lift them slightly off the concrete footing or pier. If you find dirt around the decking posts, clear away the dirt and apply roofing mastic around them in order to stop any moisture seepage, which will eventually cause them to rot. Place a piece of felt paper along the side and bottom of the dirt as well as ¾" gravel on top and around the bottom of the post. This will help keep water and dirt from settling around the post and prevent damage to the supports, sustaining the life of the posts.

Surface Maintenance

SKILL LEVEL

2

TIME

6–10 h

The time estimate is based on a deck that is approximately 150 sq. ft.

Whether you upgrade your deck or build a new one, maintenance is the key to having it last a long time. Regular upkeep like power-washing, staining, or tightening a few loose screws can keep your deck and railings safe and attractive year round.

1. Get into the habit of sweeping debris off your deck. Leaves, branches, and dirt hold moisture and will discolor and deteriorate decking material. In worse cases, the debris will cause mildew, mold, and rot.
2. If you find boards on your deck warping or cupping, carefully remove them, turn them over and nail or screw them back down. If they are too far gone, replace them.
3. Nail pops are common occurrences on wooden decks. (A nail pop is when the nail has become loose and the head protrudes beyond the lumber.) They are dangerous because someone can catch a foot

on the nail. Remove them and use galvanized decking screws to secure any loose wood caused by nail pops. Screws have a better grip and will hold down the decking boards much better than nails.

4. Splintered wood is another common problem. Use a wood chisel or utility knife to cut the splinter off and sand the area down to a smooth finish.

Hector Hint	When you're purchasing lumber for your deck, be sure to order quarter-sawn lumber and not flat grain lumber. Flat-grain lumber has a predisposition to splintering.

5. Water and termites are a deck's worst enemies. Power-wash your deck every year and coat it with a deck sealant or stain. Doing this will replenish the finish and make it look new again. The beauty of a composite deck and railing is that they don't need sealing, only power-washing.

6. If you don't want to power-wash your deck, pick up a deck wash at your local home improvement store. Apply the deck wash, wait about twenty minutes and simply rinse it off with water. The dirt and discoloration will run right off the deck and railings. After you are finished, wait forty-eight hours before applying a sealer or stain.

Railing Maintenance

SKILL LEVEL

2

TIME

4–5 h

Railings and safety go hand in hand and are just as important as any other component of deck safety. Railings help you keep your balance when going up or down the stairs and stop you from falling over the side of your deck. A safe height for railings is 42" from the top of the deck to the top of the railing. Check with your local building code official before attempting to make any major changes to your deck. Most towns have local building regulations that a code official can interpret for you.

1. Check deck railings to ensure they are sturdy and properly secured. If someone should happen to lose his balance, he should be able

to grab the rail for safety. Railings should be able to hold up to 200 lbs. of lateral pressure should someone happen to trip and fall. Many wood railings, which are the most common, are fastened with nails and after time become loose due to the constant back and forth tugging and lateral pressure they are subjected to. Also, wood can shrink over time and, in some cases, the nails will begin to pull away.

Hector Hint

There are many different types of railing materials from which you can choose. Redwood, cedar, or wolmanized (pressure-treated) are good wood selections, while there are a number of decorative plastics or stainless steel designs to choose from. There are also steel cable and glass railings that allow you to take in the landscape without ruining your view. For more selections, go to your local home improvement store or lumberyard to view samples of the many varieties of railings available.

2. Verify that the nails holding the railings in place are secure. If not, remove them and replace them with screws. Use a screw that is longer or wider than the nail for a more secure setting. Rails are attached to posts and sometimes a stainless or galvanized L bracket can be used to secure the handrail to the posts. Attaching it from underneath will make it less noticeable. If the bracket is an eyesore, paint it to match the railing. If a bracket is not practical, toe nailing—securing a screw or nail at an angle—will be necessary.

3. Make sure that the railing system is firmly fastened to the house. You can also use the galvanized or stainless steel L brackets to secure any loose rails to the structure.

4. Wood can sometimes twist with age and will need to be replaced in order to have a flat, secure setting. The 2" × 2" vertical balustrades are thinner than most of the other railing components and are subject to twisting more often than any other part of a railing system. (Balustrades are the vertical components of a railing system that fit between the top and bottom rails that prevent someone from falling through.)

5. Posts are main supports to a railing system. Occasionally, they become loose and need to be adjusted, but nailing is not a preferred way to secure a post. The easiest way is to firmly lag bolt them by drilling a smaller hole than the diameter of the lag bolt and ratchet the bolt into place. A better way is to drill a hole and using a carriage bolt, bolt them through with a washer and nut on the other side.

6. Check the bottom of the rail for rot. If rot is the issue, the post will need to be replaced.

Stair Repair

SKILL LEVEL

2

TIME

2–3 h

Depending on the width, deck stairs are made up of two or more stringers, which support the stair treads. They are attached to a double joist at the top of the deck and are supported by a concrete pad or footing located at the bottom of the stairs. Footings are concrete supports that are set in place at a minimum of 36" deep. Wood rot at the bottom of the stringer is a common problem.

Here are some tips if you are replacing your deck's stair treads:

1. Before purchasing any lumber, make sure all the stair treads in a set of stairs are equal in thickness. A small difference in stair tread width, within a set of stairs, can be a dangerous trip factor when climbing or descending.

2. Stair treads should be no less than 1" thick. A thickness less than 1" can result in deflection, cracking, or personal injury. Make sure to be consistent with the thickness of the stair tread. Using different thicknesses can cause a person to lose their balance.

3. Any stair treads 36" or wider will require a tread thickness of 1½" and may need an additional stringer centered under the tread for support.

Be sure to keep an eye on your deck's stairs as they are an important part of your deck, which needs maintenance just as much as—if not more than—any other part of a house. A well-kept deck is a great feature of any home—rural, suburban, or urban.

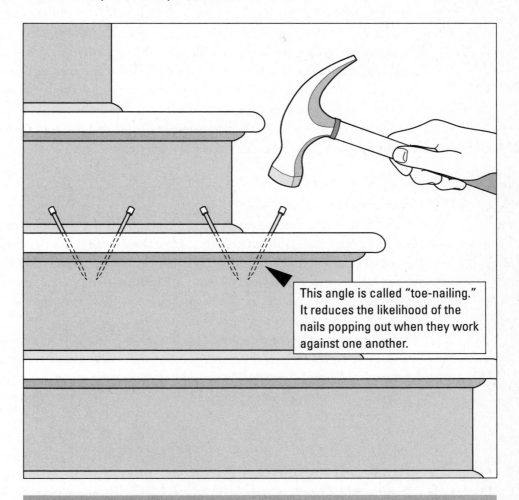

This angle is called "toe-nailing." It reduces the likelihood of the nails popping out when they work against one another.

To reduce squeaking, you can nail the tread to the riser.

Retaining the Charm of Pavers

A well-maintained patio or pool deck adds elegance and charm to most homes, making it a place where family and friends can get together, relax, or gather for a special occasion. Pavers increase the charm of any home, new or old. Whereas wood decks have classic charm, they do not have the durability of pavers. The maintenance on pavers is minimal and their useful life is limitless compared to a wood deck. Wood decks need to be cleaned and sealed every year, while pavers can easily be power-washed without having to be too careful and without worrying whether or not they will splinter. Properly maintained pavers can last a lifetime while wood, even when treated and looked after, will need to be replaced several times.

THE VALUE OF A PAVER

Compared to decks, paver stones have a more permanent feel and a richer and more stylish look to them. Since their maintenance is drastically reduced and they are more costly to install, your house value will be slightly greater, but not to the point that you should install them for that reason. Pavers should complement your home, not overpower it, and should be done for the homeowner's enjoyment.

There are many different patterns and ways you can design pavers around your yard. Your mind's eye will be the guide you need to best create an area of relaxation or play. From walkway lighting to the gentle flow of fountains and soft beautiful gardens mixed within the patterns of rigid stone, your imagination can run wild.

THE RIGHT PAVER FOR THE RIGHT PLACE

Stone pavers come in a variety of colors, shapes, and materials. Designs and layouts can be created to go with any style home and with most landscapes. Putting down pavers in a small walkway approaching your door can be attractive and add value to your home. Before installing a paver, take time to think how it will work with the style of your home and yard.

When it comes time to choose the material for your paver, you need to consider how it will be used. If it is to border your pool, be aware that the pavers do get very hot in the sun and can actually burn the bottom of your feet. A good material option for a poolside stone paver is limestone. It is cool to the touch and the stones will be much easier on your feet during the hot summer months.

Some of the concerns you will want to consider and analyze prior to installing a paver patio are:

- Does my yard have too much of an incline to easily install a paver?
- How will installing a patio affect the storm water flow in the yard?
- What will the cost be to prepare the area pre-installation?
- How much will the whole project cost?
- Do I have the physical strength and stamina needed to complete the project?

These are all important things to consider before going ahead and installing a paver.

MAYBE I SHOULD GET A PROFESSIONAL . . .

The preparation for installing pavers is extensive, arduous, and time-consuming for the professional, but even more so for someone that does not do it every day. It is labor-intensive and without the proper experience or skills, can easily become an overwhelming task. If you are a do-it-yourselfer with plenty of time and patience, it can be an awesome challenge, but I recommend starting with small 10' × 10' area first.

The preparation of a base for pavers consists of sand and compressionable stone dust (quarry process). The base must be tightly tamped to provide a solid base on which to install or reinstall the stones. Laying a solid base is the most important part of the process, and is where talent and experience come into play.

Hector Hint   Pavers do not have to fill large areas such as walkways and patios, but can be strategically placed in a garden to complement the landscape and design.

Lay or Replace an Area of Pavers

SKILL LEVEL

3

TIME

6–10 h

Laying a new paver or repairing an existing one can be an undertaking. Be sure you have enough time set aside and the necessary material ready beforehand. Adding a paver to your home's landscape is always a nice touch. And fixing heaving or sinking pavers can prevent someone from tripping as well as water from accumulating, and freezing in colder environments.

1. Pick a visible and practical area that won't be too much to tackle. For instance, it could be a small walkway from the driveway to the front steps or a square area in your backyard.

2. Clear the area that you want to place the pavers on and level it off, allowing for 4" of quarry process (a mixture of stone and dust with a high compaction factor that can be purchased at your local home improvement store or mason supply), ½" of sand, and the thickness of the pavers. Note: A minimum area of 10' × 10' should be sufficient as a staging area for your materials.

3. Once you have the level and depth set, place the stone dust down.

4. Using a 1" diameter straight pipe and level (approximately 6'–8' long), spread the stone dust evenly. Frequently check to make sure it is level. Using a pipe is recommended because wood can warp and not give a level enough area.

5. Tamp down the stone dust so that it becomes a solid base for the pavers. Larger areas require a heavy gas-powered tamper whereas smaller areas can be hand tamped.

6. Place approximately ½" of sand, making sure it is level. Do *not* tamp the sand.

Hector Hint

If you want to be unique, try something a little different than most. Think about incorporating a design into your project. A border or pattern in a different color may add that little touch it needs.

7. Place the pavers in the configuration that you want them. When doing so, try to minimize the amount of cuts that need to be made. If a wet-saw is needed, it can be rented at a tool rental center.

Make it a point to tell them it will be used to cut paver stones in order for the wet-saw and blade to be sized adequately for the job.

8. Once you are finished placing the pavers, tamp them down with a gas-powered tamper for large areas and a hand tamper for small areas. Be careful of the tamping plate and wear work shoes when performing this task.

9. Brush the remaining stone dust in between the pavers. This will lock it in place so it does not disperse like sand.

The occasional problem with pavers is that the base can fail and cause the paver to sink. If this happens, the paver needs to be removed, the base reset, and the stones reinstalled.

| **Hector Hint** | Be sure to check your local weather for any rain in the forecast. Rain can seriously affect the preoperational part of this project by washing away the sand and causing gullies in the quarry process. |

Replace or Reset Individual Paver Stones

SKILL LEVEL

1

TIME

2–3 h

Replacing individual stones in a paver is nowhere as difficult as initially setting the entire area. A little time and patience is all you need.

1. Gently pry the paver stone from its setting using a mason's trowel or flat scraper and try not to disturb the setting of the adjacent pavers. Using one trowel may not be enough, two trowels or scrapers may be necessary to get under it and lift it out. Paver stones are thick and removing them requires a little patience.

2. Once the paver stone is removed from its base, use a scraper or margin trowel to dress up the bottom and top it off by smoothing and leveling the bottom in preparation for the setting in-place of the paver.

3. When the bottom is leveled off, use your judgment to determine how much sand should be put back as a base. Putting too much

in can cause you to disrupt the other paver stones while not enough sand will require you to remove the paver stone again. After placing the sand, create a stable base by smoothing it out with a margin trowel or scraper. You will need to use some judgment of your own when defining how much sand to put back.

4. After you are sure that the base is secure, take the paver stone, place it over the open area, and gently lower it back into its setting.
5. Make sure the joints are equal on all sides and brush sand between the joints to secure the paver stone in place.
6. Using a rubber mallet, carefully tap the paver until it is secure and equal in height with the other pavers.
7. Keeping in mind that every contractor has their own preference, again, spread sand or quarry process, depending on what was previously used, into the joints and brush the excess away.

Concrete: The Paver Alternative

You may want to consider stamped concrete instead of pavers. An occasional power wash may be needed to keep it clean, but overall—if done by the right contractor—stamped concrete can be as pleasing to the eye and easily mistaken for pavers.

If you've opted to go with concrete over paver stones, here's a task to repair your concrete walkway.

Replace a Concrete Walkway

SKILL LEVEL

3

TIME

6–10 h

Concrete walkway slabs can become damaged for a number of reasons, but usually a growing tree's rooting system is strong enough to raise a concrete slab. Before someone trips, replace the concrete flag (square) with a new one.

1. Wearing work gloves and safety goggles, use a sledgehammer to break up the concrete flag in your walkway, doing one square at a time.
2. Be careful not to break the concrete square next to it. Get as close as you can and chisel any jagged edges off.
3. Remove all the debris from inside the work area and grade the dirt to match the dirt under the adjacent higher flags. You may need to add or remove dirt.
4. Make several stakes using a hatchet and a 1" × 4" × 24" piece of lumber.
5. These flags of concrete are either 4' or 5' wide. Take a 1" × 4" at least 2' longer than the flag and put one on each side of the work area, overlapping the undamaged adjacent flags.
6. Take the stakes and hammer them down on the outside of each 1" × 4" to keep them in place. Make sure they are snug so that the concrete does not seep through.
7. If you are only replacing one or two flags, use a pre-mix concrete and just add water. Use a wheelbarrow to mix the concrete. Mix the concrete as directed on the bag and to an oatmeal-like consistency.
8. Pour the concrete into the work area and with a hard rake, push the concrete into all areas, filling any voids. Get rid of any excess and make the top as level as possible before moving to the next step.
9. Lay a 2" × 4" on edge on top of the existing flags and move it from side to side, smoothing out the concrete and working toward you. Fill any voids as you work the 2" × 4" left to right. Level out the concrete to the height of the existing concrete flags.

Hector Hint	The concrete for a walkway is 4" and for a driveway it should be no less than 7" thick.

10. Once the concrete has begun to dry, using a mason's trowel, carefully smooth out the top.
11. The warmer it is, the quicker concrete dries. With that in mind, take a broom and when the water on top of the concrete begins to dissipate, lightly brush the surface of the concrete towards you. Doing this will give the concrete a rougher texture for slip resistance. If the concrete is too dry this will be difficult to do.
12. If you want a real professional-looking job, for a few dollars purchase an edger at your hardware store. After you brush the surface, run the edger along the perimeter of the flag. The edger rounds the edges and the other side gives it a border.
13. Wait twenty-four hours before removing any lumber. When removing the lumber, be careful not to chip the concrete. The concrete can take a month or more before it is fully cured.

If you are uncertain about doing this work yourself, a mason or concrete contractor can be hired to complete the project in a fraction of the time that it would take someone who has never done it before.

Pools

When first getting a pool most people don't really know what it takes to maintain it. It takes an ongoing effort to make sure that the proper chemical balance is maintained in order to keep the water safe and clear. But, with a little time and experience you'll be a pro. So, let's jump right in.

POOL CONTAMINATION

Contamination of pool water is a common problem. It is impossible to prevent bacteria and viruses from entering the water. Chlorine, used to sanitize the water, can break down quickly when there are a large number of swimmers and the sun is shining constantly. But having too much chlorine is also no good; proper balance is essential in your pool, to keep everyone safe and healthy, and your pool looking good.

Keep a Clean, Fresh Pool

Keeping your pool water clear and fresh, free of algae growth and bacteria, is a daily task. Two simple things are necessary to keep it in suitable condition:

1. Keeping the pool walls and bottom clean
2. Maintaining a safe chemical balance

Chemicals and a steady and regular filtering system are important for a pool. Pool companies have made keeping the chemical balance of a pool very easy to check. There are a couple of different ways to check the chemical balance of a pool:

1. A pool chemical testing kit comes with cells that are filled with water, changing color when certain chemicals are added as an indication of the pH, chlorine level, and other chemical levels in the water.
2. Dip sticks that change color indicating whether the pH level is in the correct range and if the chlorine is sufficient to fight off bacteria.
3. Most pool supply stores provide free digital testing services on samples of pool water.

Cloudy water can be unattractive and uninviting. This can result from several factors, but mainly from:

*   High pH levels
*   High alkalinity level
*   Low chlorine level
*   Hard calcium level
*   Algae growth

Chlorine is the main chemical that kills algae and bacteria in your pool and pH is the balance of acid and alkalinity in the water. It is essential to maintain pH levels in order for the chlorine to be effective and keep your pool safe. Water treatment helps to stabilize pH levels and stabilizers help to keep the chlorine from being burned off by the sun, providing a protective bond around the chlorine.

IMPORTANT POOL ITEMS NEEDED

- Shock treatment
- Chlorine
- Water test kit
- Soft-bristled brush
- Vacuum
- Long pool pole (for cleaning and vacuuming)

Open the Pool

SKILL LEVEL

1

TIME

6–10 h

If your pool is closed properly, you shouldn't have a problem opening it in the summer. Learning how to close it the right way comes in time and after making a couple of mistakes first.

Here's where you can begin:

1. Get the leaves off the pool cover. Doing this periodically during the winter will take the added weight and stress off the pool cover.
2. Remove the cover, let it dry thoroughly, fold it, and store it. It is essential to clean the cover and let it thoroughly dry out before storing it to prevent mold and mildew.
3. Make sure the filter is thoroughly tightened and sealed.
4. Check that the pump is connected, and that any missing plugs are back in place, and that it is primed.
5. Put the skimmer strainer back into place.
6. Fill the water level of the pool halfway up the skimmer.
7. While the pool is filling, put the ladders back and bolt the diving board back into place.
8. Walk around the pool checking that everything is all right. Make sure nothing is loose and that all screws, brackets, and tiles are secure.

9. Turn the pump on.
   There are three types of filtering systems:

   - Sand
   - Cartridge
   - DE (Diatomaceous Earth)—DE is the most commonly used these days and is the filtering system we will address.

10. Pour the appropriate quantity of DE based on the size of the pool into the skimmer.
11. Next, pour the shock in as you walk around the pool.

Shocking the pool kills the bacteria and algae. Do not enter the pool for twenty-four hours after you do this. The best time to shock your pool is after sundown, when the sun's rays cannot reduce its effectiveness.

Take a water sample in the morning and have it tested at your local pool supplier. They will let you know if you need to add anything else to the pool, before jumping in.

Chapter V

Proper Landscaping

A healthy lawn and well-maintained shrubbery not only increase the value of your investment, but also up the overall visual appeal of your home. Through proper care and attention, you can grow and maintain a lawn that will be the envy of your neighborhood, and with some additional work you can add to the overall landscape through mulching, trimming, and adding accents. Take a proactive role in the care of your home's yard and you will be able to reap the benefits of added value.

Project Worksheet

MONETARY RETURN: $750–$1,000

PROJECT START DATE: _____

TASKS COMPLETED: _____
_____
_____
_____
_____

TOOLS NEEDED:

- ❏ Brush Cutter
- ❏ Cotton (for earplugs)
- ❏ Flat shovel
- ❏ Gloves
- ❏ Goggles
- ❏ Ground cover fabric
- ❏ Leaf bags
- ❏ Pick ax
- ❏ Pointed shovel
- ❏ String trimmer
- ❏ Wheelbarrow

Lawn Basics

Lawns need good soil conditions to thrive. They need to be fertilized and aerated annually. If the soil is highly compactable, it may need to be aerated more than once a year, to permit oxygen and other nutrients in. Be careful not to overfertilize your lawn, as it can harm the soil more than help it. Take a soil sample to your local lawn and garden store and have them analyze it. They can recommend nutrients to put into your soil that will help it reach a condition favorable for lawn growth based upon your area.

So now it's time again to get outdoors and begin sprucing up what the winter washed away. The breezes are getting warmer; the buds on the trees are beginning to show and there's finally spring in the air, as well as in our step. With all of that comes some work that needs to take place on a regular basis, like mowing, watering, and caring for the lawn.

WATERING YOUR LAWN

After a long day at work, and a crowded slow commute back home, one of the last things we want to worry about is unwinding the hose and watering the lawn. Time is one of those things that most of us have little control over, if any at all. Yes, we want a nice manicured green lawn to enhance the beauty of our homes but it is, at times, a bit hard. Having to run the children to tennis, basketball, dance lessons, and football practice and then pick them up when they are finished is a full-time job. With all this going on, who can keep up? It is easy to forget to water your lawn, letting it go for days without any water.

Some people choose to stand and spray their lawn for the pure pride they take in caring for it and, remarkably, some find it relaxing. Others have moveable sprinklers that occasionally need adjustment to reach certain areas and some sprinklers mechanically move from one end of the lawn to the other. Manual watering allows homeowners to control their use of water based on recent rainfall and apply only what is necessary.

Hector Hint

If you find these tasks difficult to maintain yourself . . . share the chores.

SEMI-AUTOMATIC SPRINKLER SYSTEMS AT A FRACTION OF THE COST

Recently, walking through a hardware store I noticed a device that had connections for several hoses and attaches to the outside hose bib (faucet) on your home. This is a timer that allows each individual hose to open and shut at predetermined times. This is about as economically effective and as close as you can get to an automatic underground sprinkler system without paying thousands of dollars.

The drawback to this and to any system where the hose lays in a spot for a long period is the dead grass that occurs under the hose. The outline of the hose is noticeable once removed, and needs a little time to restore itself. This means that the hoses should be relocated from time to time, in order for these occurrences to stop from happening, or placed where there is no contact between the hose and the grass (i.e., a flower bed, or around the edge of the lawn).

TIME, PATIENCE, AND FINE TUNING

Situate the sprinkler where the spray of water can reach the majority of lawn. Develop a system of placing a sprinkler for a certain length of time in a particular place. This takes a little time, patience, and maneuvering but, if you want a healthy looking lawn, don't wait until the grass turns brown before doing something. A brown lawn negatively affects the appearance of your home.

THE BEST TIME TO WATER YOUR LAWN

The best time to water your lawn is several hours before sunrise. Watering during the day can result in your lawn becoming burned from the sun and watering at night may help grubs to reproduce. Grubs are a whitish underground parasite that feed off the roots of a lawn, leaving patches of dead grass that can easily be lifted out of place by a slight tug.

WATER PRESSURE

The use of appliances and fixtures can hinder watering during the day. For example, someone in your household taking a shower may cause a drop in water pressure, and shorten the distance of the sprinkler's spray, resulting in the insufficient watering of your lawn.

Lawn Mowing

Before each season, change the oil in the lawn mower and have the blades sharpened. Before working on your lawn mower, be sure to disconnect the spark plug. Lawn mower engines, if they are warm from use, have been known to start on their own. Keeping your lawn mower tuned prolongs its life, allows it to operate when needed, and ensures that the blade stays sharp. There are small engine shops that will service the mower, tune it up, and sharpen the blades.

MOWING HEIGHT

The height at which grass is mowed is important to the health of a lawn. Different types of grass require different mowing heights for best possible appearance. Take a small sample patch to your local plant and garden store to determine what type of grass you have and how high you should set the blades of your mower for best results. Grass blades that are too long can smother a lawn, taking away from the sunlight and nutrients that the soil needs for it to grow properly. It will also allow weeds, pests, insects, rodents, and snakes to fester in it, making it unhealthy and possibly dangerous. On the other hand, cutting grass too short can cause the soil to dry up quickly after it is watered, killing the lawn.

Hector Hint	Before mowing your lawn, clear your yard of any debris and leaves. Leaves hinder growth and smother your lawn by not letting nutrients into the soil and by soaking up the water.

Beyond Your Lawn

Preparing your lawn for warmer weather is never an easy project, especially if you have to work with difficult terrain. However, it can be a nice property-lift once you are finished.

If your yard slopes down at a steep angle, is big or small, or is dominated by rocks, weeds, poison ivy, animal holes, or any other yard hindrances, a yard design may be difficult to produce, even for the most experienced landscaper. Nevertheless, taking on and maintaining a difficult landscape doesn't have to be expensive or that difficult to do as long as you break it down into small achievable tasks. Seeing your yard as one big project can be overbearing and unattainable, but completing small affordable tasks will make it much more manageable.

Sometimes it can take a long time to figure out what to do with a difficult yard, whether it is in the front, side, or rear of your home. Eventually it will come to you. You just have to have patience and faith in your abilities. Do not take on too much at once. Put together a plan of action and timeline that is feasible, and a great looking lawn will be your reward. The key here is to keep the cost low and the job small so a person with minimal knowledge and skill can complete the tasks without too much frustration.

Get a Visual

SKILL LEVEL

1

TIME

4–5 h

Take a picture of your yard and then make a simple sketch of what you would like your yard to look like when you are finished. Easy-to-use landscape design software can be purchased at your local computer store or online. HGTV's Home and Landscape Platinum Suite is a simple-to-use software program that offers drag and drop simplicity, and tips and design ideas from HGTV's video library. This software does not require experience, will help you visualize in 3D what your landscape can look like, and makes it so much easier to get your ideas across. Remember, a picture is worth a thousand words.

1. Complete the visualization of your ideal lawn by either hand sketching or using HGTV's Home and Landscape Platinum Suite software.
2. Question local landscapers and nursery personnel regarding homes they know that may have needed similar efforts.
3. Take a ride around your neighborhood to get ideas for your home. Make notes, ask questions, and take pictures.
4. Go to your local bookstore or coffee shop and flip through landscaping magazines for ideas. It's a great way to spend a rainy day.
5. Now that you have a good idea for what it is you want to do, take small chunks of your yard at a time. Seeing your yard take shape a little at a time will make it much more enjoyable and allow you to figure out your tolerance level for yard work.
6. Place whatever it is you are planting where you think it belongs in the yard. This way you can get a better visual of how your yard will actually look. It is important to have a good visual in your mind. You wouldn't want to plant everything and have to dig it all up after all that work. Take your time when arranging your plantings. It can take a ⅓ of the time and some extreme cases, of course, depending on who is helping you, even longer.
7. Make sure you have the proper gardening tools for the smaller plants and a shovel and possibly a pick for the larger plantings. Ask the salesperson when purchasing your plants if any additional top soil or mulch is needed. The top soil will provide much needed nutrients and the mulch will sustain the moisture necessary for good growth.

Hector Hint

Keep your yard uncomplicated. Planting many items can make it look too busy. Instead, plant enough for your yard to be eye-catching.

Mulch for Effect

If you want to create a crisp, appealing appearance to your flowerbeds, try placing cedar mulch around your trees, shrubs, and plants. Trees and bushes are more attractive when a bed of fresh mulch is spread at their base. Although many homeowners put it down for its contrasting effect, mulch serves an ecological purpose as well, preventing soil from being washed away and retaining moisture for a longer period.

A benefit of using cedar, as opposed to other types of wood mulch, is that termites do not find it very pleasant. Other types of mulch can attract termites, which in turn can cause an infestation of your home, causing damage and possibly costing you hundreds or thousands in extermination services and house repairs.

1. Purchase ground cover fabric and cedar mulch. Mulch can be purchased by the bag for small projects, or you can have a truckload delivered to your home for bigger jobs. A local nursery, home center, or hardware store can provide you with bags of mulch or the name and number of a supplier for larger loads.
2. Clear the flowerbed(s) of rocks and any other obstructions that can hinder the placement of ground cover fabric. (This fabric is placed before the mulch to prevent weeds from growing through; this way you do not need to weed in mulched areas.) Overlap the edges of the fabric and place a heavy object on it to prevent it from curling and blowing around.
3. Using a wheelbarrow, distribute the mulch throughout the yard. The area of coverage should be noted on every bag.

Hector Hint

Mulch, if not bagged, is ordered by the cubic yard (3' wide x 3' height x 3' long). A 10' × 10' area will require approximately 1 cu. yd. of mulch, 2" to 3" thick. Using any less than 2" to 3" around your plantings can result in it being washed away by rain.

4. Use a hard rake to spread the mulch. The hard rake will make it easier to spread because the moisture content of the mulch makes it a

little heavier than if it were dry. Occasionally check the thickness of the mulch while spreading it and be careful not to disturb or hook and pull the fabric.

Add a Classic Touch to Your Yard

SKILL LEVEL

3

TIME

6–10 h

You may be tempted to try new and wild landscaping effects, but they should be left to the experts. Classic is better and never goes out of style.

Try placing an arch or arbor at the entrance walkway of your yard or a pergola in the backyard. Whether your home is contemporary or a center hall colonial, adding a classic area for relaxation is always welcoming. Planting a climbing ivy or grapevine to envelop and shade the area can be a contemplative addition, setting the tone for a relaxing background. These inexpensive additions can increase your home's value, as well as making a huge difference in the enjoyment it provides your family and friends.

Purchase a pre-assembled or unassembled arbor, arch, or pergola online or locally. These structures are created from different woods or vinyl and come in various sizes and shapes. As mentioned, you can either purchase one pre-assembled, or if you are an experienced do-it-yourselfer, you can opt for an unassembled one to put together on site. If you choose to go the unassembled route, be sure to follow the instructions closely.

Pre-assembled units can easily be installed by using stakes to secure them into the ground or by permanently embedding them into a bed of concrete.

1. Lay the arbor or arch on its side. Affix the stakes to the bottom, according to the instructions provided. Most manufacturers provide metal stakes with their arbors. However, if they are not provided with the arbor you can purchase ¼" diameter metal rods at your local home improvement center, cut them into 16" to 24" lengths, and bend them into a u-shape.
2. With two people, lift the arbor and set it in place, applying equal amounts of pressure to the stakes and pushing them into the ground.

Or, you can permanently affix the arbor with concrete:

1. Use a narrow pointed shovel or post-hole digger and dig out approximately 12" of dirt.
2. Once you are down to virgin, or undisturbed soil, fill the holes with 6" of gravel.
3. Making sure that the lattice of the arbor or arch is at least 4" above ground, plumb and level the arbor, setting it in the hole and onto the gravel. Use 2" × 3" × 16" wood stakes, gently tacked at the four corners of the arbor, to hold it securely in place.
4. Mix quick-drying concrete and pour it into each hole. Double-check the plumb and level of the arbor and make any adjustments before the concrete sets.

There are other elements you can add to your yard, like a waterfall running into a pond, but these types of landscaping items can run you into the thousands of dollars after you add the costs of prepping the area, setting up the electrical wiring and plumbing, and completing routine maintenance.

Construct a Gravel Pathway

SKILL LEVEL

2

TIME

6–10 h

The amount of time it takes to complete this task is directly related to the length of the path.

Tricking the eye can make a small yard look larger. Giving a small yard a boundary, like with a fence, makes the yard look smaller. So, taking away a fence or trees and shrubs that outline the property line help to give it depth and dimension, masking the actual size of it.

Adding a small 5' × 5' paver patio or small wood deck, enough for a lounge chair to read in or to soak up a few rays of the sun, is also a nice feature and is relatively cheap to do (check out page 14 on how to lay a paver). You can also trim it with solar lights, mulch, and plantings to really dress up a drab dull yard—and make it look more expensive.

Another way to trick the eye and make your yard look like it's worth big bucks is by putting in a curved walkway made from pea gravel or paver stones. The curves take your focus away from any straight peripheral lines and make it difficult to tell where your property begins or where it ends. It's an economical way to seemingly expand your yard.

1. You first need to visualize what you want to do, where you want it, and what you want the end result to look like.
2. Purchase a bag of lime from your local hardware store. Pouring the lime from a cup, outline a 3' wide path. Add shape and curves to make it interesting. Start small—you can always make it longer later.

Hector Hint

A little cotton in your ears will prevent gnats and other pests from annoying you while you work.

3. Use a flat shovel to excavate 4" of earth within the path boundaries. Remove any obstructions like roots or rocks that may get in the way.
4. Lay ground cover fabric within the path, and cut it to shape, allowing it to go up the sides slightly.
5. If you desire a border along the edges you can use stones, solid brick, or pavers to line the path.
6. Carefully pour the gravel into the pathway, making sure that the ground cover fabric is in place. Make adjustments to it as you proceed.
7. As you progress, use the flat edge of the shovel to level off the top of the gravel.
8. Use a hand tamper (this can be rented at your local rental center) to tamp down the gravel once it is in place and leveled.

Hector Hint

When purchasing gravel for a large area it is a better value for you to buy it by the truckload. Your local nursery can best guide you as to where you can purchase it in your area. They can also help you determine approximately how much you will need.

Clear It Up

If you have a yard that is overgrown and large, take your time: It won't get done overnight.

Clear a 10' × 10' or 20' × 20' section, depending on the size of your yard, at a time.

1. Using a tape measure, walk a 10' × 10' or 20' × 20' area and place something in the four corners to identify the area to be cut. Clearing out a jungle can be arduous to say the least, and seem like a job that will never get done. Taking one section at a time will make clearing up your yard much easier and make what seems like an endless project well worth your time and effort in the end. Of course, a large yard is harder to tackle, but whittling down an overgrown yard is not impossible.
2. Before starting on the next section, bag and remove the freshly cut brush. Your reward is being able to see the area you tackled, cleared. Be careful not to make the bags too heavy to carry.

Take it slow. Cutting down the brush will allow you to see the contour of the terrain and what you have to work with. At that point let your imagination go. *You* can do it and it doesn't have to be expensive.

Hector Hint
The fall is a good time to tackle outdoor work. Most plants, shrubs, and bushes have stopped growing and the bugs aren't as annoying this time of year.

Edge Your Lawn

Not edging your lawn is like getting a haircut and not combing your hair. It's an important part of grooming your lawn. It is the difference between a professionally manicured lawn and what an average lawn looks like. Edging creates a neat defined outline between the lawn, the driveway, the walkway, and the flowerbed.

An edger, which can be electric or gas powered, has a blade that spins vertically to cut a fine clean edge along the perimeter of the lawn. Occasionally the blade needs to be sharpened or replaced. Manual edgers are the simplest to use, but only if you have a very small lawn. These can be time-consuming for larger areas.

1. If you have a gas-powered edger, check to make sure that you have enough fuel to complete the job. Some edgers call for a gas/oil combination. Be sure to follow the directions and add the proper mixture when refueling. If you're using an electric edger, have sufficient extension cords to get around the lawn.
2. Adjust the blade guide on the bottom of the edger and tighten it so you don't ruin the cutting blade while edging.
3. Slowly walk the edger, cutting a neat even edge along the perimeter of the lawn. When walking the edger, make sure no one is in front of you and that you cut away from anything that can be damaged. The spinning blade sometimes catches pebbles and dirt, flinging them out and away from the operator and hitting whatever is in front of the edger.

Trim Your Lawn

SKILL LEVEL

3

TIME

1 h

A string trimmer is a tool used to trim areas of your turf that are difficult to cut with a lawn mower. Like an edger, they can be gas or electric powered, and may require a gas/oil mixture to operate.

Using a string trimmer allows you to get up close to walls, curbs, trees, and driveways. Caution needs to be taken to avoid burning the grass with the nylon trimmer cord. If you cut too low to the ground, you can burn the grass, causing a circular brown area.

1. Make sure there is sufficient nylon trim cord on the trimmer.
2. Start it as directed in the operation manual.
3. Check that there is no one around or close by. Like the edger, debris can be pelted around, hitting someone standing nearby.

4. Move the string trimmer slowly to the left and right, getting a feel for it. Hold your elbows in toward your body for better control.

Once you're comfortable with the balance of the machine, you can begin to trim the overgrown areas not accessible with the lawn mower.

Professional lawn maintenance workers use the string trimmer to edge. Professionals acquire a steadier hand than the homeowner does cutting her lawn once a week. They operate the equipment daily, and know the feel and balance required when handling it.

Some string trimmers have a blade attachment that cuts through brush, for those areas that have not been attended to for a while.

Trimming Hedges

Trimming hedges can be more difficult than it looks. Whether your hedges are square, rounded, tapered, or sculpted, they all need a keen eye and a steady hand to whip them into shape.

The more frequently hedges are trimmed, the tighter their shape and the easier it will be to maintain them. To keep hedges looking neat, they should be trimmed two to four times a year. The longer they are without maintenance the harder the job will be.

For larger hedges, trim them slightly narrower at the top, tapering them outward at the bottom. This will allow the sun to reach the bottom limbs of the hedge.

BEST HEDGE-TRIMMING MONTHS
1. March
2. May
3. July
4. September

However, if your schedule will only allow you to trim twice a year, you should trim once in April and again in September.

It is easy to tell when your hedges need to be trimmed. Remember, the more you trim them the better they will look and the easier and quicker it becomes, every time. For a newly planted hedge, do not trim for the first six months to a year. It needs to get well rooted into the soil before any limbs are cut back. In shaping it, try not to trim more than ½" for every 4" of new growth.

If the hedges have been neglected for a long period, cut them back in the spring as if they were just planted and feed them with fertilizer, using about 1lb. of fertilizer for every 20' to 25' of hedge length. Turn the soil with a shovel or hoe and work the fertilizer into the ground. Be sure to fertilize the backside of the hedge in the same manner. Keep the hedge bed clear of leaves, weeds, trimmings, and other obstructions so that the hedges reap all the benefits of the nutrients in the soil.

TYPES AND SIZES OF TRIMMERS

Hedge trimmers come in several types and sizes. For small hedges, manual hedge shears can be used.

For larger easy-to-get-to projects, use an electric hedge trimmer. These can range in size from 16" to 26" and more. For the novice I recommend a small trimmer that is easier to handle than the larger ones. Yes, the smaller the trimmer the longer it will take, but the safer it will be to handle.

Hector Hint	Have the hedge trimmer blades sharpened at least once a year. A sharp blade will allow you nicer cuts and make the job less difficult.

For homes with extensive hedges, you may want to consider a gas-powered trimmer. A gas-powered trimmer allows you the freedom to move around without worrying about the length of your extension cord. Like some other garden power tools, it may require a gas/oil combination, making it less desirable to some homeowners.

PRECAUTIONS

- When using a hedge trimmer, never put your hands anywhere near the blade. It is exposed and does not have a protective shield.

- Unplug a trimmer whenever you leave it unattended. Children can easily trigger it on.
- *Always* use protective gear. Something can happen when you least expect it.

Do the Job

SKILL LEVEL

3

TIME

2–3 h

Now that you know why you should do it and what you should do it with, here's how to do it.

1. Vertical cut—make a broad vertical sweeping motion with the hedge trimmer. Occasionally, check the straightness of the vertical edges of the hedge. Keeping a straight, even vertical edge will look much neater than a crooked uneven hedge cut.
2. Once you are comfortable with the vertical cut, slightly taper the top of the hedge to allow the sun to reach the bottom half. Cut both sides of the hedge before beginning on the top.
3. When cutting the top of the hedge, be careful not to cut downward, making a gully. Keep the blades slightly rising at a 5 to 10 degree angle, until the top has a good horizontal cut.
4. The weight of snow can damage hedge tops. Keeping a hedge rounded on the top will not allow snow to accumulate as much as if the top were flat. Starting slowly at one end, take a small area (2' at a time), and round the edges until you have the desired effect. For the handier person, cut a template out of plywood, setting it over the hedge as a guideline. Some prefer to use string, which I find can hinder mobility and can get cut by the hedge trimmer.

Be Safe

The use of protective gear is highly recommended. Power equipment can be dangerous and precautions should always be taken. Always use:

- Protective goggles
- Work gloves
- Long pants
- GFCI (Ground Fault Circuit Interrupter) extension cords

If your schedule is hectic and your lawn is too much to handle in your spare time, then you need to pay for outside lawn services. Use an established company that you have seen working frequently in the area, and speak to the neighbors regarding the cost and quality of work the lawn service provides.

When you talk to the lawn service representative, make sure to ask about other charges and whether the following services are included in your contract:

- Leaf pickup and removal
- Aerating
- Fertilizing
- Pesticides

Hector Hint

Never allow anyone that does not carry liability or workers' compensation insurance to do any work on your home. If a contractor or individual does not have the proper insurance and injures himself on your property, you can end up paying his hospital bills as well as other damages.

Every year hospitals report thousands of accidents caused by lawn equipment. Back injuries, repetitive motion injuries, and power tool accidents are relatively common. The use of chemical pesticides and insecticides also requires precautions. A person who has experience and familiarity with them should supervise the application of these chemicals.

Your third choice is to take on the projects that you are comfortable doing and know you can complete, and hire someone to do the other tasks that you don't enjoy, don't know how to do, or don't have the time for.

Once you have taken the time to observe and properly adjust your system, your time will be freed up for the many other things that need to be done around your home. Like lay in a hammock.

Your Driveway and Garage

A couple of areas that are easily overlooked, but say a lot about a house, are the driveway and garage. Since they're usually only seen by homeowners as they're coming or going, these two areas are often ignored when it comes to upkeep and renovation. Cracks, stains, and clutter are expected, but do not need to be. Proper care, maintenance, and repair will turn these oft-forgotten spots into places of pride.

Project Worksheet

MONETARY RETURN: $500–$750

PROJECT START DATE: _____

TASKS COMPLETED: _____

_____

_____

_____

TOOLS NEEDED:

- ❑ Broom
- ❑ Caulking gun
- ❑ Chisel
- ❑ Dust pan
- ❑ Flathead screwdriver
- ❑ Grease gun
- ❑ Hammer
- ❑ Hand tamper
- ❑ Hand truck and dolly
- ❑ Masking tape
- ❑ Pencil
- ❑ Phillips head screwdriver
- ❑ Pliers
- ❑ Rachet set
- ❑ Rags
- ❑ Saw
- ❑ Scissors
- ❑ Shop vacuum
- ❑ Utility brackets
- ❑ Wood chisel
- ❑ Work gloves
- ❑ Wrench

Driveway Maintenance

Repairing an asphalt driveway is not as complicated as it may sound. Here are some simple solutions that can help you save thousands of dollars and get a few more years out of your driveway.

Snow can melt during the day and freeze at night. This daily expansion and contraction puts a massive amount of pressure into existing cracks in the asphalt, reducing it to rubble. The slightest crack can freeze overnight and thaw during the day. The repetition of this process weakens vulnerable areas, causing more cracks to occur.

Repair Cracks in Asphalt

SKILL LEVEL

2

TIME

4–5 h

Repairing small cracks can prevent larger problems from occurring. Small cracks in asphalt driveways often form after water penetrates and freezing occurs. A simple preventive maintenance task can keep these cracks under control and help extend the life of your driveway.

1. Clean out and vacuum any debris that may be inside of the crack.
2. If it is a deep crack, fill it with sand to within ¾" of the top and compress it if possible.
3. Using asphalt caulking, fill the crack without letting too much of the asphalt crack repair overflow. Caulk the crack so that it is slightly higher than the existing driveway.
4. Smooth the caulking with a putty knife. Do not drive over or walk on the caulking for at least twenty-four to forty-eight hours, depending on the temperature.

Hector Hint

These repairs shouldn't be done in the winter. Spring, summer, and early fall are the best times to repair asphalt. As long as the temperature is above 45 degrees during the evening, it should be all right to perform repairs.

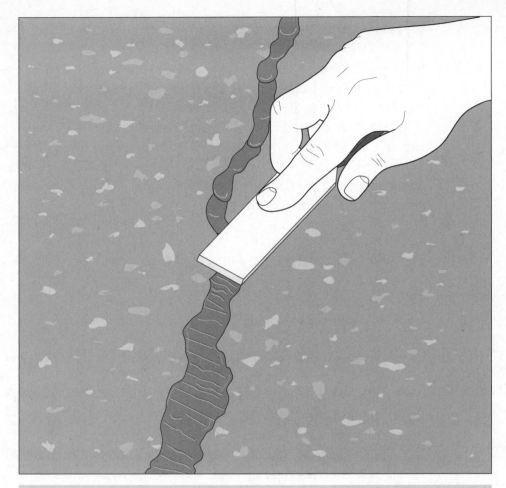

Be sure to smooth out the filler to blend it in.

Repair Holes in Your Driveway

SKILL LEVEL

2

TIME

4–5 h

If driveway cracks are ignored, they get larger and turn into small holes, allowing the asphalt to erode. Then they become potholes and eventually undermine your driveway.

1. Clean out as much dirt and debris as possible.
2. If the hole is deep, for instance 9" or more, use ¾" stone, filling the hole and allowing for at least 2" to 3" of patch to be placed on top.

This will help stabilize the bottom and allow you to use less asphalt patch.

3. Once you have filled the hole, clean around the edges. Use a chisel and hammer to smooth the edges, if needed.
4. Fill the hole with asphalt patch and tamp it down using a hand tamper or the bottom of a 2" × 4".
5. Once you have tamped it, add asphalt patch, mounding it in the middle but making sure not to make it too high.
6. Using a piece of plywood longer and wider than the area being patched, place it on the patch and slowly drive your car over it until the crowned area of the patch is flat and even with the existing asphalt and remove any excess.

Some driveways are too far gone to repair. If your driveway looks like a spiderweb of cracks, you will need to determine whether it pays to do these tasks or whether you should have a professional rip up and redo the entire driveway.

To replace an entire driveway, a backhoe is used to tear out the old asphalt, then the area is properly graded and prepped, and new asphalt is installed. Some other durable and design-flexible driveway materials that can be used in place of asphalt include pavers and concrete. If you decide to use concrete as a driveway material, it should be no less than 7" thick. Some municipalities will require you to embed wire in the concrete to help strengthen it.

Garage Doors, Openers, and Remotes

The garage door is the largest door in a home. Keeping the garage door finely tuned can help to keep money in your pocket. On average, a new garage door can cost $1,500 or more. Caution should always be used when working on a garage door. The doors are quite heavy and the powerful springs can injure you if proper precaution is not used. But, by knowing a few simple tasks, you can hold onto some hard-earned money.

Some doors are fabricated from wood and others are metal with a dense insulating foam board on the inside. These doors are very heavy, but an individual should be able to open these doors using one hand, if the door is balanced correctly.

<table>
<tr><td>**Hector Hint**</td><td>Make it a point to keep wood doors protected, clean, and sealed. The contact with the pavement and water can increase the possibility of mold and mildew growth.</td></tr>
</table>

SAFETY FEATURES

In many jurisdictions, it is required by law for garage doors to have an automatic reversing mechanism. This mechanism senses any pressure from an obstruction as it is closing and opens the door, stopping someone from getting hurt. This law went into effect in 1993, but grandfathers pre-existing openers.

The constant jerking of the door up or down can jar bolts and screws and eventually cause them to become loose. The lubrication of garage door parts is also something that should be checked on a regular basis.

Garage Door Maintenance

SKILL LEVEL

3

TIME

2–3 h

A few simple maintenance procedures can keep garage doors operating with little or no interruption.

1. Garage doors have overhead springs that help lift the door. The springs need to be inspected periodically for signs of wearing and rust. When they get old, the metal springs can become fatigued and eventually snap. Mark your calendar to check them every few months. Do not attempt to repair or replace garage door springs if you have never done it and if no one has ever taught you how to handle them. A spring snaps so fast it can cause you serious injury.

2. Rollers are bolted to the garage doors. These rollers need to be inspected regularly. Check to see if they need to be tightened, lubricated, or replaced. Loose rollers can make the door wobbly and throw the doors out of alignment. Lightweight oil should be used when lubricating them. Worn or damaged rollers can be replaced at your local home improvement center or hardware store.

3. Clean off the hinges, lubricate them, and tighten the screws or bolts holding them in place. Hinges keep the panels together and allow the garage door to fold and unfold, as needed. Applying light weight oil to the hinges will help them move freely and efficiently.

4. Check the side rails for sturdiness and strength. Make sure they are firmly attached to the wall and to the hangers, and are not bent or out of alignment. If there is cause for concern, have a professional repair the rails. The doors are heavy and rest on the rails and if the person working on them is not properly trained there is potential for injury to occur.

5. Check that the automatic reversing on the door is operating. Allow the door to come down and stop by preventing it with your hands. The slight opposite force should stop it from continuing. Do not put something rigid in its way as it may break the door and throw it out of alignment.

6. Check the photoelectric sensors that operate and bypass the openers. Make sure the sensors are aligned and firmly in place. If there is a possibility that something can bump against them or fall onto them make sure to remove or relocate it.

7. If the door fails to operate, look at your owner's manual to determine where the reset button is on the opener itself.

8. Most garage doors come with two remote openers. If you are missing one or both, they can be purchased at your local building supply or home improvement center.

Keep the Seal Tight

SKILL LEVEL

3

TIME

2–3 h

Maintaining a tight seal along the edge of the garage door will help to keep wind, rain, heat, and snow from getting into the garage space.

1. To eliminate any gaps between the garage door and the concrete floor, a rubber gasket can be glued to the floor.
2. Alternatively, a gasket can be mounted to the bottom of the door. These two different gaskets can be purchased at your local home improvement center.
3. If there is a lot of air infiltration into the garage, it may be on the outside where the garage door and doorstop meet. These side stops can be removed and relocated closer, preventing so much air from entering.

The Messy Garage: Find a Path Through Yours

SKILL LEVEL

2

TIME

6–10 h

Where does the garage begin and where does it end, you ask? In some instances, it is impossible to tell. It's almost like that movie cliché, when someone opens a closet door and everything falls out. You can make your home more livable by freeing up useful space in your garage for seldom used items. You may even find room to park another car in the garage, something you'll appreciate on the next snowy morning.

In order to reclaim your garage, you need to get rid of all those boxes, bags, and junk that have accumulated throughout the years. Pick a day and remove everything you possibly can from the garage and place them in separate piles as:

1. Items to discard that can be left by the curb for pickup.
2. Items that can be placed in the attic.
3. Things that neighbors, relatives, and charitable organizations may be able to use, such as clothes, toys, old bicycles, and the like.
4. Tools and lawn care items that may be stored in a shed or neatly placed or hung up in the garage.

5. Ice scrapers, snow blowers, snow shovels, etc., should also be placed where they can be accessible in case of a sudden snowstorm, but out of the way.
6. Anything of sentimental value should be either in a storage facility, your attic, safe deposit vault, or safe.
7. Winter and summer recreational items can normally be hung or shelved to keep them out of the way.

| **Hector Hint** | The day after you clean out the garage is a very good time to have a garage sale. Sometimes getting together with some neighbors and having a multi-home garage sale can attract many buyers. |

2 3 4 5 6 7 8

Keeping a Roof Over Your Head

The roof over your head is the most important part of your home. A roof takes the brunt of the elements' punishment on a daily basis; therefore, maintaining it and inspecting it at least twice a year is very important. A roof is not a *high*-maintenance item. (Roof shingles can last from fifteen years to a lifetime, depending on the warranty and how well they are maintained.) However, it is important to keep it routinely maintained.

Project Worksheet

MONETARY RETURN: $1,000–$1,500

PROJECT START DATE: _____

TASKS COMPLETED: _____
_____
_____
_____
_____

TOOLS NEEDED:

- ❑ Brush
- ❑ Caulking gun
- ❑ Flashlight
- ❑ Hammer
- ❑ Harness or heavy-duty rope
- ❑ Ladder
- ❑ Ladder stabilizer
- ❑ Power washer
- ❑ Pry bar
- ❑ Roofing nails

Choosing the Right Type of Roof

Picking a roof is becoming as difficult as picking wallpaper for your home—twenty-five years, thirty years, fifty years, lifetime roofs; this shade, that shade; this size, that size; this shape, that shape; this thickness, that thickness; metal roof, plastic roof (yes, plastic), clay tile roof, standing seam metal roof—it can go on and on, but at least we have the choices to meet our demands, both aesthetically and financially.

Because of the huge difference in cost, an asphalt roof is much more common these days than slate, clay, or any other type of roof. The technology for asphalt-shingle roofs has changed significantly, in resilience, style, and color. In fact, a more expensive slate-look-alike asphalt roof can be difficult to tell apart from the real thing, and is still considerably lower in price. Since asphalt roofs are the most common, we will focus on repairs and replacements to this type of roof. It is also much easier to find a roofing contractor that installs asphalt shingles than it is to hire a slate, clay tile, or standing seam metal roofing contractor.

Clean a Dirty, Stained Roof

SKILL LEVEL

3

TIME

6–10 h

When a roof does not dry promptly enough, there is a good chance that algae or moss can accumulate, leaving it discolored with a black, green, or multicolored-looking substance. A stained or discolored roof can take away from the beauty of an attractive home. The discoloration of a roof can be the result of mold, algae, or a substance from an overhanging tree. The longer it remains, the harder it is to remove.

Heights can be a bit challenging for many people, but if you are up to the challenge you can save yourself a few dollars by doing this task yourself.

1. If you don't own a power washer, rent one at your local tool rental store.
2. Set a stable ladder securely up against the lowest part of the roof.
3. Once up on the roof, carefully secure yourself to the chimney or some other stable object on the roof with a harness or rope. Use

something strong enough to sustain your weight, should you happen to slip.

<table>
<tr><td>Hector Hint</td><td>Be very careful and step around any algae, mold, or other substance growing on the roof. They tend to be very slippery.</td></tr>
</table>

4. Stand by the ridge of the roof (the peak), pick an area that is unnoticeable, and spraying downward about two feet off the shingles, begin to spray. Bring the wand sprayer closer to the shingle, until you begin to see the algae on the roof disappear.
5. Check that the granules are not being removed from the shingles when spraying.
6. Areas harder to clean may need to be brushed with detergent to loosen up the growth, but more than likely the power-washer will do the job.

Locate a Roof Leak

SKILL LEVEL

3

TIME

4–5 h

Trying to find a leak coming from your roof can sometimes can be a very challenging task, even for the seasoned professional, especially at a time it is not occurring. Water will always find the path of least resistance and will travel to the lowest spot of a ceiling before finding a place to exit. You may think the leak is right above the spot where you see the water, when actually it is coming from someplace else. It is best to wait until the rain stops before climbing on the roof. Important times to check your roof are after severe wind, rain, and hail storms. Replacing problem shingles should be done immediately; otherwise, waiting can prove to be costly in the end.

CHECKING FOR A LEAK FROM THE OUTSIDE

Begin looking for the exterior signs. The first thing is to look for obvious areas on the rooftop that may look like they need repair. For instance:

- Curling shingles—This is an indication that the existing roof has seen better days and the entire roof needs to be replaced.
- Nails popping up through the shingles—This could be a signal that there is deflection in the roof sheathing, or that the thickness of the roof sheathing that was installed is inadequate. The plywood sheathing may be deteriorating because of water damage.
- Defective flashing—Look at the point where a roof intersects with another roof or a vertical rise. Check that the flashing is not corroded or damaged.

Hector Hint

When walking and crawling in an attic be careful where you walk and watch your head. It is very easy to lose your balance and hit your head on a roof rafter or go through the ceiling.

More often than not it is not easy to see where water is entering your home and this is where a little investigative work is needed.

1. Look at vulnerable areas like the gaskets on the plumbing vents; sometimes these items can dry out and crack, allowing water to enter.
2. Deteriorated flashing is another source for water entry into your home. Look along the chimney where the masonry and roof converge. This vulnerable area should be periodically checked and maintained.
3. If you find worn shingles or multiple places of water penetration, these are signs that a new roof is needed.

Hector Hint

Sometimes it pays to have a third party come to evaluate the condition of your roof to see if a patch will suffice, or if the entire roof needs to be replaced. A fair home inspector will not charge her normal home inspection rate since she is only evaluating the roof. Getting an objective inspection may keep you from incurring a large, unnecessary expense.

4. Check for missing, cracked, or loose shingles.
5. Look at areas that may have once been patched or temporarily repaired.
6. Check that your gutters are clean. They should not cause water to back up and over into the house and enter through the eave or siding.
7. If you have a satellite television dish or solar panels mounted to your rooftop, check that the holes for the brackets are water-proofed and are not allowing water to infiltrate the attic.

CHECKING FOR A LEAK FROM THE INSIDE

If you are having a difficult time finding the problem from the outside you may need to look at it from the inside of your home.

When a problem is intermittent it is hard to find, but once it begins to rain, go into the attic and look at the obvious areas where you think the leak is allowing the rain to enter. Water always finds the path of least resistance; so, you can have a leak at one end of the house while it is spilling out some 10', 20', or 30' away, making it extremely difficult to locate. It is always easier to find a problem like this when it is happening.

1. Make sure to have a flashlight when you go into the attic. Go to the area in the attic where you think the water is entering the finished space and take a good look around. Check the underside of the roof sheathing for signs of water stains and wetness. When looking, be careful of nails penetrating the underside of the roof sheathing.
2. Observe the rafters for signs of water stains. Water stains can be very helpful when trying to locate a water problem. In many circumstances, these stains can be followed to the source of the problem.
3. Check for signs of mold on the wood and on the insulation. This is an indication that water has been there for a while.
4. If you find mold growth or wet insulation, using gloves and a respirator, remove the insulation, discard it, and replace it with new. Allowing the mold or wet insulation to stay can create an even bigger problem later requiring remediation, added expenses, discomfort, and possibly a health hazard.

Attic insulation and dust can get into your pores, eyes, and throat causing irritation, itching, and coughing. Make sure to cover up well and to wear a long sleeve shirt and long pants. A respirator will prevent you from inhaling the dust and insulation particles and the goggles will help to prevent eye irritation.

A leak from a roof can have a huge trickle-down cost effect on a homeowner. Interior, exterior, and structural repair costs can be enormous. For that reason, it pays to take care of any leak problems immediately. Rot and drywall repair, mold removal, and repainting can be very expensive and take away from the equity you accumulated in your home.

Replace Damaged Shingles

SKILL LEVEL

3

TIME

4–5 h

Damaged shingles can allow water to infiltrate your home and cause extensive damage to the interior, as well as allowing mold to flourish in the ceilings and walls. Keeping your roof clean and replacing worn or damaged shingles is important in maintaining the value of your home.

Doing this when the temperature is cold outside can be a bit more difficult than when the temperature is above 55 or 60 degrees. Asphalt shingles can become brittle and break in colder temperatures, making it easier for you to damage perfectly good shingles. Use the following techniques to replace any damaged shingles.

1. Using a hammer, gently tap a pry bar under the head of the nails of the bad shingle, making sure not to damage the roofing paper or, if it already has a layer of shingle, the shingle underneath.

Hector Hint

Make sure you have something to put the nails and debris into. The last thing you want is to have a mess blowing around onto your neighbor's yard or a flat tire because you threw the nails off the roof and onto your driveway.

2. Pry up the nails holding the damaged shingles in place.

Be careful not to damage the roofing paper.

3. Starting from the bottom, nail the new shingles into place. Keep the same overlap on the new shingle as the old, and occasionally check to see if the shingles are straight. You don't want to have to remove the new shingles you installed. Do not install the top course of shingle. The nails for the top course would need to be under the shingle above it.

4. Flip the top course of shingle upside down. Apply roofing cement to the underside of the shingle.

5. Gently slip the shingle underneath the shingle tabs above and tamp it down to hold it into place.
6. Place a heavy object on top of the cemented shingle, matting it down. Make sure the object cannot roll or slide off the roof. Wait several hours before removing.

Repair Worn Shingles

SKILL LEVEL

3

TIME

2–3 h

Shingles that are worn are susceptible to cracking and water penetration. Replacing a worn shingle can save you from costly repairs caused by a leaky roof.

Some common signs of worn shingles are:

- Granules begin to fall off and accumulate in the gutters and bottoms of the leaders and downspouts.
- The edges begin to curl and turn up.
- The nail heads begin to pop through the upper layer of shingle. At this point, a new roof is more than likely needed.

Unless they have protruding nail heads, here's how to repair worn shingles:

1. Where shingles are not too badly curled, apply a small amount of quick-setting roofing cement at the corners. A 1" diameter drop of roofing cement should be sufficient. Place it where it won't squeeze out from under the shingle.
2. Place a heavy object on top of the shingle being repaired. Make sure that it won't roll or slide off the roof. Try not to get the roofing cement on the heavy object holding the shingle down.

Patch Corroded Roof Flashing

SKILL LEVEL

2

TIME

6–10 h

Roof flashing is an integral part of a roofing system. The flashing is placed where water is most likely to meet an intersecting roof, wall, chimney, pipe, or vent.

If flashing is deteriorated, cracked, or has broken, the only thing you can do without removing layers of roofing is to patch it. If you don't have any experience, replacing it can be very difficult and possibly costly in later repairs. Roof flashing is made from aluminum or copper. The copper flashing is a much better product and can last a generation, if not more. Copper is more expensive than aluminum but well worth it if you plan on staying in your home.

1. Without harming any other part of the roof, clean the flashing with a sandpaper block or a light bristle wire brush.
2. Wipe down the flashing and clean away any debris.
3. Hammer flush any protruding nails.
4. Using a flat trowel or scraper, apply a coat of roof flashing cement. Make sure that the area is completely covered. Try to keep as straight a line as possible to give it a neat appearance.
5. Check other areas for any holes or other possible damage and apply the roof flashing cement.

Before beginning this project, check the weather. Forty-eight hours of clear weather should be forecasted before you start to do the repair. If the weather condition is unfavorable, purchase a heavy-duty tarp and cover the area so that water does not enter. Securely tie the tarp over the ridgeline (the highest part) so that water does not leak into the home and wind does not get under and pull it off.

Hector Hint

If you do not have or cannot find any roof flashing cement, a caulking gun and exterior silicone caulking can be used in its place. Be sure to push the caulking into any penetrations and to spread it over any deteriorated areas with a putty knife.

Insurance and Licenses

If you hire a roofer, make sure the contractor is licensed with the Department of Consumer Affairs in your state and has the proper liability and worker's compensation insurances. Roofs are very dangerous to work on. Even if you have friends that can do the job, make sure they have the proper paperwork. If they get hurt and are not properly insured, the liability can be yours, and that is where your friendship can easily end and the headaches begin.

These tasks do not require a great deal of skill nor a long time to perform, but the long-term effects and monetary burden, if not taken care of, can be significant.

Proper Cleaning and Drainage

Cleaning the envelope of your home and keeping rain water flowing away from it are vital elements in preventive maintenance. They are simple to do—and if done regularly—prolong the exterior life of your home for a very long time.

Project Worksheet

MONETARY RETURN: $1,000–$1,500

PROJECT START DATE: _____

TASKS COMPLETED: _____
_____
_____
_____
_____

TOOLS NEEDED:

- ❑ ¾" gravel (1 to 1 ½ yd. per 10')
- ❑ 3" or 4" perforated pipe (plastic)
- ❑ Brush with a long handle
- ❑ Bucket
- ❑ Caulking gun
- ❑ Drill
- ❑ Drill bit (size up the gutter nails so that the bit diameter is sufficient)
- ❑ Gloves
- ❑ Ground cover fabric
- ❑ Gutter nails
- ❑ Hammer
- ❑ Hose
- ❑ Ladder
- ❑ Pointed shovel
- ❑ Power washer
- ❑ Rain suit
- ❑ Stakes (enough to plot out the drainage area and trench)
- ❑ String level
- ❑ Tape measure
- ❑ Trowel
- ❑ Rags
- ❑ Safety goggles
- ❑ Sandpaper and block
- ❑ Scraper

Prepare Your Home for an Exterior Cleaning

SKILL LEVEL

2

TIME

2–3 h

Cleaning the exterior of a home is something that most do-it-yourselfers can attempt. Most home exteriors can be power-washed and the difference it makes is amazing—especially for those that have hardly ever (or never) been cleaned.

Readying the area where you'll be power-washing is a task in and of itself. It's a necessary precaution though, so be sure to follow the steps closely. Failing to take these steps to protect your property can cost you dearly later.

1. Check the windows and make sure they are closed and locked shut.
2. Know where the electric lines are coming into your home. Look around for any other high voltage lines that may be in close proximity to where you will be working. Be particularly cautious; these electrical lines can be extremely dangerous to you and others.
3. Check for anything on the exterior that may be painted. Power-washing can easily remove paint from exterior trim work around windows and doors.
4. Shutters and their parts can be loose without you even knowing about it. Check shutters and their parts for stability. Fasten and replace any loose or defective shutter parts before cleaning.
5. Cover bushes and plant life to prevent possible damage.
6. Replace broken or cracked panes of glass prior to beginning the task. If high-pressure water meets broken or cracked glass it can propel the glass like a rocket, making for a very dangerous condition.

Hector Hint   Don't try to perform this task on a windy day unless, of course, you want to take a shower.

The Cleaning Process

Start at the bottom and work your way up when cleaning, but when rinsing, start at the top and work your way down. By doing it this way, dirt will not run down and dry on another layer of grime. If you start at the top, by the time you get to the bottom, the dirt that runs down the siding can dry and cause streaking to occur. This can be difficult to remove and cause the project to take even longer to complete.

1. Become familiar with the power washer's operation. Beginning with the nozzle at a distance of 24" slowly decrease it to 12". Too much water pressure can damage your home's exterior surface, but by using common sense and good judgment, you can determine how much pressure to apply.

The angle of the water coming from the spray nozzle determines the power of the spray; the shorter the angle, the stronger the pressure. This is something you adjust as you become more familiar with the power washer.

2. Check around the house for areas that need a little extra help. Using a medium weight bristled brush and soapy water, scrub heavily soiled areas. Areas with mildew and mold should be cleaned with three parts water to one part bleach. For places that are tough, slowly increase the amount of bleach, as needed.

Hector Hint Cleaning acids are not recommended for the novice do-it-yourselfer; cleaning acids should only be handled by professionals.

3. Make sure to have a firm hold on the power-washer wand. Holding the wand with two hands is necessary, since the force of the water can cause you to lose your grip.
4. When power-washing, move your hand from side to side so that the wand is always moving and always the same distance from the

object you are cleaning. Keeping your hand in the same place and pivoting your wrist will cause the spray to be at different distances from the siding and will prevent uniform cleaning.

WORDS OF CAUTION

- A power-washer when pointed upward under siding can force the water pressure under it, ripping out the siding, allowing water to get behind, trapping it, and possibly allowing mold to grow.
- Holding a power-washer nozzle too close can damage the siding, wood, and possibly the brick mortar. Hold it away and slowly bring it closer until the dirt begins to wash off. Most of the time, you will not need to use detergent or bleach; the water from the power washer should be sufficient.
- Standing on a ladder while holding a power-washing wand can be dangerous. It is too easy to lose your balance. The force of the wand requires you to use both your hands to hold it steady.

Hector Hint

On brick or concrete block, a white matter can form called *efflorescence*. This substance is released from the minerals in the mortar between the brick or block. It is not dangerous and does not relate to a structural defect. The best way to clean this is to have a professional, using proper chemicals and protection, do the project of removing the efflorescence from the masonry.

DURATION OF TASK

The duration of this project is contingent on the type of material, the size of the area, the condition of the exterior, and how well it has been maintained. Use this timetable for every 100 sq. ft. area:

Vinyl Siding	10 to 15 minutes
Wood Siding	30 to 40 minutes
Masonry/Stucco	30 to 40 minutes

Diverting Water Away from Your Home

Water that gathers in a yard or against a house can lead to damaging drainage problems. Remove the puddles from occurring in your yard or next to your home by installing an inexpensive DIY drainage system.

A French drain (sometimes called a land drain) is simply a ditch with a 3" or 4" perforated pipe surrounded by ¾" gravel, directing surface and ground water away from a specific area to another. These systems prevent water from damaging a building's foundation, flooding the basement, or forming puddles around the exterior of the house. They are also used behind retaining walls to relieve saturated ground pressure.

Hector Hint

Many municipalities have a "Call before you dig" telephone number that homeowners and contractors should call prior to beginning any work. This service calls all the utilities in your area for you, saving you time and money. They also email or fax to you a log, should something happen (like hitting a line or pipe), confirming what utilities they notified that will verify that you took the proper steps. Compromising a utility line or your own septic system is extremely dangerous, can cost you thousands of dollars to fix, so take the appropriate steps and you will keep a few more dollars in your pocket.

Select an Area for Suitable Drainage

SKILL LEVEL

2

TIME

4–5 h

Keeping water away from your home is a standard building practice. However, some homeowners will find the standard is not always met. Back-pitched drainage can cause water to puddle around your foundation, eventually penetrating your foundation. Water problems due to inadequate drainage should be monitored regularly.

1. Try to locate an area away from your home where excess water currently drains. Judging a good drainage spot can be difficult if you don't own much land. If you're not sure of a good place, wait for rain to determine where the water naturally drains.

2. Once you locate an area where water can drain, plot it out. Using several small wood stakes, mark the outer boundaries of the area. If you have a survey available, make a copy, and on the copy draw in the area using the scale given on the survey. The scale is commonly found on the lower part of the survey, for example: 1" = 100'.
3. Next, contact your local utility companies to determine if they have any underground cables or pipes in the path or area, and let them know that you will soon be excavating.
4. If you have a septic system, contact your local health department. Most municipalities keep records of the contractor, the installation date, location of the tanks, and positioning of the leaching field.

Perfect the Pitch

SKILL LEVEL

3

TIME

6–10 h

This will likely take two full days.

Your drainage pipe needs to slope with a drop of 1' for every 100' in order to have enough of an incline for decent water flow. First you need to construct a level line:

1. Put two stakes into the ground, one at the beginning of the drain and one at the end.
2. Tie a string tightly to one end, and for now tie it off loosely on the other end.
3. Secure a line-level to the string, and fine-tune the string until the bubble of the level is between the marked level lines on the glass.
4. Tighten the string at the second stake.
5. Take the diameter of the pipe being used and add 8" to determine how wide to excavate the trench. You may need to over-excavate on the higher sides, in the shape of a V, depending on the depth and length of the trench, to help minimize the trench from caving in on you while you are working.
6. Begin digging your trench, making certain along the way that you're digging at the right depth. For example, if your drain is 100' long, it needs to be 6" deeper than the starting point by the 50' mark. Place several footage markers at different intervals so that it will be easier for you to establish a depth at a particular marker point.

Use this level line as a point to measure down from, determine the depth, and as a center line for the trench. Now you can set the pitch at the right level.

7. Before placing any gravel into the trench, line the trench with ground cover fabric. This helps to prevent any dirt from getting into the pipe, and clogging it. The object is for water to penetrate the fabric, seep through the gravel, run along the bottom of the pipe, and percolate into the stone and soil.

8. After the fabric is down, put down a ¾" layer of gravel along the length of the trench.

9. Place the pipe in the trench making sure it is pitched properly.

10. Shovel more gravel around the pipe. Be careful not to put too much in.
11. Wrap the ends of the fabric over the top of the gravel layer creating a tube.
12. Add 4" of topsoil and sod and your French drain is complete.

The damage done from standing water can be devastating to the structure of a home. It causes rot, deteriorates the foundation, can cause an environmental hazard, and attract unwanted insects. You can build a French drain by yourself, but if you are uncertain, you can hire a professional engineer to determine where to put your French drain for optimal effectiveness, or hire a professional to install the entire system.

Cleaning and Repairing Leaders and Gutters

A leader and gutter system is a very simple but important part of a home. The gutters are the part of the system that collects the water along the edges of the roof and the leader is the vertical component of the system that carries the water down the side of the house and away from the foundation. Keeping the gutters clean and the leaders from backing up can prevent water getting up under the roof shingle, entering through the fascia, and getting behind the siding. This will avoid water damage to the ceilings, walls, and floors of your home.

One way to help prevent your gutters from becoming clogged is to install gutter leaf guards. These leaf guards are installed on the top of the gutter and allow the leaves to flow over the gutter and off the roof, while the gutter collects water. Gutter guards are an easy do-it-yourself project, but only if you aren't afraid of heights. You can purchase gutter guards at a home center or your local hardware store.

The purpose of a gutter system is to capture rainwater on the roof. Water that is allowed to accumulate along the perimeter of a home can damage the structural integrity of a foundation, causing the soil to erode, and moisture and mold to infiltrate the basement. The purpose of a leader is to direct the flow of water away from the home. Letting the water accumulate around the foundation can eventually cause the soil to erode around the perimeter and back pitch it in the direction of the foundation.

What are some of the problems that can hamper the proper operation of a leader and gutter system?

- Gutters and leaders can become obstructed, causing the gutter to overflow.
- In colder climates, ice can form in the leader and gutter, causing an ice dam to occur and water to back up under the shingles and into the home.
- Gutters can become back pitched, not allowing the water to flow properly into the leaders, and in due time, creating spillover.
- The spillover can eventually lead to mildew growth on the side of the house.
- Weight from ice, snow, leaves, branches, and debris can weaken the gutter and loosen the nails attaching it to the home, causing it to detach from the house and eventually fall off.

Hector Hint

Gutters are sized according to the square foot area of the roof.

- A gutter can leak where it meets and seams with another gutter.
- Downspouts can also leak and cause water to pool around the foundation.
- It is not out of the ordinary for a falling branch to knock off a gutter, as well as damage the roof.
- The water flowing from the downspouts can erode the soil.

Clear Your Gutters

The purpose of a leader and gutter system is to direct water away from your home. Water can saturate wood siding, concrete, and masonry, finding the area of least resistance to infiltrate.

A clogged leader and gutter system defeats the purpose and renders it useless. Keeping them clean is a preventive maintenance task that should be done on a regular basis. If trees are near your house, the gutters may need to be cleaned seasonally.

1. Lean a ladder against the house at the lowest point of the roof. If the ladder is leaning on the gutter, use a ladder stabilizer (this can be purchased at your local hardware store or home improvement center) or you can also wedge a 2" × 4" into the gutter to stop it from collapsing. Some gutters are made of a thicker gauge than others and can sustain the pressure, but it is better to be sure. Do this task while holding on to the ladder. Performing this task from the roof is not advisable. It is easy to loose your balance and fall over the edge of the roof.

2. If there are leaf guards installed on the gutters, use a pair of thick rubber gloves and remove any leaves, twigs, branches, or debris that can disrupt water flow.

3. If there is dirt and debris in the gutter, remove the leaf guards. If the roof pitch is not too steep, place the gutter guards on the roof, directly above where you remove them.

4. Remove the debris from the gutters. While doing this, inspect the gutters and make note of puddles and where any debris has been gathering, that may cause it to dam up.

Hector Hint	A power nozzle is inexpensive and can be purchased at your local hardware or home improvement center.

5. If there isn't much debris, hose the gutter debris toward the leader drain. Use a hose with a power nozzle, a gutter-cleaning wand, or a power washer.

6. Look down the leader and remove any debris that is lodged in it. Point the hose, power washer, or gutter-cleaning wand down the leader to wash away debris that may later cause it to become blocked.
7. Replace the gutter guards and carefully remove the ladder.

A common problem with gutters is a leaky seam where two gutters meet. Seamless gutters are now common, eliminating the possibility of a leak occurring at the seam.

Repair Gutter Seams

SKILL LEVEL

1

TIME

2–3 h

Occasionally, water can be seen dripping from a hole or crack in a gutter. Fixing a leaky gutter is a fairly simple task. The hardest part of repairing a gutter, for most, is climbing the ladder.

1. Using a rag, clean the area that needs to be patched both inside and outside of the gutter. Make sure that both sides are perfectly dry.
2. Use a caulking gun apply clear silicone to the inside and outside of the gutter. Try not to cause an obstruction with the silicone on the inside of the gutter.
3. Smooth it out on both sides and wipe any excess off. This procedure can also be done if there is a crack in the gutter.

Do not perform this task in extreme cold or if there is rain in the forecast.

Repair a Hole in the Gutter

SKILL LEVEL

1

TIME

1 h

If you can handle a pair of snips, you can repair a hole in your gutter. Yep, it's that simple.

1. Cut a flat piece of aluminum flashing. Make sure that it is a little larger than the hole.
2. Clean the area inside and outside the gutter.
3. Press and shape the flat aluminum flashing, shaping it to match the gutter.

4. Apply clear silicone to the area around the hole and press.
5. Wipe off any excess silicone.

Complete this project when there is dry weather and no chance of rain for at least twenty-four hours.

<table>
<tr><td>**Hector Hint**</td><td>When placing a ladder against a house, the base of the ladder should not be less than or exceed ¼ of its length away from the house.</td></tr>
</table>

Re-nail a Standard Gutter

SKILL LEVEL

1

TIME

1 h

After time, gutter spikes can become loose and cause the gutter to sag, collecting water and dirt. Re-nailing the spikes into the same hole doesn't usually work very well; a new nailing area is necessary for the spike to hold. However, there are certain procedures that need to be followed so that the gutter is not destroyed in the process.

1. Remove the old nail. Wedge a 2" × 4" × 6" piece of lumber into the gutter and place the claw of the hammer around the head of the nail, lightly applying pressure to remove it. If the gutter is hanging it probably won't take much effort. If it is difficult to remove, it may be able to hold and you might be able to nail it back in with a longer spike.
2. Do not use the same hole to replace a nail. Use a drill to make a new hole in the gutter approximately 1" from the previous hole.
3. Place a nail sleeve inside of the gutter and put the nail through the hole.
4. Before nailing, check the pitch with a level so that it follows the angle of pitch for better water flow.
5. When you are sure it is right, drive the nail into place.

Gutters for residential homes are normally 4" or 6". If you find that water is a problem and there are no known obstructions, you may need to have an expert in to physically assess the problem.

Proper Masonry and Foundation Maintenance

Masonry and concrete are generally quite strong, yet still vulnerable to water, freezing rain, settlement, and other forces of Mother Nature. Being proactive in the repair of these materials will help you to keep your sanity and a few extra dollars in your bank account.

Project Worksheet

MONETARY RETURN: $1,500–$2,500

PROJECT START DATE: _____

TASKS COMPLETED: _____
_____
_____
_____
_____

TOOLS NEEDED:

- ❑ Binoculars
- ❑ Caulking gun
- ❑ Cold chisel
- ❑ Dust mask
- ❑ Flashlight
- ❑ Goggles
- ❑ Hammer
- ❑ Ladder or scaffolding
- ❑ Level
- ❑ Mason's trowel (triangular shape)
- ❑ Mixing tub
- ❑ Stiff brush
- ❑ Thin wire brush

When's the Right Time?

The spring, summer, and early fall are the best times of the year to do any work on the exterior of your home, especially masonry work. The exterior of your home takes a real beating from the heat, sun, freezing temperatures, wind, snow, and rain. All of these issues have an impact, one way or another, and some are harsher than others. There are constant changes to the exterior atmosphere during the day and night that affect the exterior envelope of our homes 24 hours a day, 365 days a year. This should cause us to make sure that periodically we review the condition of the exterior of our homes.

The Process of Pointing

Pointing is the process of removing (also known as raking) approximately ½" to ¾" of worn and loose mortar joints and replacing them with fresh mortar. Driving rain, wind, age, and temperature changes can weaken the joints, taking the strength of the mortar out and only leaving the sand. The mortar can be deteriorated to the point where nothing is left but sand and it can actually be removed by raking your finger across it. At this stage, the only thing holding the brick in place is the weight of the brick above.

Mix Mortar

SKILL LEVEL

1

TIME

1 h

Mixing mortar is a simple but very important part of doing masonry work. A consistent mortar mix will ensure that the mortar adheres properly and that strength is maintained for a long period of time.

1. Pour ¼ bag of masonry pre-mix into the mixing tub.
2. Using a shovel, work the mix into the shape of a volcano. This will help you to determine the ratio of water to mix.
3. Take the bucket of water and slowly pour it into the center of the form.

4. Moving the outside of the mix toward the middle and into the water, mix it until the consistency is a little heavier than oatmeal. Having too watery of a mix will become messy when applying to joints.

Mixing the mortar to this consistency will do for repairing defective joints in block, as well. Block foundation joints are flush and not tooled like brick joints and take away from the properties that give it strength.

Hector Hint	When mixing the mortar, mix just enough for the area you are pointing and to a thick creamy consistency. Do not make it loose or it will run off and create a mess.

Tuck-Pointing

Tuck-pointing is the task of replacing old worn mortar with a new, stronger mix. In order to apply a new mixture, the old mortar will need to be removed and the area to receive it will need to be cleaned.

1. Set the ladder or scaffolding in the work area, making sure it is secure and stable.
2. Put on your goggles, gloves, and dust mask.
3. Using a cold chisel and hammer, remove the loose mortar. Chisel out at least ½" to ¾" of mortar below the face of the brick.
4. Dip the wire brush into the bucket of water and brush out any loose debris. The water will help to make the mortar adhere better to the masonry and existing mortar.
5. Using the mason's trowel, scoop up enough mortar for ½ of a mortar joint and place it up to the joint. Take the pointing tool and push the mortar off the trowel and into the joint.
6. Smooth out the mortar with the pointing tool and move on to the next area.

When Is It Time to Rebuild?

If you see a section of loose brick, have a mason remove the section. If the old brick cannot be used, then it will have to be matched as close as possible and the section will need to be rebuilt. This is a common occurrence in chimney repair. The top of the chimney is vulnerable to age, wear and tear, and water will freeze in the cracks and cause more water to penetrate making the condition worsen every time it thaws and refreezes. In the colder months this happens daily. Water can get far enough down to crack the flue liner, which then allows fumes to enter the home, making for a potentially life-threatening problem.

Another common problem is when gutters back up or the leaders leak onto the exterior of your home. This can cause water to overflow and the continuous effect of washing up against an area will wear out the mortar and discolor the masonry. Repairing your leader and gutter or having them replaced will solve that problem.

Lintels support the masonry above the doors and windows and occasionally need to be maintained or replaced. A lintel is a steel or concrete support above a window or door opening. A steel lintel should be painted and free from rust. If the steel is riddled with rust and flaking, it is time to have it replaced. An experienced mason contractor will need to safely change it out if it is structurally unsound.

If cracks are visible on a concrete lintel it is time to replace it.

Another sign that there may be a problem is when cracks have formed in the joints of the brick, or worse, when a crack splits a brick. They are noticed, at times, above windows and doors. Sometimes these are caused by the settling of a home (which is a common occurrence) or, in some cases, they can be caused by something more serious.

If sagging is obvious above an opening, a more serious problem could be in the making and should be immediately addressed.

Monitor these cracks and if you see them getting longer or wider have a professional take a look at them. The best way to find a reputable contractor is through references who have had a pleasant experience with a contractor and found his or her work to be satisfactory and professional.

Hector Hint

Although the look of ivy growing on a home has a particular old-world feel, the ivy weakens the mortar joints and makes it difficult to determine the condition of the brick and mortar holding your home together. Many homeowners do not notice these affected areas, and allow them to expand year after year. Unfortunately, notice is not taken until water infiltration or a major structural problem occurs, costing thousands of dollars in unexpected repairs, aggravation, and inconvenience.

Seal Up and Secure Your Foundation

Water infiltration through a foundation is a common event, more often happening in older homes or where water flows toward your foundation, saturating the surrounding soil. After time, water can enter between cracks in the foundation or from under the concrete slab. Settling and age can also contribute to the penetration of water, further causing mold and mildew to develop.

Look for signs of:

- Crumbling of interior foundation paint
- Water marks on the walls
- Cracks in the foundation
- Cracks below and above windows and doors
- Eroding mortar joints
- The smell of mildew

When possible, correct problems on the outside of the foundation first. Doing this will diminish the possibility of water absorption into the foundation, and of additional lateral pressure being exerted on the foundation, and allows any wet areas inside to dry prior to working on them.

Seal Your Stone, Brick, or Block Foundation

SKILL LEVEL

3

TIME

6–10 h

A porous foundation, cracks, and worn mortar joints are all places where water can penetrate a foundation, causing it to weaken, a basement to flood, or a possible environmental problem, like mold.

1. Using a flashlight if needed, examine the foundation for signs of damage from the inside.
2. If you find water penetration inside, define an area of reference in order to inspect the outside of the foundation for any possible signs of entry. A shovel may be needed to dig below grade (below the top of the soil) and locate the point of entry.
3. If the point of entry is above the ground, continue to step five.
4. Assuming it is below grade, dig out the area exposing the void, so that you can comfortably work.
5. Clean the area using a stiff brush and remove any loose mortar and debris.
6. Using pre-mixed mortar, mix an amount enough to fill the voids found.
7. Fill in any poor joints, cracks, or holes and make the mortar joint flush with the foundation wall.
8. Making note of the drying time, allow the mortar ample time to dry.
9. Once the mortar is dry, apply a generous amount of foundation flashing, using a trowel.
10. Apply and secure foundation membrane over the area, trowel on another coat of foundation flashing over the membrane, and smoothe it out.
11. Carefully put back the earth and make sure to pitch it away from the foundation.

Hector Hint	Make sure all possible cracks are thoroughly sealed and that the smallest of areas are addressed. Continual freezing and thawing will enlarge small cracks over time.

A bowing in a foundation wall and a widening of horizontal cracks could mean there is lateral pressure from the earth, weakening the foundation wall. This can be due to improper construction methods or a poor design. A structural engineer is recommended to provide you with a scope of work (guideline for removal and repair) for the situation.

Cracks in a concrete foundation need to be tackled in a different manner than stone, brick, or block foundations. In the previous project I discussed using mortar to bond stone, brick, and block together, but expandable concrete is used to repair problems in concrete foundations. Expandable cement expands and seals water out, whereas regular cement shrinks. Although cement shrinkage is not necessarily visible, it can allow water to penetrate.

Seal a Concrete Foundation Crack

SKILL LEVEL

3

TIME

6–10 h

A thin crack in a concrete foundation is enough to allow water to enter a home. Although it may seem like a difficult job, a little patience and elbow grease can seal this problem up.

1. Put on work gloves and safety goggles.
2. Use a cold chisel to cut an inverted V along the crack, making the narrowest part at the face of the foundation.
3. Mix a small amount of expandable cement.
4. If it is a vertical crack, start at the bottom and use a mason's trowel to apply the expandable cement into the crack. Make sure it is well compacted. The inverted V will stop the expandable cement from coming out when it expands.
5. Scrape off any excess, leaving the cement flush with the walls of the foundation.

Do the joints of the block line up or are they shifting apart? Foundation settling is normal to an extent, but when a foundation continues to settle and the cracks continue to get wider, it could be the result of a weakening and shifting below the foundation; a declining state of mortar between the stone, block, or brick; or lateral bowing caused by the commanding pressure of the earth and/or uneven settling in the foundation sometimes caused by an underground stream or unstable soil. In this case, it may require a structural engineer to monitor the condition and make the necessary recommendations for repair.

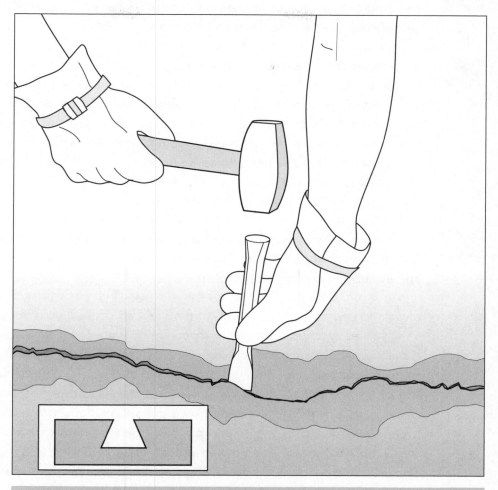

Do not be afraid to use some force when working the chisel into the concrete.

Check Your Concrete Slab

SKILL LEVEL

3

TIME

1 h
for 5' length

Concrete slabs are part of a foundation and need to be inspected occasionally. Areas where cracks sometime develop are where column supports or pipes penetrate the slab. To help correct the problem:

1. Cut an inverted V with a chisel.
2. Fill the crack with expandable cement as you would with a crack in a concrete foundation. The cement will expand, filling the void and sealing the crack. (A silicone sealant can seal the crack, but can shift with any movement, disguising a possible problem. A rigid cementitious sealant, however, is more probable to crack again, exposing a potentially more serious problem.)

Look at the concrete slab in your basement. Check for signs of heaving. This can be a sign of a high water table, exerting upward pressure. The joint between the foundation wall and concrete slab is an area of least resistance and a likely place of water infiltration.

An underground stream or a broken sewer line that is eroding the soil away and carrying the dirt through the line can cause a void under a slab. This is fixed by chopping out the concrete at the area of the broken pipe, repairing it, backfilling the soil, and patching the concrete. If you are subject to a high water table, getting a professional opinion will help to determine the cause and the solution. Relieving the pressure with a sump pit, sump pump, and a French drain system is a common solution to a high water table. When water fills the sump pit, it triggers a flow-switch that pumps the water out through the pitched French drain and away from the home. The French drain pipe has perforations that will also carry water by gravity through the line.

Be sure to get comparable pricing (at least three estimates), and local references from the contractor. If extreme damage is visible, a structural engineer may need to be consulted to provide a solution and some may be able to refer contractors to remedy the situation. If the engineer also provides the contracting, make it a point that he or she breaks down the cost of providing a scope of work and the contracting. This will allow you to get other contracting prices and be able to compare.

In the winter months, the warming of daytime air and freezing temperatures in the evening constantly force cracks to become larger until the structure or foundation is too weak to sustain the weight. The structural integrity of these foundations and structures themselves become undermined, begin to crumble, and can cost homeowners thousands of dollars to repair.

When you have a wall bowing or pulling away from the main structure, look at the beams and joists, and check to see if they are securely resting on the foundation. A wood beam or joist should be bearing on at least 3" of the foundation wall, whereas steel and stone should bear a minimum of 6".

PART II

Your Home's Interior

4   5   6   7   8   9   10   11

Doors, Locks, and Hinges

Doors, locks, and hinges serve more than one function in a home. Safety is their primary purpose and aesthetics is their secondary responsibility. They can be visually appealing, making a statement with their style, color, and finish. However, doors and their hardware take quite a bit of abuse and should be regularly maintained in order to avoid costly repairs. Simple maintenance and quick changes to doors can refresh a home and add to its interior and exterior appeal. If you're open to the idea of working with the doors in your home, read on to secure some additional value.

Project Worksheet

MONETARY RETURN: $750–$1,000 *This estimate is based on an average size home.*

PROJECT START DATE: _____

TASKS COMPLETED: _____
_____
_____
_____
_____

TOOLS NEEDED:

- ❏ #8 common nails
- ❏ Drill
- ❏ Drill bit (check the slotted hole for the size)
- ❏ Drywall nails
- ❏ Drywall saw
- ❏ Drywall screws
- ❏ Extension cord
- ❏ Flathead screw driver
- ❏ Hammer
- ❏ Handsaw or circulating saw
- ❏ Ladder
- ❏ Level
- ❏ Masking tape
- ❏ Measuring tape
- ❏ Pencil
- ❏ Phillips head screw driver
- ❏ Pry bar
- ❏ Rags
- ❏ Reciprocating saw
- ❏ Sandpaper
- ❏ Screw gun
- ❏ Screws
- ❏ Small block plane
- ❏ Stud finder

- ❏ Taping knife
- ❏ Utility knife
- ❏ Wood chisel

Doors Leave Quite an Impression

Take a look around and see what is available. There are many different types of doors: raised panels, flat panels, and many diverse configurations. There are various doors that have half moon panels; some are detailed with square panels; some doors contain unusual detail to the panels. The choices are many and so are the prices.

Deciding on how to trim a door can be a challenge because styles vary dramatically, and can make a world of difference in the look of your home. There are many beautiful ways to decorate around your doors. You can have a thick colonial 3½" casing with a beautiful plain or an ornate crosshead which looks like crown molding over the top of the door.

DOOR PROBLEMS

Once a door is warped, it is impossible to correct. There isn't much you can do to un-warp a door. In fact, it is usually easier and faster to change out the entire frame and door by ordering a pre-hung door than to change a door without the frame. It will also cost you less for the installation.

If a door swings by the force of gravity, then you probably have a problem with the way the door was installed. The edge of the door should be within 3/16" of the doorjamb (the jamb is the frame holding the door in place) and parallel from top to bottom. It should not swing open or close by the force of gravity. That means it is out of plumb. The door and frame will need to be reinstalled.

There may be other reasons, more serious, that cause you to have problems with doors not closing or swinging by gravity. If there are any sagging beams or rotted posts in your home, this may be the cause and should be inspected. If you are not sure what to look for, have a professional inspect the situation for you.

Unstick Sticky Doors

SKILL LEVEL

1

TIME

2–3 h

Swelling can cause doors to hit or rub against the doorjambs, scraping the paint off the door and jamb. It can also cause the doors to not latch properly. Follow these few simple tricks to remedy this problem in no time.

1. Take a flat piece of wood, place it against the inside of the frame where the door is rubbing, and gently tap it with a hammer. Continue to hit it and check it until the frame allows the door to close properly.
2. Once the door closes, check that it latches. If the door does not latch, the strike plate will need adjustment. To make this correction, see: So, the Strike Won't Latch (page 101).
3. If the door still rubs on the jamb, it will be necessary to plane it. Mark the door where it was rubbing.
4. Remove the door.

REMOVING THE DOOR

1. Using a nail and hammer, place the nail in the hole under the hinge.
2. Tap the nail with the hammer, which will pop the hinge pin up.
3. Pull the hinge out from the top.
4. Repeat for the second hinge (and third hinge if there is one). Be sure someone or something is bracing the door so it does not fall over once all the hinge pins are removed. Carefully remove the door.

5. Straddling the door and using a block plane, plane the door from the outer edge in, but going with the grain where the door was marked. Make it a point not to take off too much. You do not want to plane a gully into the door's edge.
6. Reinstall the door and check its alignment. Also check to make sure that the lock and the strike plate are not hitting.

Remedy a Problem Bi-fold Door

Bi-fold pivot hardware has a habit of becoming loose. This causes the doors to come off the pivot and fall. On occasion, the pivot will slide and the door will rub against the wall closest to the pivot, damaging the drywall or wood jamb.

Adjustments can be made to the pivots on the bi-fold doors or on the tracks. If the pivots on the door and track are not lined up properly or are loose, that could cause them to come out of the pivot frequently.

1. Remove the screw on the track holding the pivot.
2. With a sharpened pencil, mark where the setscrew should be positioned.
3. Using a bit, drill a hole for a longer setscrew. If the setscrew cannot be removed, drill on both sides of the pivot to stop it from going back and forth.
4. Slide the pivot back into place and set the screws(s).

Do this wherever the pivot gets loose.

Are Pocket Doors Rubbing You the Wrong Way?

A pocket door is a door that slides into the wall and saves space by not having to swing into a room. These doors can normally be found in older homes, since they are more expensive to purchase and install.

The problem that sometimes occurs with a pocket door is that the 2" × 4" framing members in the pocket are flat against the wall and not on edge, as normally done when a wall is framed. Framing lumber is kept outside in the lumberyard and when transported is exposed to moisture on flatbed train cars. Having soaked up moisture because of exposure, they begin to dry out during the first heating season inside a home, which can lead to shrinking and then warping.

Pocket doors commonly rub against the framing members or stick and come off the tracks. If the 2" × 4"s are warped, the only thing left to do is to remove the door to get to the heart of the problem.

1. Using a utility knife, carefully cut along the caulked edges of the door trim and the wall. By not cutting between the trim and wall, the caulk can pull the paper and paint off the wall.
2. Use a small pry bar to remove the door trim. Do this very carefully so that you don't crack the trim and so that the trim can be reused.
3. The next step is to take the door off the track. Disconnect the door from the rollers or roll the door to the edge and remove the rollers, along with the door, from the track.
4. Inspect the door to see on what side and where it has been rubbing. There should be a worn horizontal area on the door.
5. If you can, try getting your hand and a small plane in the opening to shave down the area on the 2" × 4" where you think the problem is occurring.
6. If planing the 2" × 4" does not work, you will need to remove the wall to repair the problem. Removing the wall to get at the problem may be beyond your capabilities. If so, you can hire a local carpenter or repairperson to complete the task.

Hector Hint

Pocket doors can be adjusted for height where the rollers attach to the door. Although some come with a special tool, a pair of pliers should be able to do the job.

Rollers are meant to last for a long time, but sometimes a lack of lubrication can shorten their lifespan, causing them to wear prematurely. Make sure when you go to the hardware store or home improvement center that you take a sample with you. There are also door hardware stores online. Search Google for "pocket door hardware."

Adjust a Storm Door

SKILL LEVEL

1

TIME

1 h

Your screen door is probably the most abused door in your home. A storm door swings open and closed anywhere from ten to one hundred times per day. Taking the beating it does, it shouldn't surprise you if it is in need of repair, adjustment, or replacement.

Some storm doors have screens that permit fresh air to flow throughout your home in warmer weather. During the colder time of year, fixed and moveable glass allow these doors to provide additional protection from cold air infiltration and loss of heat.

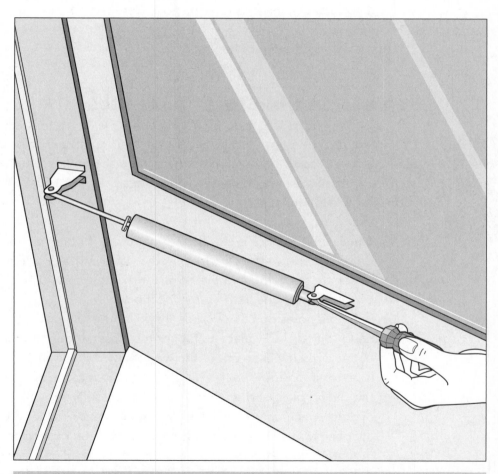

The adjustment is simply made with a screwdriver to fine-tune the tension on the door. It's that easy and fast.

1. Adjust the existing closer to see if this is all that is needed prior to replacing the existing one. These closers look like a 12" tube that connects the door to the frame, and can be located at the top, middle, or bottom of a storm door. Heavier storm doors may require two closers. Over time, they can become less operable and the tension can cause screw holes to wear out.

2. Closers have adjustment screws that can tighten or loosen the pressure on the door. Most closers have + and − signs to indicate the direction of adjustment to obtain the amount of tension required. If you want to slow the speed of your door closing, turn toward the +. If you want to make your door close faster, turn toward the −.

If that doesn't do the job then read on.

Replace an Old Storm Door Closer

SKILL LEVEL

3

TIME

2–3 h

After years of use, storm door closers lose their compression and do not close the door properly. When this happens a replacement is required. These storm door closers can be purchased at your local hardware store. The installation is simple and neat.

1. Make sure the door is closed and that there is no tension on it.
2. Carefully remove the old closer. If the holes in the door for the old closer are still good and the holes for the new closer line up, just install the new one in the same location.
3. If the old holes don't line up or are no longer any good, you will need to find a new place to mount the closer. Mount it on the top of the door. It will be out of the way of any child's hand. If there is no room on top, see if it will mount in the middle. Because of the sliding glass and screens, it is sometimes hard to put it in the middle, which only leaves the bottom of the door. Due to the lack of space anywhere else on the door, I have seen many closers mounted on the bottom.

4. Once you have found a spot to put it, you will need to mount the brackets on the door and doorjamb, while the door is closed and latched.
5. Make sure the closer itself is straight and level. Using the torpedo level (some have magnets attached), position the closer and brackets and mark where the holes will need to go.
6. After the holes are marked, remove the closer from the brackets by removing the pins that hold them together.
7. Drill the holes with the appropriate size drill bit (check the screw size). A little smaller is better for this type job. When you drill the door, make sure not to drill all the way through and come out the other side.
8. Once the brackets are in place, fit the closer back into the brackets and attach it to the brackets by sliding the pins back down and in place.
9. Now, adjust the closer so the door doesn't swing too fast or too slow, but just right.

Taking Care of Your Locksets and Hinges

Locksets play a vital function in a home and, if not maintained, can be an unnecessary expense repeated over and over and cost you time and money. However, these issues can easily be avoided with proper maintenance. The steps for maintaining your door locks are easy and quick to do.

Lubricate the Locks in Your Home

SKILL LEVEL

1

TIME

1 h

Performing these tasks once a year will prolong the life of the locksets and prevent you or someone in your home from possibly becoming locked out, or worse, in an emergency, locked in. Having an easy way in or out can mean the difference between being safe or at risk.

1. With the long spray tube on the nozzle of a graphite lubricant can, carefully spray the strike (the part of the lock that keeps your door from opening) on the outside.
2. Turning the doorknob so that the strike is inside of the door, lubricate it while turning the knob several times. This will ensure that the lubricant is worked into the mechanism.
3. Wipe any excess off the door and lockset. Spraying too much can get messy. A short spray is sufficient to do the job.

Adjust the Lockset

SKILL LEVEL

1

TIME

1 h

Sometimes a simple thing like a loose screw can stop a lockset from operating properly or at all. Periodically checking that all the screws are tight will help to ensure that access in and out of doors is possible and give you an opportunity to make sure the rest of the locksets are functioning the way they should.

1. Check the doorknobs to make sure they are snug and not flimsy. Fixing a loose doorknob can just be a matter of tightening the screws. If there is an emergency and the knob is not properly secured, you can have a problem getting in or out.
2. Adjust the knob and faceplate before tightening the screws. Make sure that the faceplate and knob are properly aligned with the lock.
3. When the latch retracts and releases easily, tighten the screws for the knob and faceplate.

Lubricate Key Cylinders

SKILL LEVEL

1

TIME

1 h

The most important thing you do before you step foot inside your home is to put the key in the lock and turn the handle. What if you can't get your key out? How about breaking the key inside the cylinder, because you can't turn the key to open the door, or you can't get the key out, or the knob comes off when you try to open the door? Well, these are just a few of the things that do happen and can happen, but can also be avoided.

1. Locksmiths consider graphite a good lubricant for cylinders, so a pencil can be used to lubricate a key cylinder. Since lead poses a health threat, graphite is now used in pencils instead. Rub a pencil along the notched and smooth edges of your key and put the key into the cylinder, repeating this several times. The graphite from the pencil will lubricate the cylinder, preventing it from jamming or your key from being stuck.
2. From the inside of the door, using a screwdriver, remove the screws holding the faceplate of the thumb latch.
3. Expose the interior latch mechanism and neatly spray it with silicone. Remove any excess spray from the face of the door.
4. Replace the cylinder and cover plates and tighten the screws.

Whenever using a graphite spray, be sure to use it sparingly and have a rag to wipe off the excess overspray.

So, the Strike Won't Latch . . .

SKILL LEVEL

2

TIME

1 h

When a home settles it will sometimes throw off the alignment of the latch and strike of a door. A simple solution is to realign the door strike with the latch, allowing the door to latch and remain in the closed position.

1. Remove the two screws holding the strike plate in place, and remove the strike plate.
2. Slowly closing the door, look at the correlation of where the strike and the strike hole align. With a pencil, mark the top and bottom of where the strike on the door aligns with the frame and the strike hole.
3. Using a wood chisel, chisel out the space needed to align the strike hole with the strike.
4. Use masking tape on the top and bottom to hold the strike plate in place.
5. Close the door to see if the strike latches. If it doesn't, repeat the task.

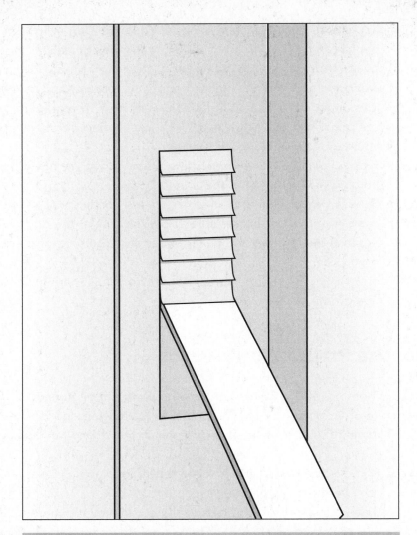

Work slowly with the chisel. It's better to chisel away too little than too much.

Hector Hint

So that the screws don't cave in, fill the old holes with wood splinters and glue, and let them dry.

Silence Door Hinges

So, you think you're not going to wake anyone up . . . then you open a door and the hinges give a horrible creak and now the baby's crying, the kids are up, all heck is breaking loose—and all you wanted was a glass of water. Here is a simple solution to your problem.

1. Close the door and latch it. Doing one hinge at a time, place a nail under the hinge, hammer it up and pop the hinge pin out.
2. Lightly spray inside both leaves of the hinge and the pin itself. Be careful not to overspray.
3. Immediately wipe off any excess from the hinges and the door.
4. Replace the hinge pin by tapping it back into place. Swing the door back and forth to ensure that it is lubricated.

Keep the Doorknobs Uniform

When trying to make your home attractive, having three or four different doorknobs on your doors is not visually comforting. Charm, symmetry, and order make a home appealing. Having different locksets, like a glass doorknob, a chrome knob, a brass knob, and a nickel knob, doesn't add any character and gives the home an inconsistency to its design. Keeping your knob choice consistent is not an expensive task, and one you can do yourself.

Changing or replacing a doorknob is a simple task:

1. Match the knob with the manufacturer of the lockset. To find out who the manufacturer is, look on the edge of the door at the strike part of the lockset. The stamped name of the manufacturer can normally be found there. Once identified, visit the manufacturer's website or your local hardware store to choose one of their knobs.
2. Find the setscrew and determine what type of screwdriver you will need. Some of the newer type knobs have a pin that can easily be pushed in with a screwdriver allowing you to easily remove the knob. Older homes may have knobs that screw on to the stem (the shaft that the knob is attached to).

3. Once you have removed the old knob, simply install the new knob reversing the actions you took to remove the old one.

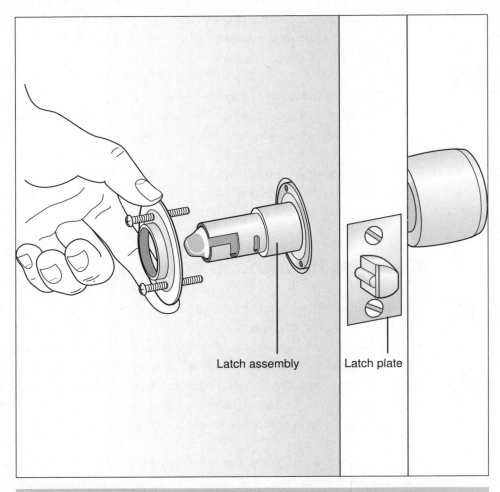

Latch assembly   Latch plate

Be careful not to misplace any of the pieces of the new doorknob during your assembly.

Hector Hint   If you go online, you may be able to find doorknobs that you can buy from the manufacturer, costing you less because you eliminated the intermediary.

Clean a Gummed Lockset

SKILL LEVEL

3

TIME

1 h

Over time, locksets can either stick or become difficult to unlock or open even after they are lubricated. They can become gummed with dirt and dust and lubricating them just isn't enough.

1. Remove any screws holding the strike mechanism and the door-knobs in place.
2. Remove the strike mechanism by pulling it out from the edge of the door.
3. Using a rag and light machine oil, rub down the mechanism and all other interior moving parts.
4. Use a cotton swab dipped in oil to get into the hard-to-reach places and remove any gummy residue that is preventing the lockset from operating freely. Push the strike in and out. This will allow you to test it and loosen it.
5. With a dry rag, wipe off any excess oil.
6. Replace the strike mechanism, the doorknobs, and the screws.
7. Lubricate the interior mechanisms before replacing the knobs.

This task should take no more than fifteen minutes. The amount of time will vary depending on the quantity of doors in a home, the type of locksets, and their condition. Most of the time, any needed adjustment on a lock is minor.

Windows

Windows are the perfect way to let the outside in. A home's windows provide light to brighten rooms, warmth on a sunny day, and a breath of fresh air when opened. However, inefficient and poorly cared for windows can be a drain on your home's energy (and mean an increase in your bills) as well as a poor reflection on your home's upkeep if they are dingy or broken. Completing the tasks covered in this chapter will keep your windows in the best shape possible.

Project Worksheet

MONETARY RETURN: $1,000–$1,500

PROJECT START DATE: _____

TASKS COMPLETED: _____

_____

_____

_____

_____

TOOLS NEEDED:

- ❑ Flathead screwdriver
- ❑ Hose
- ❑ Ladder
- ❑ Long-nose pliers
- ❑ Masking tape (½" roll)
- ❑ Permanent marker
- ❑ Power washer
- ❑ Scissors
- ❑ Silicone spray lubricant
- ❑ Spline roller
- ❑ Utility knife
- ❑ Vacuum and hose

Replace a Broken Screen

A broken screen can happen for any number of reasons. It can be the result of your dog's hot pursuit of the neighbor's cat, your kids horsing around, or when someone in your household forgets his key and works his way through the screen to open the window. There's no need to buy a new screen; you can easily repair the one you have.

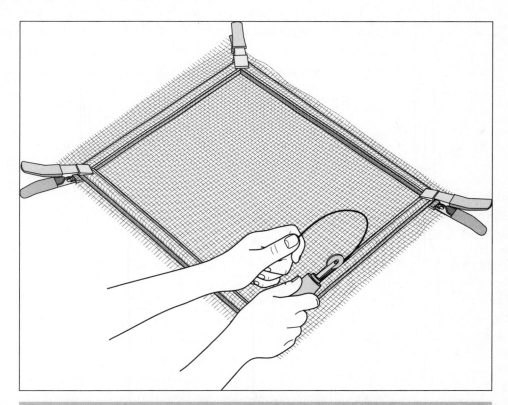

Clamps help to keep the screen in place during your repair.

1. Remove the old screen by finding the end of the vinyl spline. This is the gasket in the groove of the frame that holds the screen in place. Once you have located the end, take your screwdriver and pry out the end.

2. Use long-nose pliers to remove the rest of the spline. If the spline is in good condition and not dry rotted, you can use it again. Once you remove the entire spline, the screen can easily be removed.
3. Place the new screen fabric over the frame and cut a piece along the outside edge of the frame.
4. Cut the screen fabric diagonally across the outside groove where you plan to begin installing the vinyl spline.
5. Using the spline roller, push and roll the spline and screen into place, making sure to stretch the screen into the spline groove of the frame.
6. Cut the excess screen with a pair of scissors or a utility knife.

Once you complete this task on one screen, the others will be much easier.

Most hardware stores repair screens and will charge you a small fee to put a new screen in the frame for you.

Clean Your Screens

This task is very simple to perform and speaks for itself.

1. Remove one screen at a time and mark a window number on the frame's edge with a fine-point permanent marker. Start at the top floor of your home and work your way around clockwise and down to the next floor, numbering each screen.
2. After the permanent marker has dried, line the screens up so that you can easily spray each one down.
3. Use a power washer or power nozzle for your garden hose to clean the screens.
4. Allow the screens to dry before placing them back.

Replacing Inefficient Windows

Windows bring the outdoors in and keep the harsh cold of the winter and intense heat and humidity of the summer from invading your home and workspace. Windows provide security from the harsh climate changes in our environment and the opportunity to take in warm refreshing breezes throughout your home.

The windows in many older homes are constructed with single-pane glass. These windows are outdated, waste energy, and cost you money. Changing these windows to energy-efficient windows can save you in heating bills, paying for themselves sooner than you may think. Energy-efficient windows are manufactured several different ways, and have different energy-saving degrees of efficiency.

Beside the energy savings related to double-pane windows, sound attenuation is another added aspect of thermal-pane windows. The air barriers between the double-panes of glass are what gives these windows their thermal resistance, and provide sound resistance to make noise from the outside less of a bother and the inside of your home more comfortable. This may not be an issue in the rolling hills of the countryside, but is a great benefit in a big city, keeping screeching sirens, horn-blowing cars, and noisy truck engines from invading and dominating the sanctity of your home.

On average, if you are not a trained carpenter, installing a replacement window may not be advisable. There are some people that can catch on to this task fairly easy, but most people may want to get estimates for this work to be done.

FOUR DIFFERENT TYPES OF ENERGY-EFFICIENT GLASS PANES

When you do choose to replace your windows, there are a number of different window options available. If you want to cut down on your utility bills though, you should opt for energy-efficient windows. There are several different types to choose from:

1. **Double-pane Glass:** These windows have a vacuum thermal barrier between the two panes of glass, reducing the amount of heat

loss. In combination with several other options, these windows can become even more cost-effective.

2. **Low-E Glass:** Lets the light in but reduces heat transmission. This option is used with double-pane windows, increasing its energy-efficiency.

3. **Argon and Krypton Gas:** These gases have different insulation values and are sealed between the panes of glass to reduce heat transmission.

4. **Triple-pane Glass:** A system of three sheets of glass in a sash. This type of glass uses the same principle as double-pane, except the three sheets of glass are separated by two air spaces. These windows are primarily used in colder climates because of their added thermal performance.

Know What You're Getting

When energy-efficiency ratings are calculated for a window, both the glass and frames are taken into account. However, certain frames are not insulated and a homeowner needs to be aware of what a contractor or supplier is providing. Before purchasing, make certain to ask if the window frames have an air cavity and whether or not the cavity is insulated.

NEWER OPTIONS MAKE A BIG DIFFERENCE

Newer windows come with options that can add to the style of your home and make life a little easier. Sure, these options add to the cost of the window, but depending on your budget and how meticulous you are, some or all may be worth the investment.

Tilt-wash Windows: This type of window makes cleaning much easier by tilting the sash into the home instead of the homeowner getting on a ladder or hanging out of the window to clean the outside of the sashes.

Interior Blinds: Another special feature that some window companies provide as an option are interior window blinds. These blinds are in between the glass panes, saving you the arduous task of having to clean the dust and dirt off them while making them environmentally safer. Though they are housed between the glass, they can be opened and closed by a thumb crank on the outside of the interior sash.

Interior Grilles: Grilles between the glass panes are another available option. These save you time, making it possible to clean one large pane of glass rather than having to clean smaller panes in between each grille.

Hector Hint	Remember, you get what you pay for and if it is not stipulated in the contract, you may not get it.

WINDOW REPLACEMENT OPTIONS

Replacement Windows: The configuration of a replacement window is different from that of new construction windows. Replacement windows fit into the frame of the old windows, reducing the size of the window and amount of light that enters your home. There are many different manufacturers of replacement windows from which to choose. These windows are fabricated from aluminum, wood, and vinyl. No matter what window you are considering, the warranty, price, and energy-efficiency are all deciding factors.

Sash Replacements: Another energy-efficient alternative, without reframing or having to trim the exterior and interior of your home, is a sash replacement. This method is where the old window sashes and tracks are removed, tracks for new sashes are attached to the existing window jamb (the frame), and new energy-efficient thermal pane sashes are installed. This method will allow for the same amount of light to enter, but no interior or exterior trim work is required, and they can be installed in a fraction of the time it would take to install a replacement window.

Up front, these window sashes, tracks, and hardware are a little more expensive than replacement windows, but after factoring in the labor and materials for the interior and exterior carpentry, they are comparable. If you decide to tackle this task yourself, it is important to follow the manufacturer's installation instructions for the brand of sash replacements you choose.

Hector Hint

Beware of the lead-time when ordering new windows. The lead-time is the difference between the time you order the windows and when you receive them. If you order replacement windows, they can take two to four weeks depending on the manufacturer. New windows and sash replacements can take a few more weeks, depending on the time of year and demand.

INSTALLATION TIME

On average, a replacement window installation should take approximately two to three hours and a sash replacement should take about twenty minutes overall once you get the hang of it.

Different types of windows in order of how commonly they are used:

1. **Double Hung:** Consist of an upper and lower sash that can be raised or lowered.
2. **Casement:** These windows pivot on the top and bottom of one side and crank outward on the other side.
3. **Gliding or Sliding:** These windows slide left to right in separate tracks.
4. **Hopper and Awning:** Operate with the same principle. Hopper windows push out and up, hinging on the bottom; awning windows push out and down, hinging on the top.

This is a task that requires a homeowner to deliberate whether it is cost-effective to replace the windows.

Preventive Window Maintenance

SKILL LEVEL

1

TIME

6–10 h

Time goes by extremely fast and before you know it, things that should have been done a year or two ago haven't been done yet. We are all stressed, and time is of the essence, for us all. Even the little things, like maintaining your windows, are important. Whether the windows in your home are double-hung, casement, gliding, awning, hopper, or jalousie, take one day a year to help extend their life a little more and help keep that hard earned cash in your pocket a little longer. Pick a day to tighten, vacuum, and clean up those windows.

1. Depending on the type of screws holding the window hardware in place, use a screwdriver to tighten the window locks, hinges, and window pulls, making sure not to strip them in the process.
2. If the windows are newer, look to see if the tracks are screwed into the frame; if they are, check to see if they are loose and tighten them if not.
3. Use a rag and soft bristled brush to clean the tracks and around the window sashes.
4. Open the windows and vacuum the sill, removing any dirt particles that may interfere with the seal of the window when it is closed.
5. With a soft cloth and mild detergent clean the locks and any other exposed parts. Make sure the detergent is mild. Abrasive cleaners and window hardware are not a good combination. Abrasive cleaners will scratch the finish on the hardware.
6. Lubricate the locks, hinges, and tracks of the windows. Use a silicone spray with a long spray attachment that comes with the can, to avoid overspray. Wipe down any parts on the locks that are adjusted manually.
7. Clean the glass panes of the sashes using a window cleaner and paper towels.

Unsticking Your Window

Sometimes when a home is painted, the window sash along with the window gets painted shut. The ease of fixing this problem is a direct result of how many times the window was painted and how thickly the paint was applied.

1. Simply tapping around the sash may jar it enough to free it, but if that doesn't work. . . .
2. Using a utility knife, slowly score a line between the window sash, the frame, and all other areas that may be painted shut.
3. Tap around the sash, loosening any part that may still be painted shut.
4. Try lifting or lowering the sash.
5. If that doesn't work, spray a silicone lubricant in the sash tracks to help it move freely.
6. If this is an older home, there may be layers of paint on the window and you may need to cut deeper around the sash with the utility knife.

Hector Hint

When a seal is broken between thermal panes of glass in a sash, an ugly hazy film will obstruct the view through the glass. This haze is caused by moisture that was able to enter through a broken vacuum seal. After time, the haze can become imprinted into the glass. A glazier with the right equipment or the window manufacturer can repair the window or replace the sash.

Out with the Old Caulk and In with the New

The window is shut but I still feel a breeze. . . . Caulking is a task most anyone with a little fortitude can achieve.

1. If the window is not easily accessible and a ladder needs to be used, make sure it is stable and that you feel secure before attempting to complete this project.

2. Use a sharp utility knife to cut between the old caulking and the trim around the window.
3. Pull the caulk from around the window and scrape off any residue still stuck to the wall and trim. Pieces of old caulk may interfere when you smooth out the new caulking.
4. Have an exterior waterproof caulk, caulking gun, utility knife, and rag to continue this task. Cut the tip of the caulk tube at a 30- to 45-degree angle using the utility knife.
5. Puncture the inner seal of the tube through the tip using a long nail or rigid thin piece of wire.

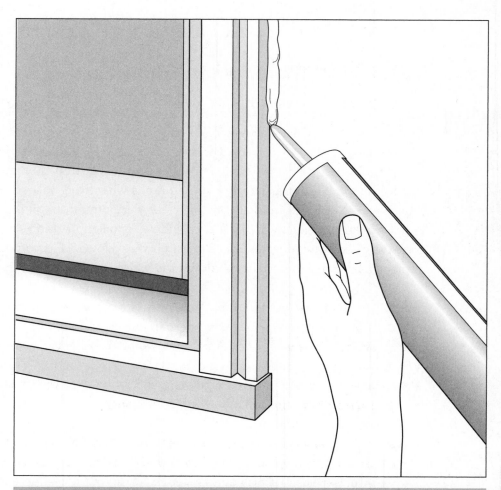

Be sure to apply the caulk evenly to the seam.

6. Firmly place the caulking tube opening between the trim and window at the angle cut on the tube. Squeeze the trigger very slowly until you see it working its way through the tip. Move the caulking gun and squeeze the trigger so that there is smooth movement and the line of caulk is neat.

7. After a neat bead of caulk has been laid in place, wet your finger and lightly smooth the caulk applying pressure to keep it uniform.

Hector Hint When you've finished caulking, quickly disengage the caulking gun so that the caulk does not continue to flow.

Insulating Windows in Older Homes

SKILL LEVEL

3

TIME

2–3 h

When installing replacement windows, the old window sash, storm window (if there is one), pulleys, ropes, and weights, should be removed, and the old caulking and paint will need to be scraped clean. Well, the storm window, caulk, and paint are obvious, but what is forgotten by many or are just left alone altogether are the voided areas where the pulleys, ropes, or chains where housed. Cold air can infiltrate your home through these areas, reducing the efficiency of the new window installation. Many of the old sash-weighted windows have access panels that allowed the homeowner to replace a broken rope or chain holding the weight to the sash.

1. If you can access the removable panels, unscrew or unfasten the side jambs to expose the voided area used for the passage of the weights. Make sure to remove the weights and anything else that may hinder the placement of insulation.

2. Take some blanket type insulation and stuff it into the voided areas. Note: Make sure to stuff it with something stiff enough to fill it well at the sides and bottom.

3. The upper end of the jamb is the most difficult to access. If you have difficulty placing the insulation in this area, purchase Hilti CF-116-14 Reusable Insulating Filler Foam at your local home improvement center. This insulating foam will not get messy and continues

to expand like regular can-type foam insulation. When applying foam insulation, the nozzle needs to be far enough into the voided area so that even the smallest of crevices are filled and air cannot penetrate. If you have many windows to do it will pay to purchase the filler and foam from Hilti.

Hector Hint	Using regular foam insulation can become a mess. It can keep expanding out of any hole or crack and drip down, making it messy and difficult to clean up. Once it dries, the foam can be tricky to get rid of, and leave tough marks to remove.

Eliminating the Draft Around Your Windows

SKILL LEVEL

3

TIME

2–3 h

There's more than one way to skin a cat. So, here's to getting rid of that chill when there isn't a panel to remove.

1. Remove the window stop that seals the space between the replacement window and the old window jamb.
2. Drill into the voided area vertically from top to bottom every 6" to 8". Make sure the drill bit is just wide enough to be able to get the long nozzle into the hole.
3. Use the Hilti CF-116-14 Reusable Insulating Filler Foam and make sure to fill the space entirely.
4. When you pull the nozzle out of each hole, be sure to wipe the excess off and immediately cover with a small piece of duct tape.
5. After a few hours remove the duct tape and replace the stop.

Floors

The condition of the floor in a home can tell a story about how well the home was maintained, or not. These days hardwood and carpet are the most common types of flooring and fairly simple to care for and repair. The floors in a home are constantly taking a beating. So, no matter what type of floor is in your home the upkeep of it should be on a fairly regular basis. This chapter walks you through some simple maintenance tasks that will stretch out the lifespan of your floors by making up for all the wear and tear.

Project Worksheet

MONETARY RETURN: $1,500–$2,500

This chapter is based on an average size home and average damages.
For larger homes and above average damages the return will be greater.

PROJECT START DATE: _____

TASKS COMPLETED: _____
_____
_____
_____
_____

TOOLS NEEDED:

- ❑ 1½" × 1½" wood blocking
- ❑ Broom
- ❑ Bucket
- ❑ Double-sided tape
- ❑ Finishing nails
- ❑ Furniture glides
- ❑ Gloves
- ❑ Hammer
- ❑ Ladder
- ❑ Mop
- ❑ Rags
- ❑ Saw
- ❑ Screw gun
- ❑ Screws
- ❑ Utility knife
- ❑ Vacuum cleaner
- ❑ Wood glue

Hardwood Flooring

The beauty and character of hardwood flooring has become so popular over the years that many homeowners are also having it installed in their kitchens, mudrooms, and bathrooms. This would not have even been a consideration back in the '70s or '80s when contemporary homes were in fashion, but a homeowner can never go wrong with this classic look. However, a wood floor can augment the look of non-contemporary or contemporary homes.

Like older homes before linoleum, composition, or ceramic tile, the concern for many was the potential damages to the floor as a result of spilling, dropping objects, and wear in high traffic areas. This is not the case any longer. Harder urethanes do a much better job of protecting wood floors and last much longer than they did years ago.

A wood floor throughout the home has a warm appealing feel and look. There is something distinctive about the warmth of wood and the old world charm it lends to a home. It looks attractive and, if installed properly and cared for, has a beauty that can be enjoyed for a lifetime.

Wood flooring comes in many styles and widths. The different types and colors of wood flooring vary significantly, which can make it difficult when the time comes for you to make a selection. But suitably selected, wood flooring can significantly enhance and flatter wall colors and furnishings in a room.

WHAT TYPE WORKS FOR YOU?

Not only do we have to choose between the many types of wood floors, but now we also have to decide whether we want a regular ¾" floor, a laminate floor, or an engineered floor in our home.

Engineered floors are less expensive than solid hardwood floors, and easier and cheaper to install, but require regular maintenance like hardwood floors. Engineered floors can be installed over concrete and in basements because they can easily adapt to changes in humidity.

Laminate floors are composed of a durable vinyl and are fabricated to look like wood and ceramic. They are less expensive than engineered and natural wood floors and don't require as much maintenance.

During installation of an engineered or laminate floor, dust is significantly reduced. These floors do not need sanding. Although today, for natural wood floors, they have floor scrapers that vacuum up the dust as the floor is being scraped for relatively the same price.

Odor and the potential for a fire hazard with the application of polyurethane is a nonfactor, since polyurethane for an engineered floor is applied at the factory. Pre-finished floor applications are done in environmentally controlled areas, making the application much more sustainable and uniform.

It takes one day to install a pre-finished floor in a standard size room, whereas unfinished natural wood floors can take up to a week before they are ready to be used. There is a three-coat application process of polyurethane for natural wood floors. Each coat needs to dry and to be screened (very light sanding) before the next coat is applied.

Another important consideration when having your floor installed is the humidity and temperature in the home. Natural wood floors need at least three days to acclimate to the temperature and humidity in a home, prior to being installed. If this is not done the floors can buckle and the expense to repair them can be extensive, to say the least.

Erase Minor Scuffs and Stains

SKILL LEVEL

1

TIME

1 h

1. Start by working a pencil eraser over the darker scuffmarks.
2. Pour some oil soap like Murphy's Oil Soap on a clean rag.
3. Rub the rag in a circular motion over the scuffmarks and stains. Work from outside of the stain to the middle.
4. Wipe the target area clean with a dry rag.

Buff Your Hardwood Floor

SKILL LEVEL

1

TIME

2–3 h

Here's how to buff your hardwood floor without wax to bring back the natural shine.

1. Purchase an inexpensive manual hand buffer from your local home improvement store.
2. Use a wet mop to evenly spread an oil soap like Murphy's Oil Soap across the area you intend to buff.
3. Start at the farthest point in the room from the doorway and work the manual buffer evenly across the floor. Be sure not to trap yourself in a corner as you buff.
4. Do not let anyone walk on the newly buffed floor for at least one hour.

For floors that are severely damaged, a more extensive repair may need to be done and a wood floor professional should be consulted.

Here's what you should and *shouldn't* do in order to maintain the great look of your hardwood floor:

SHOULD DO

- Sweep or vacuum the floor on a weekly basis; clean the floor with a cleaner suggested by the manufacturer.
- Wipe up spills immediately, eliminating any chance of the floor absorbing the liquid, which will cause swelling and destroy the finish.
- Place a mat in front of your sink (if you have wood floors in the kitchen) to eliminate water getting on the floor. If water puddles on a floor for long periods, it can damage the texture and finish.
- Lay a runner or throw rug at the doorway to prevent tracking dirt from your shoes onto the floor, which will scratch and wear down the finish.
- Install window treatments to minimize the sun's direct ultraviolet rays from destroying the finish and making the sheen dull.

SHOULDN'T DO

- Do not use wax on a wood floor as it damages the finish.
- Do not wet mop a wood floor regularly; it can destroy the finish.
- Do not slide heavy furniture across the floor when moving it. Sliding can scratch the finish and remove the polyurethane.

Natural wood floors never go out of style and are very easy to clean. Wood floors hold their value well and can easily return your investment when you decide to sell your home.

Hector Hint	Oak flooring is the most common hardwood floor installed and is very hard to drill or nail through without first pre-drilling a hole.

A Quick Wood-Floor Transformation

SKILL LEVEL

2

TIME

6–10 h

If your floors are worn and tired looking, a quick fix is all they may need. If done properly, it can help to add life and sheen to your wood floors. Nevertheless, if your floors are damaged beyond what is considered standard neglect, you may need to resort to a more expensive, messy, and time-consuming method of sanding, staining, sealing, and coating your wood floors.

Let's get started . . .

1. Remove all the furniture from the room you'll be working in.
2. Sweep the room thoroughly.
3. Use a clean mop and plain hot water to wash down the floors. A damp (not soaked) mop should do the job. The hot water will clean and evaporate quickly so there will be no moisture left in the wood. Water should not be used regularly on the floors.
4. Once the floor is dry, open the windows. Apply polyurethane to a clean cloth and, starting at the farthest part of the room, work your way across the room wiping the polyurethane on the floor in a pattern you'll be able to distinguish. Keep the polyurethane uniform, and be careful not to miss any spots. Polyurethane has a watery

consistency, and a light coating is all that is needed, and if a brush or roller is used it can make a mess.

<table>
<tr><td>Hector Hint</td><td>Before you purchase the polyurethane, determine if you want a matte or gloss finish on your hardwood floors. Polyurethane also comes in a water or oil base finish. The oil base finish has an overbearing smell and is highly flammable, but the water base, although a little more expensive, is much easier to handle and odorless.</td></tr>
</table>

5. As you finish each room, close the door and lock it if you are able, or put a piece of painters tape across the door opening to prevent anyone from stepping on the floor while it is drying.

In twenty-four hours, your floors will look shiny and new.

Take the Squeaks Out of Your Floors

It's late at night when you're walking down the hallway and suddenly a loud creaking sound is heard throughout the house. That's right—you forgot to step over that spot, *again*. Don't worry, here are some solutions that may help to correct that noise and make it less of a problem.

A squeaking floor is usually the result of a finished floor rubbing against the sub-floor or the sub-floor rubbing against the floor joist.

Fix the Squeak from Underneath

SKILL LEVEL

1

TIME

4–5 h

If access from below is possible and there is blocking or bridging (metal diagonal strips) between the joists, look to see if there is any space between the floor joist and the sub-floor. If you encounter spaces between them:

1. Purchase wood shims at your local lumberyard or home improvement store.

2. Tap the wedges into place at the affected areas that have a space until the squeak is gone. This will fill the space, avoiding any rubbing and prevent any further squeaking.

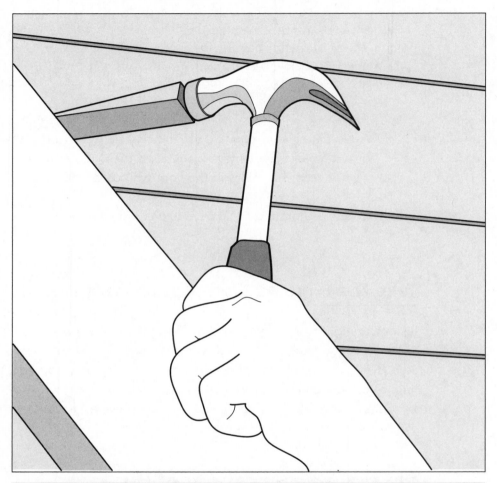

Wood glue will help to keep the wedge in place.

3. If you are comfortable that the problem has been resolved, remove the wedge, apply wood glue on both sides, and re-tap it into place. Make sure to have paper towels handy to catch any excess glue that might drip.

If you cannot find any areas where there is space between the joist and sub-floor but know the thickness of the sub-floor and the finished floor and have access from below:

1. Purchase screws that are shorter than the sub-floor and finished floor combined. The thickness of a standard hardwood floor is ¾" and the sub-floor should also be ¾" thick, although sometimes a builder may skimp on the thickness of the sub-floor in order to save money.
2. From below the floor, screw upward into the sub-floor and finished floor. This will pull the two tight eliminating any squeaking that may be caused by them rubbing together.

Fix the Squeak from Above

SKILL LEVEL

2

TIME

1 h

If you can't access the floor from underneath, go to your local hardware store and purchase finish screws, a tip for your drill or screw gun, a drill bit slightly narrower in diameter than the shaft of the screw, and wood putty that matches the color of the floor. A natural hardwood floor is typically ¾" and the sub-floor should be ¾". A 1½" finish screw should be sufficient to penetrate the finished floor and sub-floor.

1. Find the location where the squeak in the floor is coming from by walking slowly across the floor and putting pressure on and off the area to confirm the spot.
2. Pick a place in the area of the squeak and in the grain of the floor that will be least noticeable and pre-drill a hole approximately ¾" deep. Try to prevent drilling through the sub-floor in order for the screw to have a good hold when it goes through.
3. Using a drill or screw gun, screw the finish screw into the hole and slightly counter-sink it (which means to make the head of the screw go slightly below the surface). This is accomplished by moving the drill in a circular motion to allow space for the screw head to enter.
4. Use the wood putty to cover the screw head and wipe off the excess.
5. Use a rag to smooth it over and to apply a dab of polyurethane.

Get Rid of a Noisy Stair

Most of the time, a squeaky stair is caused by the nosing of the stair rubbing against the riser of the step and is a fairly easy problem to solve.

1. Locate what step is causing the noise.
2. Drill two equally distant holes into two 3" pieces of 2" × 2" (actual size is 1½" × 1½") wood blocking.
3. Slather a generous amount of wood glue on the top and side of the blocks.
4. One at a time, place the blocks underneath the corner of the stair where the riser meets the tread.
5. Take two screws that are sufficient to penetrate the entire 2" × 2" block but only a partial thickness of the riser which, on average, is ¾" (a 2" wood screw should do the job), and screw the blocks in place.

Try not to put any pressure on the step for at least twenty-four to forty-eight hours until the glue dries.

Carpet Installation Woes

Improper installation of carpet can result in discoloration or unsightly seams. When carpet is installed, it is not considered abnormal for some seams to be visible. The style of carpet, its manufacturer, and its thickness are all directly related to the visibility of the seams. However, excessive gaps at the seams, lack of carpet padding, and discolorations are definite concerns for the homeowner. As time goes on and the carpet receives some wear, these issues will become more prominent.

The flooring contractor should address any of these issues and an honest effort should be made to examine the situation and make a direct attempt to correct it. Stretching and re-seaming the carpet may correct the problem, but not in all cases. A carpet with a thicker pile helps to better conceal a seam, but if the quality is poor and the carpet is old, there is nothing you can do about it.

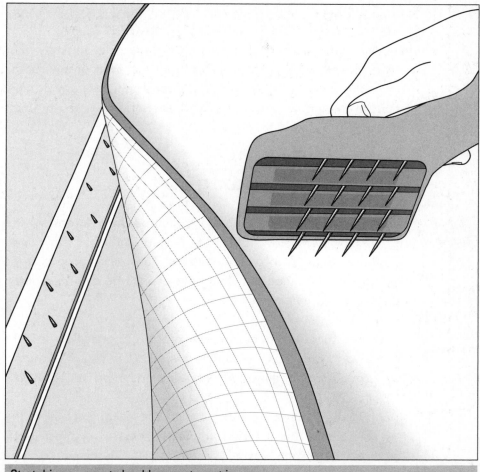

Stretching a carpet should correct most issues.

WHERE'S THE PADDING?

A lack of padding or two different thicknesses of padding under a carpet is absolutely unacceptable. This is where the installer is wholly responsible. Wherever there is carpet there should be padding. If the padding is missing in any area, the carpet should be pulled back and the padding replaced or repaired. If the padding is missing, the installation definitely does not meet standard practice for residential installation.

THINKING OF REPLACING THE CARPET?

If you happen to have discolored or faded carpet you may want to change it. A drab and dingy carpet will dampen the spirit of any room, no matter how it's decorated. Before putting money into furniture or paint, consider replacing a worn carpet as the most cost-effective way of improving your living space.

Replace the Padding

SKILL LEVEL

3

TIME

4–5 h

Padding is an important component of carpeting. It keeps our feet insulated from a cold floor below, it helps to cushion an infant's fall, and it prevents premature wearing on certain carpets. The only reason a carpet may not need to have padding is if the carpet needs to be directly glued to the floor, as in some commercial carpet.

1. The tool used to secure the carpet to the tackless (the thin strip of wood with the nails to hold the carpet in place) along the perimeter of a room is called a kicker. A kicker can be rented at your local tool center.
2. To remove the old carpet, place the kicker just before the tackless, gently kick with your knee to release any pressure that may be on the carpet, and pull up the carpet. Do this until you have gone around the room or closet and released the carpet from the tackless, allowing you to roll it back. Make it a point to roll the carpet and not to crease it.
3. Remove any undersized padding and staples.
4. Cut a small square piece of the proper thickness of padding and go to your local home improvement store or carpet showroom and purchase the amount needed to replace what was removed or missing. Padding is manufactured in different thicknesses and needs to be replaced with the same thickness. Carpet and padding

are measured in square feet for smaller areas and square yards for the larger areas.

5. Using a staple gun, cut and staple the new padding into place. Make sure to replace the small piece used to get the proper thickness and don't use too many staples.

6. When you are finished putting down the padding, roll the carpet back down.

7. On your knees, gently kick the carpet back onto the tackless. Be careful not to kick the carpet too hard or it will tear. Also, don't be concerned with excess carpet at the wall once you finish. Take a screwdriver, run it along the edge of the carpet between the tackless and the underside of the base molding. Doing this will tuck the carpet under the base molding.

Install a Carpet Patch

SKILL LEVEL

3

TIME

6–10 h

If you think a patch will be sufficient to repair damaged carpeting, cutting out the bad section and replacing it may be all that is necessary. Patching is effective as long as the damage isn't located in the middle of the room, and you have an extra piece of carpet big enough for the job. Take note that the shorter the pile, the more obvious the repair will be. If it is a longer pile it will be easier to conceal the repair, but the pile nap of the patch needs to be running in the same direction as the existing carpet. You can check this by brushing the carpet pile so that the shading is in the same direction.

Hector Hint

Be careful with the type of spot removers that you use on carpet; some spot removers will discolor and even ruin a decent quality carpet. So make sure to look in *Consumers Digest* or your nearest flooring store for the latest and least damaging carpet cleaning product on the market, and observe the manner in which it should be applied.

1. Cut the piece of a matching remnant. Make sure it is a little larger than the damaged area and that the shading and wear are about the same.

2. Place the remnant directly over the carpet so that it covers the damaged area. Before cutting the patch, check that the pile, when brushed, is in the same direction as the nap of the existing carpet.

3. Taking a utility knife with a new blade, carefully cut through the patch and the damaged carpet. Doing it this way will make the patch very snug.

4. Place four pieces of double-faced tape along the edges and halfway under the existing carpet.

5. Firmly press the remnant patch into place.

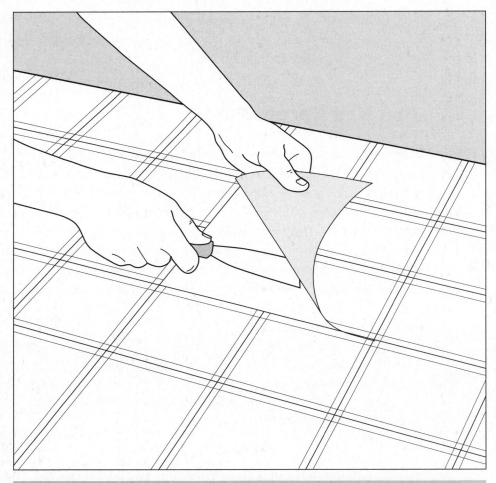

If you're working with a carpet that has a pattern to it, be sure to match the pattern exactly when you place the carpet patch.

Fix a Squeaky Carpet

SKILL LEVEL

1

TIME

1 h

Finish nails have a very small head that makes them harder to see and will easily penetrate the carpet and padding without causing any damage to them.

This task will use a technique for nailing called toe-nailing. Toe-nailing is when the nails are driven toward one another or away from each other. This technique causes the nails to work against each other, holding the wood down and preventing the nails from popping out.

| **Hector Hint** | Trying to use screws may damage the carpet by catching the thread and quickly unraveling it. |

1. Using 2" #6 finish nails, toe-nail the finish nails at a 65 to 70 degree angle toward each other through the carpet and padding where the squeak is heard. Make sure the heads of the nails are into the wood and not sticking up through the carpet. The heads on finish nails are very small and are not visible once they pass through the carpeting and padding material.
2. With a nail set, countersink the heads of the nails so that they cannot be felt through the carpet and padding, should someone step on them without any shoes.
3. Adjust the area of the carpet where the nails penetrated.

CHAPTER
V

Walls

Imperfections such as holes, cracks, and dirt are easy to spot on the walls. Cooking, moving things around, and the wear-and-tear from kids playing all make it necessary to give the walls a periodic facelift.

Project Worksheet

MONETARY RETURN: $1,000–$1,500

PROJECT START DATE: _____

TASKS COMPLETED: _____
_____
_____
_____
_____

TOOLS NEEDED:
- ❑ 1½" drywall screws
- ❑ 9" and 12" drywall taping knives
- ❑ Caulking gun
- ❑ Drop cloths
- ❑ Drywall nails
- ❑ Drywall saw
- ❑ Drywall screws
- ❑ Extension cord
- ❑ Fine metal file
- ❑ Flathead screwdriver
- ❑ Hammer
- ❑ Joint compound
- ❑ Level
- ❑ Mesh and regular paper drywall tape
- ❑ Rags
- ❑ Roller and extension
- ❑ Roller cover(s)
- ❑ Sand paper (fine and medium grit)
- ❑ Sandpaper block
- ❑ Screw gun
- ❑ Spackle
- ❑ Tapered brush
- ❑ Utility knife
- ❑ Vacuum cleaner
- ❑ Wood putty

Sizing Up the Job

When taking on a painting job, try to break rooms down or have an idea of what you want prior to entering the store. The size of the room, the amount of natural light the room receives, and the intended ambiance are some of the things you need to keep in mind when looking for a paint shade.

When picking a brand to use don't skimp. Buy more than you need so you don't need to stretch the paint and can barely cover the walls. Make sure the coverage is good.

The colors we choose have a lot to do with how large a room appears. Lighter colors give a room a more spacious look and a darker color will make a room appear smaller. Ceiling height is most definitely something to take into account. With low ceilings, a very bright white ceiling and light-colored walls will enhance the room and lighten it up, giving the illusion that the ceiling is higher and that the room is larger

| **Hector Hint** | Latex paint is much easier to clean up and cheaper because it doesn't have an oil base. Paint brushes, roller covers, and other painting tools clean up easier with latex. Not having to clean them up with turpentine and mix them with a paint thinner also makes them much safer to use. |

Clear, Patch, and Clean

SKILL LEVEL

2

TIME

6–10 h

Proper preparation is almost as important as the paint job itself. Clearing the work area will help to prevent damage and allow you enough room to work comfortably. Taking the time to patch nail holes and caulk the trim seams will result in a job you will be proud to say you did. The last item, but not least, is the cleanup. Although it is tedious, cleaning up after completing a task is a vital step and should not be taken lightly. Getting dried-up paint off the floor, vacuuming the sanded wall patch, hanging the pictures, and organizing the room, are the final steps in this task before opening the door.

1. Clear out the room of as much furniture as possible. If necessary, put the furniture in the middle of the room.
2. Roll up the rugs and place them in another area or in the middle of the room.
3. Make sure to have enough drop cloths to cover the furniture. Secure the drop cloths so that they do not come off while you are painting.
4. Remove all the outlet and switch cover plates and place them in a safe place. Cover thermostats and wall-phones that cannot be removed.
5. Remove the door hardware or cover it so that you don't get paint on it.
6. Cover the light fixtures and chandeliers. Use masking tape to cover the base and secure the plastic.
7. Remove pictures, drapes, shades, Venetian blinds, and anything that may be hanging on the walls or windows.
8. Place tape over the baseboard, on the glass around the windows, and on the outlets and light switches.
9. Prepare the walls by scraping off loose paint and patching any holes or cracks with quick-drying spackling compound, then lightly sanding to a smooth finish.
10. Patch the woodwork with wood putty and sand it once it is dry.
11. Wipe down walls with a slightly damp rag and vacuum the windows, sashes, sills, baseboard, door trim, window trim, and floor.
12. Caulk between all painted woodwork and walls and smooth the caulk over with a wet rag. Make sure not to make the cut on the caulking tube too large. It could become very messy, so the smaller the cut, the better.
13. Apply stain sealer wherever there are water marks or other stains.

Hector Hint	When purchasing paint, you are better off getting a little more than you need. This way there is less of a chance of having a difference in the dye lot or color mix.

Prime and Paint

A home, on average, needs to be painted every three to four years. Using a paint that covers well is better than an inexpensive brand that may require you to paint an area several times and possibly cost you as much, if not more than a better paint. A more expensive, higher quality paint can be a better value.

1. Cutting is the art of using a paintbrush to get at the areas the roller can't. Use a comfortable brush at least 2" wide to cut in the corners. Some people affix painters tape to edges for a neat, even line.
2. There is a method to rolling paint onto a wall. When using a paint roller, a pan is needed to dip the roller into. Roll it down the incline of the pan, just enough that it doesn't drip. Apply the paint in the form of a large "N" (this will help to distribute some of the excess paint onto the wall). Then go back over the area with vertical up and down strokes. When using the roller, precede the end without the handle to smooth out any lines that may have formed from the end of the roller.
3. Prime the ceiling first and once the ceiling is dry, prime the walls.
4. Once you have completed the priming and it is dry, you can then begin to apply a finish coat of paint. Again, start at the ceiling, wait for it to dry, and then begin on the walls.

Hector Hint

Covering a dark color with a light color can be more difficult than covering a light color with a dark color. In some cases covering darker walls may require additional coats of paint.

5. After the walls are completely dry, remove the masking tape from any woodwork that was protected. Lightly sand to remove any possible splatters.
6. Using semi-gloss paint, paint the woodwork and windows. When painting the wood windows, use a small 1" brush on the grilles and sashes.

7. Lightly sand the doors to remove any paint splatter or imperfections and wipe them down with a slightly dampened rag.
8. Apply a semi-gloss paint to the doors, using smooth, even strokes. Do not apply too much pressure to the brush and don't skimp on the paint.

If you really want to get done quickly, you may want to consider a painting party, but leave the party part for after the painting is complete.

Hector Hint

If the doors are new, they will need to be sealed prior to being painted. If they are not sealed the grain can open, giving the door an unfinished or damaged look.

Drywall

Drywall is gypsum covered on both sides with paper, giving it a smooth texture. Drywall is available in sheets of 4' x 6', 8', 10', 12', and 16'. The larger the board the fewer seams and fewer problems you are likely to have with them. Drywall reduces the amount of labor and time required in building a wall, applying a finish, achieving a smooth ready-to-paint surface, and a shorter application period than that of plaster walls.

Naturally, the thicker and longer the board the heavier it is, and the flimsier it is to work with. But, a thicker and longer board offers more protection and sound reduction, and fewer seams. Drywall is installed by nailing or screwing it to wood-stud-framed walls or screwing it to steel-stud-framed walls.

Taping and compounding the seams is the next step in the installation process. This is a three-step process:

1. Applying the tape with a thin coating of joint compound is the first step.
2. So that there are no signs of a transition between the boards of drywall, a second coat of compound is applied.
3. The third coat is applied, allowed to dry, and sanded.

Humidity plays a big part in the drying process of the taping compound. In some cases it can take several days for one coat to dry.

As a construction consultant, I have often been asked, "Why do walls develop cracks?" This mostly happens during the first heating season. The moisture accumulated in the drywall during the summer dries out in the winter when the heat in the home is turned on. The drywall may crack about $\frac{1}{16}$" to $\frac{1}{8}$", but once patched, it doesn't normally crack again. If the crack is larger than that, it could be a more serious problem, possibly structural.

DRYWALL FIRE SAFETY

Drywall has a moisture component that allows it a fire rating. The fire rating is determined by the length of time it would take a fire to burn through it. A fire rating on drywall is increased when installed in conjunction with other layers of drywall, or insulation, and air space. The boards come in different thicknesses, such as $\frac{1}{4}$", $\frac{1}{2}$", $\frac{5}{8}$", and $\frac{3}{4}$" and each thickness increases the fire rating. The thicker the board the higher its moisture content and the longer it will take a fire to burn through it.

DRYWALL AND BACTERIA

In bathrooms, kitchens, and other places where water problems are possible, mold- and moisture-resistant drywall or a cementitious board is best used. The paper sides of drywall are treated to help deter water damage and bacteria growth.

CRACKS, POPS, AND BOWS

A common problem found with drywall is that if not installed and taped properly, cracked seams, nail pops, and loose corner beads (the metal strip that is installed on the outside corners joining two sheets of drywall together) are likely to occur, and will continue to get more noticeable as time goes on.

Wood studs are normally transported by train and are stored outside, exposing them to plenty of rain and moisture. Once indoors, the wood is in a controlled heated environment that causes it to shrink and makes the drywall susceptible to nail pops, cracked seams, and loose corner beads.

Patch Nail Pops

Nail pops are common in many homes unless screws were used to fasten the drywall. Nail pops are caused by twisting or shrinking of the wood stud or banging from the opposite side of the wall.

1. Tap the nail back into the wall just enough to make a slight indentation, making sure not to break the paper.
2. With a screw gun or a drill with a clutch, put a 1¼" screw 1" to 2" above and below the nail pop, drawing the sheetrock back in without weakening the area of the nail pop.
3. Using a wide taping knife, apply a careful coat of compound.
4. Let it dry and sand to a smooth finish.

Repair Cracked Seams

Cracked seams do not mend themselves, and will progressively spread with age. Prior to any painting in your home it is good practice to take care of any cracks you may find.

1. Using a utility knife, carefully cut a line at the edge of the existing tape and remove it.
2. Apply a coat of compound where the tape is.
3. With the appropriate length of drywall tape and starting from the top, begin to apply the tape, smoothing over it with a wide drywall taping knife.
4. Spread compound over the tape, feathering it. After the first coat of compound is dry, apply a second and third coat.
5. Gently sand for a smooth finish.

Hector Hint

Once a wall is painted with a finish coat it is very difficult to fix and will require you to re-prime the wall before any repairs can be done. A higher gloss paint used on the walls and ceiling makes it even harder to repair and will require a primer to be applied before being compounded, taped, and sanded.

Fix a Gouge in a Wall

SKILL LEVEL

2

TIME

1 h

Look at drywall work as an art form requiring patience, a steady hand, and practice. Sure, some people catch on quicker than others, but it just can't be fudged.

1. For small gouges, use a wide taping knife; apply a careful coat of compound. For larger gouges, apply a piece of mesh tape first.
2. Let it dry and carefully sand to a smooth finish.

If you don't know how to do it, learn from someone that knows how or take a scrap piece of drywall and practice on it.

Hector Hint A patch larger than 6" to 7" will require a back support to screw the drywall to.

Mend Drywall Cracks

SKILL LEVEL

1

TIME

1 h

Patching a drywall crack is probably the simplest drywall task to do. Getting in your car to purchase the materials is actually more difficult.

1. Cut a one ¼" V along the area that is cracked.
2. Fill the crack with compound and sand as necessary.
3. Run the taping blade to smooth out the compound. For quick drying, use a lightweight compound.

Fix Small Drywall Holes

Doorknobs are to drywall what bones are to dogs. Unless you have door-stops installed behind a door, your knob will devour the drywall, creating a bigger hole every time it hits it. A big hole requires either a blow patch or mesh patch depending on the size.

A blow patch is a square piece of drywall with a 1" perimeter of paper. Cut the wall to the size of the gypsum so that the square piece of drywall fits into the hole, leaving the paper to overlap the wall. The overlapping piece acts as the tape. Now tape the patch as though you were taping a seam. The process works for holes that are no larger than 6". Any hole larger than that will require securing of the drywall from behind.

1. Using a small level, draw a square box around the hole. Draw the box at least one inch beyond the hole on all sides.
2. Use your drywall saw and cut out the drywall on the line.
3. Taking another piece of drywall and using your utility knife, cut a piece of drywall at least 2" larger than the height and length of the hole.
4. Again, using your utility knife, cut the paper on only one side of the drywall, remove the cut side of the paper, and remove the gypsum, leaving a flap of paper on the other side to act as the piece of tape.
5. Run the edges of the hole. Apply a 2" coating of compound along the edge of the cut-out.
6. Set the drywall patch piece in place and with compound and taping knife patch the seam and let it dry. A second and third coat will be needed.

Repair Large Drywall Holes

Fixing large holes in drywall requires a little more work than the small ones, but with a little patience it can be accomplished.

1. Repairing a large area of drywall requires that you use a drywall saw and cut out a rectangle or square around the existing hole. The procedure is typically for holes that are larger than 6".

2. Secure a stud or two (depending on the size) to the adjacent dry-wall. Leave half of the stud into the open space so that the new replacement drywall can be screwed to it.

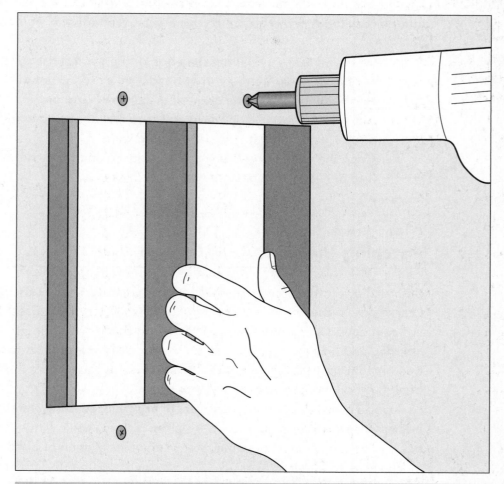

These additional studs will help stabilize the patch.

3. Tape and compound the perimeter as you would any other drywall seam. See the previous entry, Repairing Cracked Seams (p. 144), for more detailed instructions.

Restore Damaged Wall Corners

SKILL LEVEL

3

TIME

6–10 h

Dented corners are a little more challenging than cracks and gouges, whereas small dents in the metal corner bead are pretty easy to fix. File them back into place without doing too much damage and re-tape the area.

1. When a crack is evident at the edge of the vertical rise of the corner bead, re-secure the corner bead with a drywall screw.
2. Apply compound to the edge of the corner bead and space.
3. Cut a long enough strip of drywall tape and apply it over the compound, smoothing it out with a taping knife.
4. Once the compound is dry, apply a second and third coat, allowing it to dry each time between coats.

Patching Plaster

Before the introduction of drywall, plaster was used for walls in homes. Cracks due to the age of a home, shifting of walls (caused by settling), and the contraction and expansion due to climate changes, all contribute to the cracking and unsightly veins found on plaster walls. It is difficult to find contractors that specialize in plastering these days, because of the introduction of high-production drywall construction.

A good plastering job requires years of experience; however, the average homeowner should be able to do a simple plaster repair with a little practice and patience. There are many steps to the installation of plaster, but it's much easier to repair.

There are different ways plaster is applied: over wood lathe (½" × 2" lateral strips of wood), wire lathe, or masonry. Plaster usually requires three coats, but these days they make it a lot easier, needing less time and effort to complete a project.

Repair a Crack in Plaster

SKILL LEVEL

3

TIME

6–10 h

Plaster is not as user-friendly as drywall; therefore, it calls for a little more for-titude and artistic contact. The components of plaster soak up water, caus-ing it to dry quickly and crack as a result. Experience is the key to patching large areas of plaster, but a novice could easily accomplish this task.

1. With a scraper, make the crack a little wider. It should not exceed ⅛", if possible. Remove any loose paint, plaster, and plaster dust, using a brush or vacuum cleaner, and wipe clean.
2. Slightly dampen the area to be repaired and let it dry.
3. Apply a plaster primer on and around the area to be patched.
4. Make sure to read the directions on the plaster patch before filling the inside of the crack with plaster. Note: Plaster has a tendency to dry quickly. If you see that happening, add a little water.

Hector Hint

Do not get discouraged. It takes practice to apply plaster smoothly and consis-tently and to get used to its properties.

5. Smooth it over with a wider layer of spackle until it is even with the rest of the wall. If the area is a little wider than normal or there is a hole in the wall, use mesh tape, slightly indenting it, applying a coat of plaster and then a second coat after the first is dry.
6. Once you are sure it is dry, sand it down to a smooth finish. Plaster takes a little more work to sand. If you are satisfied, wipe off any dust, prime it, and now you are ready for your finish coat paint.

If the plaster is actually falling off the walls or ceilings, you may want to take on the task of removing all of the plaster and replacing it with drywall.

Before attempting to patch a large area watch someone tape, and get a few pointers. There are quite a few tricks of the trade, which only practical experience can teach you. Also, find an area in a closet for practicing, before attempting to try it elsewhere. Your local library or a home improvement store is a good resource to help in furthering learning.

Remove the Wall to Get at the Problem

SKILL LEVEL

3

TIME

6–10 h

Removing a wall in a finished space is where patience, a steady hand, and your ability to think ahead come into play. Taking a step back and seeing the whole picture is crucial to not damaging other areas in a space while removing a wall. Protect the space before beginning any work.

1. Using a stud finder, locate the stud that is furthest away from the door edge and beyond the stud you think is warped.
2. Take a long level and place it on the stud until the horizontal bubble is between the lines, indicating that it is plumb. Allow enough room on the stud for the drywall to be secured to it.
3. Draw a straight vertical line along the stud side of the level.
4. Using a drywall saw or reciprocating saw (for plaster), cut from top to bottom, along the vertical line.
5. Remove the drywall or plaster from the wall between the door frame and your cut. Discard any debris, maintaining a clean work area.
6. Take out any nails or screws from the studs.
7. Use a hammer and pry bar to remove the warped stud.
8. Measure the length needed and cut a new 2" × 4" to replace the old one. Make sure the new stud is kiln-dried lumber. Kiln-dried means that it is already dried out, minimizing a chance of it warping.
9. Toe-nail #8 common nails on both sides and at the top and bottom of the stud. Toe-nailing is to diagonally hammer the nail into the stud.
10. Once you have secured the stud, measure the area of drywall that is needed, cutting a sheet of drywall to that measurement.
11. Nail or screw the drywall to the studs every 8" to 10" on every stud. Make sure that the nails or screws are recessed but not breaking the paper on the drywall. To finish the drywall see Chapter 10.

In most cases, a simple adjustment and a little touch up is all that is needed. A few simple repairs can retain the beauty in an older home sustaining its character and charm for many years to come.

The Kitchen

The kitchen is probably the most popular room in your home. It sure is in my house. It seems to be the place where people most often congregate or go to. A kitchen is the command center for a home. The place where the notes and reminders are posted, where we fuel up with food, and, out of all the rooms in your home, that is the most expensive to repair. Therefore, it is very important to keep your kitchen well maintained and really think through any improvement or renovation projects.

Project Worksheet

MONETARY RETURN: $1,500–$2,500

PROJECT START DATE: _____

TASKS COMPLETED: _____
_____
_____
_____
_____

TOOLS NEEDED:

- ❏ Adjustable wrench
- ❏ Caulking gun
- ❏ Construction adhesive
- ❏ Extension cord
- ❏ Flathead screwdriver
- ❏ Joint fastening bolts
- ❏ Paint brush
- ❏ Phillips head screwdriver
- ❏ Pipe wrench
- ❏ Pliers
- ❏ Pry bar
- ❏ Putty knife
- ❏ Reciprocating saw
- ❏ Rubber mallet
- ❏ Safety glasses
- ❏ Screw gun
- ❏ Small bucket or can
- ❏ Tape measure
- ❏ Utility knife
- ❏ Wood shims

Countertops

If you're planning to upgrade your kitchen, getting a handle on the different types of countertops can be quite a challenge, to say the least. There are many different colors, styles, and combinations made more complicated by the rate at which surface technology progresses. Here is a brief overview of a few different types, some of their characteristics, and a few things you should consider.

Hector Hint

If you are thinking about getting granite and picking from a selection of slabs, make it a point to mark the slab you want. Ask the person you are dealing with to mark the back and make sure that it will be enough for your kitchen. Remember that two different slabs may not properly match, and there could be noticeable differences at the seams.

The prices of countertops range from $95 per lineal foot for a plastic laminate top to over $100 per square foot for a stone or manufactured countertop. The range can be a thousand dollars to over five thousand for a 10' long countertop. A thousand here and another thousand there and before you know it you have taken a hefty chunk out of your equity. Do your homework, take your time, and ask a bunch of questions to determine what will meet your needs, and in particular, your budget constraints.

Hector Hint

If a countertop is complex and intricate in shape, expect to pay more than usual.

SEAMS

Seams are an important obstacle when it comes to countertops. Nobody likes to see them, but unfortunately, with most countertops, a seam may be necessary.

EDGES

The type of countertop edge that you get also impacts its price. You can choose from several types.

Here are a few common types:

- Bullnose
- Half-bullnose
- Demi-bullnose
- Ogee
- ⅜ bevel

MATERIALS

Countertops come in many colors, styles, designs, and materials. Whether you are going for the commercial look of stainless steel, granite for its resilience, or plastic laminate for price there are other factors that also need to be considered. For example, your return on investment, durability, and the style of your kitchen. No matter which one you pick, a new countertop in any kitchen makes a big difference.

Here are the advantages and disadvantages of some of these materials:

Plastic Laminates: This is a plastic sheet glued to either plywood or flake board and susceptible to water damage at the seams and edges much easier than any of the others I will be mentioning. It is the least expensive of all countertops. Many choices of colors and styles are available and, if properly maintained, can last a long time. The worst thing is to leave water sitting on or near a seam without wiping it up immediately. The liquid can weaken the glue and swell the wood, delaminating the surface. Laminate also scratches much easier than the others do.

Marble: First, let me say that marble, unless you have someone who can constantly monitor and care for it, is totally out of the question. Why? Because it is so porous that water, soap, detergents, or other household foods or items that are placed on it can easily cause stains; and with a house full of children, I would definitely not recommend it. True, marble is beautiful but unless you are ready to properly and continuously care for it, don't consider it.

Corian: When Corian was first introduced to the market, I had it installed in my new kitchen. I found it to be durable to a degree, but since they only had solid colors at the time, stains or burns were not as easy to remove as they said they would be. However, since then the product has developed a wide selection of colors and blends making it easier for the homeowner to maintain and harder for one to notice any imperfections, blemishes, or burns.

Stainless Steel: This is a more commercial- and professional-looking countertop. These are not usually utilized in someone's residence, but as of late with the trend of "gourmet kitchens" on the rise, you will see more and more of these in higher-end kitchens. I have seen a combination of stainless steel and granite and the look was fantastic. The problem with stainless steel is that it can scratch, dent, and show fingerprints. The dents and scratches are impossible to remove, but do give some character to the kitchen.

Ceramic Tile: I am not personally fond of tile countertops. The grout, if not sealed properly, can accumulate bacteria, discolor, and if you want to throw some flour on the counter to roll out some dough, it isn't so easy or sanitary. Ceramic tile can be very decorative as a backsplash but not for food preparation.

Granite: In my opinion, nothing beats the durability, natural beauty, available choices, density, and classiness of granite. The colors, blends, and natural patterns can enhance any cabinet style.

There are other countertops like Silestone, quartz, or concrete, which are quite popular, and, which you can see at your local kitchen design store.

Remove an Existing Countertop

SKILL LEVEL

3

TIME

6–10 h

A number of countertops are vulnerable to burns, chipping, gouges, and, at some point, swelling from water penetration and may need to be replaced. It may sound like a tough task, but once you begin, it all comes together like a simple puzzle.

1. Remove all the items you have in the lower base cabinets.
2. Thoroughly check the backsplash to see if it is attached to the countertop or if it is independent from it.
3. If the countertop has tile applied to it, remove as much of the tile as possible to reduce the weight and make it easier to lift out of place.

Hector Hint Make sure to remove drawers from the cabinets before beginning to do any work.

4. Protect the areas adjacent to where you are working, especially the floor.
5. Turn off the hot and cold water lines and disconnect them from the faucet.
6. Detach the waste line from the sink at the P-trap. The P-trap is the U-shaped drain line under the sink.
7. If you have a cooktop, turn off the gas before disconnecting the gas line.
8. Turn off the circuit breaker to the cooktop and unplug or disconnect the electric.
9. Disconnect the waste line and electric to the dishwasher.
10. Remove the sink, look underneath the countertop and disconnect the mounting screws.
11. Next, remove any screws holding the countertop in place. They can be found holding the counter to the cabinets. If it is difficult, it could be that the countertop was glued down as well.
12. Once all the screws are removed, gently try to lift the countertop off the base cabinets.

13. For a countertop that is glued down, get a pry bar into an area between the countertop and the base cabinets. Without cracking the cabinet, pry up an area into which you can fit a reciprocating saw blade.

14. Using the reciprocating saw, slowly and carefully cut between the countertop and base cabinets. Be very careful not to damage the base cabinets. Use a metal cutting blade in case there are nails or other screws that may be holding it in place.

15. Carefully lift the countertop out from under the tile backsplash, if there is one, and away from the base cabinets.

Depending on the size of the countertop, you may need two people when removing and replacing it with the new one.

Get the Countertop Right

SKILL LEVEL

1

TIME

2–3 h

When measuring a countertop, make a diagram and note the dimensions on it. Show reference points from where you are taking the measurements so that you can refer to it when needed.

1. If you are a novice, take a picture of the existing countertop while it is in place, and bring it along when you are ordering the new one. It may make it easier for you when ordering the new top, should any questions arise.

2. Measure the length of the existing countertop(s).

3. Measure from one edge of the countertop to the centerline of the cut-outs and make note of what side you are measuring from. Remember any holes that need to be cut have to be measured to the center of the cut-out, not the edge.

Hector Hint	Be uniform and clear when marking down the measurements. You will need to refer to the drawing at a later date and don't want numbers all over the place. The countertop should overhang 1" on the front and $\frac{1}{16}$" to $\frac{1}{8}$" where the countertop butts against appliances.

4. If you are purchasing a new sink, faucet, or cooktop, have their dimensions on hand when ordering the new countertop. Whoever is making the cut-outs will need to know how many cut-outs, where to locate them, and the dimensions of the cut-outs.

Install a New Laminate Countertop

SKILL LEVEL

3

TIME

6–10 h

Plastic laminate is the most common material used for countertops in the kitchen and bathroom. The benefits of plastic laminate are its low cost and durability. While it doesn't have the durability of some of the more expensive materials, it also doesn't have the hefty price tag. It's a smart choice because of the variety of colors, shades, designs, and edges available.

1. Place the new countertop on the base cabinets. When handling the countertop be careful not to damage the walls.
2. Check to see how the countertop sits on the cabinets and that it is level. If it is not level, the base cabinets will need to be shimmed and leveled prior to installing the top.
3. If there are two countertops that meet at 90 degrees, they will need to be flush on top and aligned evenly.
4. Pull the two tops apart, apply silicone caulk to one of the tops, and push them together, making sure not to have it come out through the top.

Hector Hint

Purchase the caulk to match the plastic laminate applied to the top of the countertop. If you cannot find the same color, use a clear silicone.

5. Using the fastening bolts, connect the two tops. Do not tighten the bolts too much.
6. Use a small 2" × 4" on edge and gently tap it until the two tops are flush with each other.
7. Tighten the bolts once the sides and top are flush.

8. Insert shims approximately every 2' between the countertop and base cabinetry and apply a bead of construction adhesive.
9. Before removing the shims, check the level of the countertop and adjust the shims or remove them as appropriate.
10. Remove the shims and gently set the counter down. Allow the adhesive to dry.
11. Horizontally caulk the top of the backsplash where it meets the wall, if it was connected to the countertop or the back edge of the countertop, where it meets the wall.

Everything Is Hinging on the Cabinets

Kitchen cabinet hinges are something most of us at one time or another try to fix. "Frustrating" is probably the word we would use to describe adjusting them. The type, the company, the style, and cost of the cabinet determines how they are made. That determines the type of hinge that will be used, and the amount of adjustments that are possible.

The more adjustments on a hinge, the more they will cost. Some are exposed on the exterior of the cabinet and others are concealed on the interior side of the cabinet. Hinges come in various styles. There are decorative hinges, adjustable hinges, and plain hinges, along with brass, nickel, chrome, and many more types available.

Adjustable hinges can move a door nearer or farther away from another door, closer or further away from the cabinet, and adjust the door higher or lower on the cabinet.

Problems can often occur. The hinges may need an adjustment so that the door opens and closes properly. Or, the door can swing too far open, pulling the hinge screws out of the cabinet door. This will make the screw holes too large to hold them.

Repair a Stripped Cabinet Hinge and Door

SKILL LEVEL

2

TIME

2–3 h

Sometimes a screw holding a hinge on a cabinet door can become loose and the screw hole is no longer able to retain the screw. The following fix may be able to secure the screw to the door.

1. Remove the door from the hinges and cabinet, and place the cabinet door on a flat surface. Lay a towel underneath to protect it.
2. Using small splinters from another piece of lumber, put splinters into the screw hole tightly with wood glue. Gently tap them into place, filling it solid.
3. Use a utility knife to cut the wood splinters and wipe any excess glue from the hammer and cabinet.
4. Let it dry for at least forty-eight hours.
5. Replace the hinge and hang the door.

Change the Look by Painting Your Kitchen Cabinets

SKILL LEVEL

3

TIME

6–48 h

(based on a 10' length of wall or base cabinets)

If the finish on your cabinets is dull, dark, and dreary, painting them a light bright color is probably what they need. The cost of painting your kitchen is much less than purchasing new cabinets or re-facing. The object is to make your home as attractive as possible while retaining as much equity as you can.

1. Remove all the doors, drawers, and hardware.
2. Place all the hinges, pulls, knobs, and screws where they won't get lost. Now is a good time to replace the hardware with stylish hardware that fits into the existing holes.
3. Using masking tape, mark all the drawers and cabinet doors so that it will be easier later when it comes time to put them back. For example, mark the base (B) cabinet doors left to right—B1, B2, and so on—and the wall (W) cabinets left to right—W1, W2, and so on.
4. If you are changing the cabinet hardware and will not be using the existing holes for the hardware, fill them with putty and allow it to dry before sanding it flush to the surface. When filling the holes,

make sure there are no voids. The ideal thing would be to find pulls and knobs that fit the existing holes.

5. Prepping the surface of the cabinets can make all the difference in the finished product. Although stripping the cabinets is the best way to prep the surface, it's possible to get a good result without going through this process. Prepare the surface of the cabinets to receive new paint. Thoroughly clean the surface of the cabinets with a trisodium phosphate (TSP) or an equivalent and rinse, allowing the cabinets to dry before continuing.

6. Repair any dents or gouges with wood putty. Allow it to dry before sanding.

7. Once the cabinets are dry, use fine-grit sandpaper and sand the surfaces, wiping off any dust when you are done.

8. Prep the adjacent walls and countertops by using painters tape to border them off. Place drop cloths on the floors and on the countertop. Make sure all areas are protected before commencing.

9. An oil base paint will give you a much better finish, but a decent latex paint will be sufficient for a nice finish, and will be a lot easier to clean up and remove paint splatters and drips.

10. Paint the inside of the cabinets first. Use smooth continuous brush strokes. If a second coat of paint is needed, use a wet/dry 220-grit sandpaper to lightly sand the cabinets. Wipe or vacuum any dust off before applying a second coat of paint.

11. Install the hinges on the doors and the doors on the cabinets. Put all the drawers in place and install the new hardware.

Install an Under-Cabinet Light

SKILL LEVEL

2

TIME

2–3 h

It is difficult to prepare food with shadows on your work area. A simple solution can give you added lighting for your prep space and add ambiance at the same time. It is under-cabinet lighting. These lights wash down onto the countertop and backsplash from the underside of the wall cabinets, brightening up your work area and softly lighting and enhancing the space between the countertop and backsplash.

Although under-cabinet lights do an excellent job of lighting prep space during the day, the nighttime is when it functions as a visual assistant and also helps to set the mood for relaxation. These lights can be adjusted for mood by using a dimmer switch to brighten or to dim the lights.

Under-cabinet lights come in several types and styles. The most common are:

- Fluorescent strip lights
- Individual halogen "puck" lights
- Halogen strip lights

Fluorescent under-cabinet lights are simple to install, but provide an artificial-looking light. At one time, halogen under-cabinet lights were more difficult to install but technology has made the installation process as simple as plug-in fluorescent fixtures and as affordable. The added feature of a halogen is its similarity to natural sunlight.

Mounting a puck light or fluorescent strip to the underside of a cabinet is simple. They are small, easy to mount, and basic to wire.

1. Remove the contents of the bottom shelf of the wall cabinet.
2. Remove the lens cover of the light to expose the mounting screw holes.
3. Place the light in the desired location and mark the holes on the underside of the cabinet. Some people recommend positioning the light in the rear of the cabinet; I recommend housing it toward the front where it will be seen the least.
4. Use an awl or a nail to start the hole for the mounting screws.
5. Mount the light(s), using short screws that will not stick through the top side of the bottom cabinet shelf.
6. Utilize cable clips to run and conceal the wires. Neatly stretch the wire, insert it into the clip, and plug it into an outlet.

Hector Hint

Some of the terminals have a place to plug in a touch-sensitive on/off dimmer switch. The switch does not have to be recessed and can easily mount directly to a wall or cabinet.

Hardwiring lights may not be something you want to do if you have never done it before; concealing the wires with cable clips should be sufficient.

Drip, Drip, Drip . . .

One of the many things taken for granted in the kitchen is the faucet—only noticed when it's the dripping faucet. The sound will drive you out of your ever-loving mind. Like everything else in our homes, faucets need some TLC and preventive maintenance too.

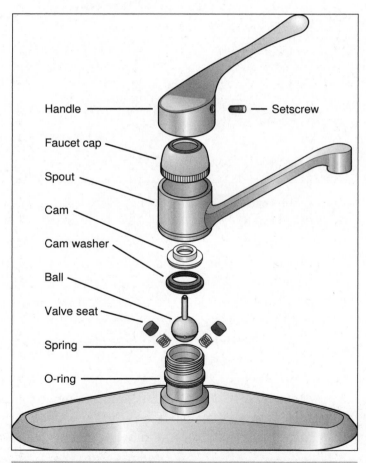

Handle — — Setscrew
Faucet cap —
Spout —
Cam —
Cam washer —
Ball —
Valve seat —
Spring —
O-ring —

Kitchen faucets are more complicated than you might think.

Change the Washer in That Faucet

Changing out a washer in the kitchen faucet should stop the dripping.

1. The first thing you want to do is shut off the water supply line leading to the faucet. If you don't you can find yourself with a geyser and no way to immediately stop it. You can usually find the shut-off valve within the water supply line leading to the faucet. Most shut-off valves are located under the sink, but in a rare situation or an older home, you may not find one there. If you cannot find the shut-off valve under the sink, the water main supply line can be found close to the water meter.

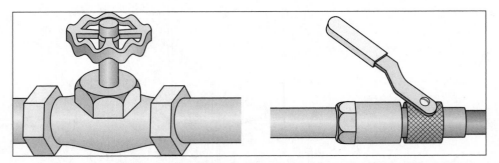

If you cannot locate the shut-off valve under your sink, you will have to turn off the main supply line.

2. On some faucets, the handle must be removed to get at the faucet cap, or bonnet. In order to do this, undo the screw on the top of the faucet and remove the handle. Now, make sure to lay out all the parts in the order you remove them. This is so that you don't forget where they came from, and you can put them back in the same order in which you took them off.

3. The next thing you will see is what is called the faucet cap, or bonnet. With an adjustable wrench remove the bonnet. By doing this, and then removing the spout, cam, and cam washer, you will expose the valve stem and ball.

4. You can remove the valve stem by rotating it clockwise, in the same direction as you would to shut off the water. Once it is loose, the assembly should pull straight up.

5. Pry off the old rubber O-ring washer without damaging the seat that is securing the washer. Be sure to replace the washer with the same size and type. If the washer is not the same size and type, reverse the worn washer so that the bottom is now on the top. This is just a temporary solution and doesn't always work because the washer may be too worn.

6. When you have replaced the washer, replace the parts in the reverse order.

Now, turn the water back on, try the faucet.

The Bathroom

Be realistic when estimating your talents and capabilities when it comes to improving your bathroom. Think simple and consider how much you can afford to spend without breaking the equity bank. Remember, you want to build equity, not blow it. Choose projects like the ones covered in this chapter that will have a large impact, but require as little money out of pocket as possible. And beyond renovation ideas, this chapter provides troubleshooting advice for the leaks and clogs that can come up.

Project Worksheet

MONETARY RETURN: $750–$1,000

PROJECT START DATE: _____

TASKS COMPLETED: _____
_____
_____
_____
_____

TOOLS NEEDED:

- ❏ 14" pipe wrench
- ❏ Adjustable wrench
- ❏ Auger
- ❏ Awl
- ❏ Broom and dust pan
- ❏ Brush (small- to medium-bristled)
- ❏ Bucket
- ❏ Caulking gun
- ❏ Cold chisel
- ❏ Drill
- ❏ Drill bit (¼" in size)
- ❏ Flashlight
- ❏ Flathead screw driver
- ❏ Goggles
- ❏ Hammer
- ❏ Hole saw
- ❏ Hose
- ❏ Level
- ❏ Masonry bit
- ❏ Notched trowel
- ❏ Pencil
- ❏ Phillips head screw driver
- ❏ Pliers
- ❏ Plumber's snake
- ❏ Plunger

- ❏ Pry bar
- ❏ Rags
- ❏ Rubber gloves
- ❏ Screw gun (or screw tip for drill)
- ❏ Shop vacuum
- ❏ Sponge
- ❏ Stud finder
- ❏ Teflon tape
- ❏ Toothbrush
- ❏ Tube clamp
- ❏ Utility knife
- ❏ Wall glue
- ❏ Wood shims
- ❏ Work gloves

Remove an Old Vanity

SKILL LEVEL

2

TIME

4–5 h

Replace an old dilapidated vanity with a new one or, better yet, if you have the room, replace it with a larger one or a double sink vanity. Do you have enough room where the existing vanity is to add an additional sink? Since you already have the supply and waste lines in place, the savings for the additional sink is cut by the additional plumbing costs. Whenever children are part of a household or your spouse is a bathroom hog, this is a time-saving and cost-effective addition to any home.

Before we embark on installing a new vanity or pedestal, we need to remove the old, outdated vanity taking up that valuable space in your bathroom.

1. First, measure to make sure there is enough room for two sinks in your bathroom. A space about 24" wide and 27" deep, without having an obstacle in the way, is sufficient for a vanity base, a pedestal sink, or wall-hung sink.

Hector Hint

If the new sink and base is next to the existing sink, you will want to use a double vanity base. This allows the two sinks to share a common vanity and vanity top, permitting more drawers and storage space. Assuming there is enough room for a double vanity, the old vanity and sink and top will need to be removed.

2. Open the vanity base doors and locate the hot and cold water cut-offs.
3. Once you've located the cut-offs, turn on the hot and cold water in the sink.
4. Reach underneath the vanity base and turn both cut-offs clockwise until the water stops running out. If the water continues to run, you will need to have the cut-off valves replaced by a professional before continuing.
5. Disconnect the hot and cold water supplies to the faucets and the drain assembly from the sink.
6. Unscrew the base cabinet from the wall. These screws are located inside the base cabinet.

7. Using a utility knife, cut any caulk attached to the countertop and vanity.
8. Gently lift the base cabinet up and out, clearing the drain and cut-offs. The vanity top, sink, and base should come out in one piece.
9. Clean off any old caulking left on the wall.

Install a New Vanity Base

SKILL LEVEL

3

TIME

4–5 h

Planning and double-checking measurements are important steps in doing any task. The added effort can save you time and money.

1. Measure the width of the space required for the new vanity. Check that the doors, when opened, will not interfere with anything else in the bathroom. The last thing you want is to install the vanity and discover that the bathroom door can't be opened or that the vanity doesn't allow enough space for one of the other bathroom fixtures.
2. Next, make sure the new vanity fits through the doorways and that you're able to maneuver it around corners, if you have to.
3. Whether the cabinet is being placed in between two walls, centered on a wall, or butts up to the left or right side, you need to have a point of reference for measurements. Measure the cabinet. Using a pencil and level, lay out the cabinet on the wall, where you want it. Check that the horizontal line on top is level and the vertical lines on the sides are plumb.
4. Take horizontal and vertical measurements from the hot and cold supply lines and the stub out for the drain line to the horizontal and vertical layout lines on the wall.
5. Transfer the measurements onto the backside of the vanity cabinet and mark where to drill the holes for the pipes. Using an electric drill and a ¼" drill bit, from the outside of the box in, make three pilot holes.

| **Hector Hint** | Make the holes a little larger to compensate for the possibility of the floor being slightly out of level. |

6. Remove the handles from the supply lines and measure the diameter of the three holes needed.
7. Use a hole saw bit and electric drill to make the holes for the two supply lines and drain stub-out.
8. Using a stud finder, locate and mark the studs behind where the vanity is to be placed.
9. Slide the vanity base into place and check to see if it is level.
10. If the base is not level, slide wood shims under the base to level it.
11. When you're sure it is level, secure the base to the wall using 3" galvanized wood screws.

Hector Hint

Wood screws are not able to penetrate ceramic tile. If the wall has tile on it, you will need to drill through it with a masonry bit before putting the screws through it. If the studs are difficult to locate, a toggle-type anchor may be necessary to hold the vanity base to the wall. However, if there is no ceramic tile on the wall, locate and secure the cabinet to the studs.

12. Cut the shims using a utility knife or a wood chisel.
13. When a gap is obvious between the vanity base and the floor, apply a bead of caulk or cove base to hide it.
14. Attach the faucet to the sink, following the instructions accompanying the faucet.
15. Place a bead of silicone caulk on the top edge of the vanity and set the countertop in place. Apply downward pressure to the top and allow it to dry.
16. Set the sink into the vanity top.

In some cases, you may need to remove the cabinet doors before setting the cabinet in place, to allow for workable room in the base.

Replace an Old Vanity with a Pedestal Sink

SKILL LEVEL

3

TIME

2–3 h

Removing the old vanity and adding a pedestal sink will give a small bathroom the appearance of being larger. For removing an existing vanity, refer to *Remove an Old Vanity* on page 169.

1. Put the pedestal base and the sink in place. Making sure that the sink is level, mark the mounting holes with a pencil. If there aren't any tiles on the walls, check to see if the studs line up with the mounting holes and make sure to catch them when securing the sink.
2. If tiles are on the walls, a masonry bit is needed to penetrate them. Place several strips of tape on the spot and remark it, and the tape should be able to help keep the drill bit centered. This step should also be used to mount the pedestal to the floor.
3. Install the faucet and drain line assemblage.
4. Following the instructions for the pedestal sink you are installing, secure the sink and base using the fasteners provided, and make sure it is firmly set in place.
5. Once it is set, connect the drain lines and hook up the hot and cold supply lines.

Following the manufacturer's instructions will help to insure the warranty. Most manufacturers will include the mounting brackets and screws.

Hector Hint Never overtighten the screws and bolts. Doing this can crack the pedestal or sink.

Privacy Can Make a Nice Difference

If you are handy, constructing a small privacy partition for the toilet area can add a sense of comfort to your bathroom. Having a separate toilet area allows someone privacy while still allowing someone else to use another area of the bathroom and is a nice feature for a home, particularly if you forgot to lock the door.

When people in a household get up in the morning at the same time, it's an inconvenience for all, but splitting the bathroom helps to accommodate more than one person. Many newer homes on the market have the sink area in one part of the bathroom with a separate toilet room.

If you can split a bathroom into one and a half or better yet, two bathrooms, you add value to your home. Sometimes this can be done by using a walk-in closet or other space that is already in the house without the expense of adding on to the structure of your home. It is a consideration when figuring whether or not it is to your advantage in the long and short term.

Simple changes can make a big difference.

Install a Crescent-Shaped Shower Curtain Rod

SKILL LEVEL

2

TIME

1½ h

Think about removing the old shower curtain rod and adding a crescent-shaped shower rod. This will add space to the inside of the tub area, taking away that claustrophobic feeling that standard shower curtain rods present. These rods can be used with standard shower curtains so there's no need to purchase new ones. Shower doors don't give you more space but these rods do. Even the more upscale posh hotels use them, making for a comfortable bath and shower experience. Pick one up and let's get down to business.

1. Remove the shower curtains and straight rod.
2. Take the new rod out of its packaging and neatly lay everything out.
3. Assemble the crescent-shaped shower rod on the floor according to the instructions in the packaging.
4. Measure from the ceiling to the top of the old shower rod bracket. Record that measurement.
5. Along the crease where the wall meets the ceiling, measure back 3" from the start of the tub. Mark with your pencil.
6. From the pencil mark, measure down the recorded distance the old shower rod bracket was from the ceiling. Mark with your pencil. This is where your new bracket should be placed.
7. Hold the new bracket in this spot and mark where the bracket holes will be with your pencil.

8. If mounting directly onto drywall, use an awl or nail to make the hole for the plastic anchor. Be sure not to make the hole too big. The anchor should fit tightly after being tapped into place. If you are mounting the brackets onto ceramic tile, you will need to tap through the glazed part of the tile before drilling into it and then the plastic anchor can be installed.
9. Once all the anchors are in place you can screw the brackets into place and mount the shower rod.

Counter space has always been a problem in small bathrooms. Replacing a counter with one that extends over the toilet tank, for example, can give you much needed space, 2 to 3 sq. ft. in some cases, making it seem as though the bathroom is bigger. When doing this, the vanity top must not interfere with the workable space required should the toilet need repair. Some vanity tops can be hinged to lift if necessary. Others, like granite or marble, could be separate and configured to lift out of place as needed.

You can never have enough mirrors in a bathroom. Not only do they make the space look larger, but are practical when getting dressed and putting on makeup, adding to the reflective qualities of lighting, and letting you see yourself from many different angles.

Good Bathroom Lighting

Lighting in a bathroom is as important as pots and pans are in a kitchen, especially if there isn't a window. Lighting in a bathroom can emulate daylight and nighttime lighting, which is important to men and women whether preparing for work or a night out. Therefore, placement, intensity, and effect all play a part when choosing lights for your bathroom.

Lighting sconces on each side of the mirror create better lighting, but if that is not possible, mounting a multiple bulb fixture above the mirror will help to illuminate the area in front of it without causing any shadowing.

Showers and tub areas require waterproof lights that keep moisture from entering the electrical components inside the casing. Heat lamps are also an added feature to help you warm up when drying off.

A change in color can make a major difference in the lighting of a bathroom. Small bathrooms should be lighter. This will give your bathroom a sense of space and openness. Larger bathrooms can afford to be darker in color. Be careful with the type of paint you use in the bathroom. A semi-gloss will better reflect light given off by light fixtures and an enamel paint will help protect the bathroom walls from moisture.

Change Out an Old Water Closet

SKILL LEVEL

2

TIME

2–3 h

Depending on the bathroom, an old discolored toilet bowl can either take away or add charm to a bathroom. It all depends on its condition. If the bowl is not operating properly, the internal mechanisms may need replacement. However, if it is too far gone, it may need changing.

Before purchasing a new toilet, you may want to consider an elongated bowl. These are roomier, stylish, and can be very quiet when flushed. Some are one piece units, making them easier to handle and install.

To remove the old toilet:

1. Shut off and disconnect the supply line leading to the toilet.
2. Flush the toilet to empty the tank of any water that may be inside.
3. Use a plunger and plunge out of the bowl whatever water is left.
4. Take the lid off the tank and bail out whatever what you can and soak up the balance of water in it using an old towel or rags.
5. Remove the tank by unscrewing the two bolts located on each side.
6. To soak up the water left at the bottom of the bowl and in the curved outlet, stuff it with rags.
7. Gently lift and remove the tank from the bowl.
8. Remove the caps holding the bowl to the floor and with a wrench, loosen and remove the bolts holding it in place.
9. Shift the bowl left to right to loosen it from the flange. If possible, use two people to lift it. Place rags in front of the bowl to catch water when it is removed.
10. Scrape the old wax gasket off and check the flange for corrosion. A replacement gasket and wax ring can be purchased at your local hardware store.

11. Replace the old wax gasket and change the flange if it's corroded. Be careful not to let the wax fall into the drain line.

To install the new toilet:

1. Position the flange bolts facing upward in the flange slots. Make sure the wax seal holds the bolts in place.
2. Place the bowl over the flange and the bolts through the bowl holes. Firmly seat the bowl over the flange, tighten the bolts, and snap on the bolt covers.
3. If the toilet is a two piece set, set the tank into place over the gasket and bolt the tank to the bowl, making sure not to overtighten the bolts. Connect the water supply line to the tank and turn the valve counterclockwise.
4. While the tank is filling up, check for leaks where the tank and bowl meet. In addition, look around the bottom of the bowl and floor. After flusing the toilet several times and when you are sure there are no leaks, caulk or grout between the bowl and floor.
5. Attach the toilet seat to the bowl using the plastic bolts provided.

Hector Hint

Toilet tanks and bowls can be cumbersome for one person to maneuver. Setting the tank in place is much easier when two people handle it.

Maintain, Remove, and Replace Ceramic Tiles

SKILL LEVEL

1

TIME

1 h

Ceramic tiles are hardened durable surfaces, made of baked clay that is glazed and polished for a shiny glossy or a matte look. Stone, like granite, is sliced from mined areas, polished, cut for a specific use and professionally installed, whereas ceramic tile is easier for a novice to install.

Ceramic tile is commonly installed on shower walls, bathroom floors, and at times, the other walls in the bathroom, as well as the ceiling in the shower. One cracked tile stands out in a sea of ceramic like a sore thumb. So how do you remove individually cracked or damaged tile without destroying the entire wall in the process? Good question.

1. Find the tiles that are loose or cracked and look for replacements that are the same, or match as close as possible. You may need to try several places before you are able to find a match. Better quality tile may have a stamp on the back indicating the brand name or number. That does not mean that you will be able to find that exact color. Different dye lots have different shadings and sometimes certain colors are discontinued due to style changes.

Hector Hint

If you cannot find tile to match what is already there, you may want to place accent tiles where the damaged tiles where. This may require you to remove additional tiles in order to get the design the way you want it or to scatter a few accent tiles on the walls, making it a point not to put them on the same horizontal and vertical grid lines.

2. First, remove the grout surrounding the tile. Grout helps quite a bit in holding the tile in place. If you try to remove the tile without removing the grout around the tile, the adjacent tile can crack as well. Your local hardware or home improvement store should sell a grout scraper. These work very well.

3. Removing the tile should be done gently. If you are removing the tile from a wall, try not to rip the paper backing off the drywall. Ceramic tile is much easier to remove from Backer board or cement board than drywall. You do not need to be as gentle when the tile is mounted on plywood or cement board or cement on the floor, but always scrape the grout out before beginning.

4. Score the tile with a glasscutter, making an X shape and breaking through the glazed finish. Carefully tap and break the clay part of the tile in the scored area, prying the tile out without damaging adjacent tiles. Occasionally you cannot help but rip the paper backing on the drywall. In that case, apply a paint sealer, let it dry at least twenty-four hours before gluing tile on the wall.

Be careful not to damage any of the surrounding tiles.

5. Use a flat board to align the tile with the other surrounding tiles and use spacers to match the existing joints where the grout is to go. Now you must wait another twenty-four hours to let the glue set before grouting the tile.
6. When applying the grout, try not to get it all over the place. Make it a point to fill all voids around the tile.
7. Wait about fifteen to twenty minutes and remove any excess grout that may be on the tile. The best way I found to remove grout without getting a film on the tile is to wipe with a single long stroke, rinse the sponge, and wipe again, repeating the process until all

the grout film is gone. Doing it this way will avoid smearing the grout around.

8. Using the shower or stepping on the grout before it dries completely will weaken the bond and may cause it to fall out or become uneven. You must also give the grout at least sixteen to twenty-four hours to dry.

9. Wait several weeks before applying a grout sealer. A sealer will help to keep mold and mildew from growing and keep the grout clean. Maintenance should be done annually.

Grouting tiles can be messy. Therefore it's best to wear rubber gloves when working with grout.

Match Finishes and Styles

Older bathrooms have ceramic wall toothbrush holders and soap dishes, but that's not so much the case these days. Homeowners are using separate toothbrush holders and soap dishes that sit on the vanity top. The metal finishes in a bathroom should match, including the toothbrush holder, soap dish, towel bar, shower door, toilet lever handle, shower curtain rod, and light fixture(s). This helps to keep things uniform and consistent. Another way to keep things in step is to match the least difficult to replace items, like a towel bar or shower curtain rod, with the more permanent things, like shower body trim or a faucet.

After time, like any other fixture in your home, faucet handles become outdated, tarnished, and just don't look good any longer. Since faucet handles are subject to constant use, they are likely to eventually show signs of wear. Matching up handles for a vanity faucet and shower is a very simple task that can make a huge difference in the look of your bathroom.

There is a wealth of bathroom lavatory parts on the Internet, from old-fashioned glass faucet knobs and classic porcelain handles, to many different modern-day styles and finishes. Replacing them is simple and makes a world of difference. So think about changing your bathroom hardware finishes and/or faucet handles to match what's in style today.

Replace a Ceramic Soap Dish or Toothbrush Holder

SKILL LEVEL

2

TIME

2–3 h

Ceramic toothbrush and soap holders can occasionally fall out or crack, leaving a big ugly space in the wall. Although it may look a little difficult, they are fairly simple to replace. The hard part is matching the color and shade of the original. Dye lots vary and colors are sometimes discontinued over time. Therefore, finding the exact shade and color may not be possible. But if you are diligent and creative you should be able to find something to fit the scheme.

1. Clean out the area where the ceramic fixture had been fastened.
2. If you are using the old ceramic fixture, scrape off any adhesive or plaster that may be stuck on the back.

3. Cut a strip of duct tape and keep it within reach.
4. Using a small amount of premixed thinset or plaster, apply it to the back of the ceramic fixture and set the fixture in place.
5. Tape the fixture back and wipe any excess thinset or plaster off.
6. Wait at least twenty-four hours before removing the tape and grout the area around the fixture using the same color grout.

Add Charm with a Few Accents

Many newer baths, with the exception of the shower and bath walls, do not have wainscoting. Wainscoting is the tile on the walls outside of the shower and bathtub walls. It is more common in older homes to have wainscoting on all walls, but with the cost of building materials it is often considered an option. Wainscoting can be installed floor to ceiling or partially up the wall. The standard is 48" above the floor.

With the look for classic homes always in demand, some homeowners have opted for wood wainscoting on their bathroom walls instead of tiles, giving it a warm, classic-country look. When installing wood wainscoting, an oil-based paint will give it a rich look and protect it against the harmful effects of humidity.

Fix a Leaky Shower Door

SKILL LEVEL

2

TIME

2–3 h

Shower doors, if installed correctly, do not usually leak, but occasionally an improperly prepped area can prevent silicone waterproof caulking from adhering properly. If not maintained, water can also penetrate between the tub or shower and the door frame. This is not a difficult repair to attempt and can easily be fixed by a novice do-it-yourselfer.

In most cases, shower door frames have a bead of waterproof silicone caulking between the frame and the shower or tub interior and some frames have a rubber gasket between the frame and the tub or shower.

Preventing mold or mildew smells, and even rot, which a leak could cause in the sub-surface of the floor or wall in your bathroom, will be well worth your time and effort.

If caulking the exterior of the door frame is not enough:

1. Carefully remove the shower doors and place them securely against the wall so they are out of the way.
2. Remove the screws holding the metal frame of the shower in place.
3. Gently remove the caulking bead between frame and shower or tub.
4. Remove screws rusted in place by drilling them out or lightly tapping them counterclockwise until they are loose.
5. Using a small pry bar with a soft cloth underneath to prevent scratching the surface, gently loosen the frame of the shower door.
6. If you are replacing a rubber gasket, use a piece of wood under the frame, place the rubber strip down, line the strip up with the metal bar and punch holes in the strip using a hammer and awl.
7. Insert the screws through the metal bar and through the rubber strip. Trim the rubber strip along the outside of the door frame to fit, and peel away the backing.
8. Replace the strip and tighten the screws to secure the bottom of the shower door. Apply silicone sealant to prevent future leaks.

Hector Hint

Never apply silicone caulking to the tub or shower side of the frame. This can clog drainage ports, preventing water from escaping from the inside of the track.

Remove Corrosion from a Shower Door Frame

SKILL LEVEL

1

TIME

1 h

Like many other areas in your home, shower doors need to be maintained and cleaned periodically. After time, caulking can shrink, allowing water to infiltrate and make its way to the other side.

1. Using a bleach solution of ¾ cup of bleach to 1 gallon of water and a small medium-bristled brush, scrub the door. Make sure to wear gloves to avoid skin irritation, and open the windows and use an exhaust fan to remove any fumes.

2. Making sure not to scrape the finish off the frame or doors, carefully scrub any corrosion off the metal. When you are finished, dry the surface with a soft towel.

Clogged Bathroom Drains

We have all, at one time or another, had a clogged drain. Tubs, showers, and vanity sinks are the most common places to get clogged. Hair and soap scum are usually the culprits, but in a kitchen we can generally blame a stopped-up drain on food particles. And the toilet, as we all know, is usually clogged by toilet paper, or if you have little children, a ball, or a toy.

Hair, food, and toilet paper are much easier to clear than a ball or a toy in the toilet bowl. In most cases, if a ball or a toy becomes lodged in the toilet bowl, the toilet bowl may need to be replaced.

WHERE DOES IT ALL GO?

Looking under your sink you will find a U-shaped pipe connection; this is called a P-trap. This U-shaped connection catches sediment and holds water, creating a seal and preventing any noxious odors, that are a direct result of waste, from entering your home. The configuration of pipes that empty the dirty water into the sewer or septic system is called the waste line system. Easily spotted, these pipes are larger than any other pipes in a home.

PLUNGING RIGHT IN

The key to clearing a clog with a plunger is to create a vacuum in the waste line you are trying to clear.

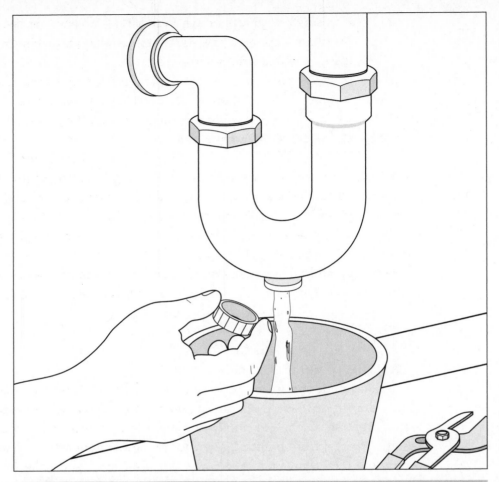

A typical P-trap will look something like this.

Clear Your Bathtub Drain

Techniques used to unclog a sink vary slightly from that of clearing a bathtub drain. You may need to repeat the steps in this task a couple of times before the object becomes dislodged.

1. Remove the overflow plate located above the drain.
2. Make it as airtight as possible by stuffing it with rags. Make sure that no rags fall into the drain. If a rag does fall in, make a small

hook from a wire hanger and try to fish it out. Move the mechanism for the drain stopper to the side before stuffing it with rags.

3. Fill the tub with at least 4" of water.
4. Make sure there is water in the toilet bowl and close the stopper in the bathroom sink. If there is no stopper, stuff it with a rag.
5. If there is a bathroom above or below, repeat the process in them, as well, in order to create a better vacuum.
6. Making sure to have good suction, place the plunger directly over the drain, secure the plunger and push and pull several times, creating a better vacuum and immediately remove it. Creating pressure and immediately releasing it can dislodge a clog drain. This process may need to be repeated several times before the clog dislodges.
7. Once the task is complete, you can remove the rags and replace the overflow cap.

Unclog Your Toilet Bowl

SKILL LEVEL
1
TIME
1 h

1. Place a plunger firmly over the inlet of a toilet bowl.
2. Push and pull the plunger to create suction and after several times, immediately release it. The water should go down the waste line. After several times, if it does not, you will need to try an auger or a plumber's snake.

Clear Your Tub's Waste Line

SKILL LEVEL
3
TIME
2–3 h

The purpose of an auger is to drill through any sediment build-up in a drain or to snag whatever may have fallen in.

1. Use a screwdriver to remove the overflow plate.
2. Slowly feed the auger into the overflow inlet. Once the auger is about 2' to 3' into the drain or if you hit a blockage, begin to turn the auger clockwise so that it cuts through the blockage. If it fails to dislodge, try reversing the auger, counterclockwise.

Unclog a Toilet Bowl with an Auger

1. Place the bent part of the auger into the inlet. Turning the auger clockwise, feed the auger into the toilet bowl inlet. This may take a few tries because of the trap at the bottom of the bowl.
2. Continue to turn the auger until the object or stoppage clears. If the auger fails to clear the clogged bowl, you may need to use a plumber's snake in order to get far enough in the waste line. A plumber's snake is longer than an auger, but utilized in the same manner.

If you still cannot clear the stoppage, you probably need to call a plumber.

Fix a Leaking Showerhead

Check for water dripping or spraying out from the threaded area of the head. Sometimes tightening the showerhead will be enough, but if that doesn't do it, it may need Teflon tape or replacement.

1. Unscrew the showerhead counterclockwise, using an adjustable wrench or pliers.
2. Apply Teflon tape to the pipe stub-out, clockwise.
3. Screw on the old or new showerhead using the adjustable wrench, but be sure not to overtighten it. An older stub out can crack at the elbow if too much pressure is applied.
4. Test the showerhead.

Replace a Worn Tub Diverter

Tub diverters allow water to flow to the showerhead or to the tub spout. If water is diverted to the showerhead and leaks out of the spout into the tub, it is time to replace the diverter with a new one. This means the internal mechanism of the diverter is worn and the entire tub spout needs to be replaced.

1. Much like a showerhead, a tub spout can be removed by turning it counterclockwise. It may need to be lightly tapped to help loosen it from the pipe stub.
2. Clean any corrosion off the stub-out by lightly brushing it with a steel wool pad. Make sure to clean all the particles of the steel wool off the stub-out.
3. Wrap Teflon tape around the stub-out two or three times, clockwise.
4. Making sure not to strip the threads on the stub-out, hand tighten the new tub spout.
5. Run the water and check that the spout does not leak back onto the wall when the diverter is in either position.
6. Applying waterproof silicone around the spout at the wall will help to prevent water from running down the wall and getting behind the spout and ruining the wall.

Inspect the Caulking and Grouting Around Your Home

SKILL LEVEL

3

TIME

2 h

(for a standard size bathroom)

Caulking is very important in preventing a leak and keeping water from infiltrating vulnerable places.

Caulking should be somewhat flexible, and not be cracked or blackened with mildew. If it is, replace it with a tub and tile type silicone-based waterproof caulk.

Check the following areas for cracked or missing caulking in need of repair:

- Around the bottom of the toilet
- Along the wall at the edge of the tub or shower
- At the inside corners of the tub or shower
- Between the countertop and backsplash
- Where the tub meets the shower
- At the base of the tub or shower along the floor
- Where the shower door meets the wall and tub or shower base

To patch cracked and old caulking in your bathroom tub and shower:

1. It is important when purchasing caulk to buy a silicone-based caulk. This type of caulk is waterproof and adheres very well and for long periods. There are several colors to choose from; it is best to use the same color previously there.
2. For repairing small cracks and voids, cut the caulking tube at about a 45 degree angle, just enough to allow for a hanger to puncture the inner seal. For areas that do not have any caulk at all, a ⅜" cut will need to be made.
3. Install the caulk tube into the caulking gun.
4. Position yourself close to where you will be working and be sure to have a wet rag with you.
5. Slowly begin to apply pressure to the trigger on the caulking gun until you can see the caulk beginning to exit the tube.
6. Gently apply the caulk, keeping the gun moving along the path requiring caulk.
7. Once the spot needing caulk is complete, quickly release the pressure from the caulk or it will continue to ooze out. If you've never done this before you may need to practice a few times first.
8. Using your finger or a wet rag gently smooth out the freshly caulked area without removing too much.

KNOW WHEN TO CALL IN THE PROFESSIONALS

There are some things that need to be fixed by professionals in order to avoid future or additional damage. Call a plumber if you find the following problems and feel as though you are in over your head.

- Leaky or stuck water supply lines and valves
- Leaks present in the shower pan
- Recurring mold or mildew on the walls

Stop That Constantly Running Toilet

SKILL LEVEL

2

TIME

1 h

Hundreds of gallons of water are wasted in a single household per day from a constantly running toilet. In some cases it is easily heard and detected, but in others it may not be.

Adding several drops of food dye into the tank and waiting thirty minutes for the dye to find its way into the bowl without flushing is one way to find out if you have a problem. If you detect a problem, follow these simple steps to stop a toilet from consistently running.

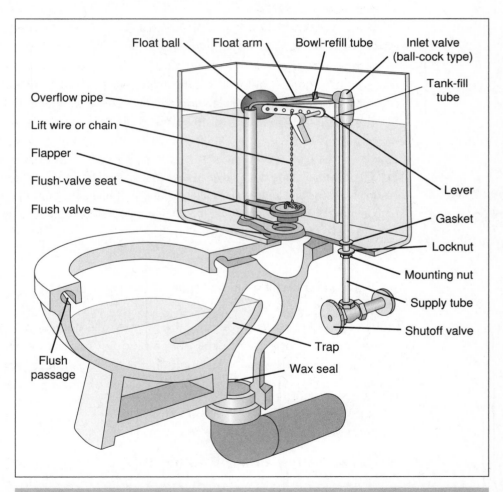

Here is a diagram of the various parts of a standard toilet.

1. Jiggle the toilet handle to see if the running water stops.
2. If that doesn't take care of it, check the chain or solid guide. In some instances they may be tangled, deteriorated, or out of position.
3. Also, see if the flush handle fits comfortably against the tank. A loose handle can offset the guide and stopper.
4. Stoppers are located at the bottom of the tank and are lifted by the handle, allowing water into the bowl to flush. Check that the stopper sits squarely on the opening and has not deteriorated. A replacement stopper can be purchased at your local hardware or home center and easily installs the same way it is removed.
5. Since tanks function by gravity, water level in a tank plays a big part in how well the toilet will flush. Look at the water level to see if it is no more than 2" below the top of the overflow tube. The overflow tube stops water from reaching the top of the tank and redirects the excess water into and down the drain line.

Hector Hint

The float arm adjusts the water level in the tank. The adjustment for the arm is at the arm pivot. An adjustment screw allows the arm to pivot up or down. If making an adjustment is not sufficient, hold the float arm near the pivot point and gently bend it to make the adjustment.

6. If the water is still running, replace the float arm and mechanism.

If these procedures do not remedy the problem, a replacement tank may need to be installed or a service call from a plumber may be necessary.

If you need to replace the entire unit, install a 1.6-gallon capacity water-saver toilet. The standard toilet uses 5 to 6 gallons of water per flush.

Hot Tubs, Spas, and Whirlpools

After a long day at work or just to relax and unwind, there's absolutely nothing better than the massaging warm waters of a hot tub. Hot tubs can be enjoyed in the summer or winter. It doesn't matter what time of year it is; the relaxing effect they have on us is not seasonal. It could be 20 degrees outside and as long as you have a robe waiting for you outside the tub, you'll be so relaxed it won't even matter. These large pools of relaxation are normally found outdoors because of their size. Occasionally you will see one indoors, but only if the space allows.

What is the difference between a hot tub, spa, and whirlpool? Hot tubs can accommodate from two to as many as eight or even more people. They are usually located outdoors and have water jets, a water heater, and are not drained. When not in use they are covered, minimizing heat loss and reducing the amount of energy used. Hot tubs also need to be checked for proper pH levels and require the use of chemicals to do so. The jets are adjustable to different settings by the touch of a button. Some come with speakers and a television or audio system. Spas are very similar to hot tubs in size and location except they do not have water jets.

Whirlpools, on the other hand, are installed in a bathroom and ordinarily accommodate one person. The hot water is provided like that of a regular tub. Between uses the tub is drained and chemicals are not needed to maintain a sanitary environment. Whirlpools are therapeutic and use water jets to massage your body.

These units can be very expensive, but preventive maintenance will keep your investment sound.

What are some common problems that can occur in hot tubs and spas?

1. The hoses can leak.
2. Pumps can leak and may need to be replaced.
3. The jets can become clogged.
4. Chemicals may need to be balanced for proper pH levels.
5. Fiberglass can become dingy and fade without proper care, especially in direct sunlight.
6. Tubs and spas can leak in several places. For instance, anyplace that penetrates the fiberglass may be vulnerable to a leak.
7. Thermostats may need to be replaced or adjusted.
8. Electrical wires can become corroded, loose, or faulty.
9. Plastic jets can break.

10. Gaskets and connections can become loose over time and may need to be replaced or tightened.
11. Heaters may need to be changed or adjusted.

Unless you are experienced with this or handy, you may want to call a repair person who knows about these tubs or your local spa dealer and have him or her repair these problems for you.

Hot Tub and Whirlpool Maintenance

To keep up with them:

1. Shut the breaker off or remove the fuse whenever checking or working on the tub.
2. With a flashlight or droplight check for any signs of water outside of, under, and around the tub and tub floor.
3. If there are signs of a leak, try to locate the source.
4. Look and feel around any tubing or hoses at unions or connections to see if there is any water that may be leaking from these areas.
5. Check the wiring for any frayed wires, loose wires, or missing wire nuts.
6. Make sure the wire connections are tight.
7. Verify that the heater is operating properly.
8. Make certain the jets are not clogged, that they are properly adjusted, and not cracked or broken.
9. Clean the fiberglass and wax with a manufacturer-approved cleaning and waxing product.

Heating and Cooling

Make sure that your heating and air conditioning units are functioning at optimal performance in order to save yourself utility and maintenance dollars. Something to keep in mind: If you sell your home and the heating or cooling systems are substandard and ill maintained, it will be noted on your home inspection report. That will be another negotiation tool your buyer would have in reducing the price of your home. Take proper care of your heating and cooling systems in order to stay in control of your home's temperature and value.

Project Worksheet

MONETARY RETURN: $1,500–$2,500

PROJECT START DATE: _____

TASKS COMPLETED: _____
_____
_____
_____
_____

TOOLS NEEDED:
- ❑ Awl
- ❑ Can of air-dust remover
- ❑ Hose
- ❑ Pipe insulation
- ❑ Screwdriver
- ❑ Shop vacuum or regular vacuum
- ❑ Soft-bristled brush
- ❑ Utility knife
- ❑ Wire ties or aluminum tape

Your Air Conditioning System

We need to spruce up and prepare our air conditioners to keep the humidity out of our homes and keep us cool-headed during the warm months. It is not a pleasant experience, after you have worked hard all day, to come home to an air conditioner that is barely alive, leaving you to a sweaty, uncomfortable evening at home.

We want to be proactive about this and get our air conditioners ready now! Whether it is a wall unit or central air, we need to do a few simple things to make sure they are operating efficiently and effectively.

Hector Hint

Before doing any maintenance on your air conditioner, *always* make sure that it is unplugged and that the circuit breakers are off or the fuses are removed. Never remove the housing and attempt to repair the unit yourself.

Air Conditioner Maintenance

SKILL LEVEL

1

TIME

1 h

Like trying to row a boat into the wind, a poorly maintained air conditioner will need to work harder to operate and use more electricity.

Here are some tips to help keep your air conditioner running well and your home comfortable.

1. Plug in your window unit to make sure it is operating before the season begins. You don't want to wait for a hot sticky day to find out it no longer works or that the circuit breaker is off, causing you to wait for hours for the house to cool down.
2. Unplug the unit and remove the filter. The filters are housed behind the front grill area of the unit. Replace the filter if it has deteriorated beyond use. A home improvement store or your local hardware store usually stocks these.
3. Clean the filter by using a mild detergent, rinsing it thoroughly and letting it dry before replacing it. This should be repeated monthly during the cooling season.

4. Using your vacuum or shop vacuum, gently vacuum the front grills on the air conditioner and the rear condenser coils. Be careful not to destroy the condenser coils when cleaning. Gently brush and vacuum the dust and dirt from the coils. Make sure to straighten any bent coils. Use a plastic comb or something that cannot puncture any of the condenser tubes.

5. After you have completed the cleaning process, turn the unit on. If it is not blowing out cool air, the freon may need to be replenished. You will need a service professional to do this.

Central Air Conditioning Maintenance

SKILL LEVEL

2

TIME

2–3 h

Central air conditioners are meant to function proficiently and last for a long time, but only if they are properly cared for. Following are some things you can do to keep your air conditioner functioning the way it should.

1. Change the air filters. These units have filters and will need to be changed monthly during the cooling season. Filters can sometimes be found in the air handler, which blows the air through the ducts, or in the return air grills. Return air grills are found in the ceiling or high on the wall, and are usually rectangular in shape. In most cases, these filters are replaced instead of cleaned.

2. Hose down the condenser unit, found outside your home, making sure to remove any leaves or debris that may have gathered during the colder months. These units are meant to sustain exterior elements so getting water on them will not damage the unit.

3. Air handlers can usually be found in the attic. These units should periodically be checked for leaks. They have drip pans to catch any water that may otherwise leak onto the ceiling below.

4. Check the batteries in your thermostats. If you use a timer on your thermostat, make sure the unit is turning on and off at the pre-set times.

It is important to have your duct system cleaned by a professional every one or two years. Look in your local yellow pages or call your local air conditioning company.

What to Do If Your Furnace Is Not Running

In many parts of the world, oil and gas are the main source of energy for furnaces. There are forced-air furnaces, hot-water type furnaces, and steam furnaces. These furnaces are usually fueled by oil or gas. Oil is dirty and very expensive to use, whereas gas is a much cleaner and a more efficient fuel. In some cases, it is difficult to convert these furnaces from oil to gas due to logistical reasons and cost. But more and more homeowners are switching and, in some cases, get a financial incentive to do so by the utility company.

WHERE'S THE FUEL?

Oil furnaces operate using a low-quality petroleum which is delivered to the home and stored in an oil tank above ground. At one time, oil tanks were placed underground, but because leaking tanks are environmental hazards they are no longer installed underground. Natural gas is piped into a home from a utility company, while propane gas is stored in tanks outside the home.

INSIDE A GAS AND OIL FURNACE

The oil or gas is sprayed into a burner and ignited by an electric spark or pilot light. The furnace heats air for a forced-air system, water for a hot-water baseboard system, and a steam system boils water to create steam for the radiators.

ZONES

Depending on the size of a home, there can be more than one zone on forced-air and hot-water baseboard systems. Steam heat systems are less likely to have multiple zones.

HOW THEY HEAT

Here are several ways that a home is heated in the colder months:

Hot-Water System: A hot-water heating system heats and maintains water at a specified temperature. When a thermostat senses a drop in the room temperature, a zone valve opens, distributing the hot water to that particular zone in the house. The hot water then heats the elements in the baseboard. Baseboard heating elements are located by or under windows to offset any cold air that may penetrate. The hot water is recirculated back to the boiler, reheated, and redistributed through the system. Once the zone that is calling for heat has reached the desired temperature, the zone valve then closes.

Forced-Air System: A forced-air system heats air and blows it through a series of ducts. The air is released through adjustable registers located throughout the rooms and different locations in the house. The air is returned through a return air duct system, reheated, and distributed once again. A thermostat regulates the amount of heated air that flows through the registers. Once the room has reached the temperature it was set for, the system either shuts down or a damper closes, stopping any more heated air from entering the area controlled by the thermostat.

Boilers: This system is the oldest of the three. This type of furnace heats water to create steam. The steam rises through a series of angled pipes to radiators throughout a home, heating the rooms. The pipes are slightly pitched upward to make the flow of steam easier. The return pipes are pitched slightly downward from the radiators in order for the condensation from the steam to return to the boiler, where it is reheated. Radiators have a pressure valve that releases the pressure of the steam and can be heard hissing at times. The radiators and steam pipes can get hot enough to cause a serious burn. Although steam is considered to be the best form of heat, it is the toughest to control.

Hector Hint	Due to several factors, some homes need to use propane as a source of fuel. Here is a little extra precaution that needs to be taken: Never place a propane tank under a tree. If the tree should happen to get struck by lightning, become rotted, or weakened by any other means, a branch can fall, hitting the tank, severing the gauge and connections, and possibly catch on fire and explode.

FURNACES

Furnaces are generally quite reliable and last for a long time. There are also regular maintenance tasks that a homeowner can do to stop from having to spend buckets of money on repair bills. Occasionally, furnaces may not run or fire up, or may cycle on and off.

Hector Hint	Make sure the filters on a hot air system are changed on a regular basis. Dirty filters do not allow the air to flow freely, or the furnace to operate as efficiently as it should.

What to Do If Your Furnace Is Not Running

SKILL LEVEL

3

TIME

2–3 h

Here are a few simple steps you can take to check your system before calling for service.

1. If you have an oil furnace, check the amount of oil in the tank. If it's low, but you are still getting a reading, the tank may have sludge in the bottom. The sludge cannot be burned and the tank will need to be filled.
2. Press the reset button. An overload may have caused it to trigger off.
3. The thermostat may not be operating properly. If this is happening, the thermostat may need to be adjusted, cleaned, or replaced; see What to Do When Your Thermostat Fails (page 204).

4. A circuit breaker may be tripped or a fuse may be blown. Your circuit breakers are located in a panel usually opposite the electric meter where the electricity enters the home. If you cannot tell which circuit breaker was tripped and the circuit breakers are not labeled, try switching all of them off and back on again.

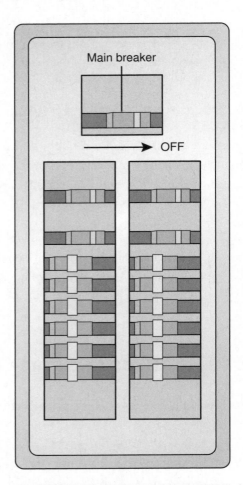

Turn off all the circuit breakers if you cannot tell which one relates directly to your problem.

5. Circuit breakers can go bad and may need to be replaced. Since high voltage electrical power can be very dangerous if you are not familiar with it, it may be best left to a professional.

6. Fuses are also usually located where the electricity enters the home opposite the electric meter. Look for the fuse labeled "furnace." Check for a severed band by looking at the top of the fuse through the viewer. If the band is broken, the fuse is blown and will need to be changed. If the fuse locations are not labeled, you will need to check them all.

7. The pilot may not be providing a spark for the furnace to fire up. Follow the instructions in the owner's manual for your particular furnace.

8. When the furnace recycles on and off frequently, it could be caused by a faulty thermostat or a dirty filter in a forced air system.

SAFETY SENSORS

Oil and gas furnaces have several safety devices:

- **Low water shut-off:** If the water gets too low in a hot-water or steam system, the low water switch is activated and the furnace automatically shuts itself off.
- **Flue backdraft or flue blockage switch:** In the event that there is a blockage or a backdraft, the flue backdraft switch is triggered, causing the furnace to shut down.
- **Reset button:** When the furnace senses a malfunction or overload, the system will shut down and will need to be reset in order to fire up.
- **Pilot light gas shut-off switch:** If for any reason the pilot light should go out the gas is automatically shut off, preventing a buildup of gas.

Note: Before doing work of any kind, make sure the circuit breaker is off or the fuse is removed.

Replace a Forced-Air System's Filter

To replace a filter:

1. Open the unit and remove the blower access door. The filter can usually be located on the front or side of the furnace housing.
2. Take the filter out by either sliding it out or holding it firmly and pulling it out.
3. Using a vacuum cleaner, remove any dirt and dust from the area around the filter housing.
4. Replace the filter with the type that is suggested by the manufacturer.
5. Close the blower door and make sure that it interlocks and is closed properly.
6. Check that the blower blades are clean and wipe off the fuel pump.

Replacing a filter should be done monthly during the heating season.

FLUES

Inspect the flues for proper connections and pitch. The flue pipes should be angled upward to allow for the exhaust and carbon monoxide to be removed from the home. This is overlooked many times and can be a dangerous, if not fatal, situation.

ELECTRIC FURNACES

Unbelievably, in some parts of the country it is actually more economical to use electric heat than it is to use gas or oil to heat a home. The use of an electric furnace may be due to a preference of the builder, the cost of electricity, or both. These furnaces use electric elements to warm the air and distribute it throughout a home. Electric forced-air heating systems distribute air throughout a house from what is called a ducted system. Once it is distributed, the heated air is recaptured and recirculated. This process creates what is called positive airflow throughout a home and saves on energy bills, since the circulated air is already warmed. The difference between this type of system and the forced-air one is that this one only heats homes and does not function as an air conditioner. Like any other mechanical system in your home, these units do require adjustments, part replacement, and preventive maintenance.

Reasons that a repair may be necessary include:

- The furnace may cycle on and off over and over again.
- The unit may not come on at all.
- The blower may continuously operate.
- The furnace or fan may be noisy.
- The system may not produce enough heat.

Hector Hint   Do not to try to repair these heating elements or other major electrical components by yourself; call a licensed repairperson.

If the furnace does not run, make sure to check for a blown fuse or tripped breaker. Verify that the switch for the furnace is on. Many units have a reset button, built-in breakers, and fuses right on them.

NOISY FURNACES

If the furnace is noisy, check that the access panels are locked and fastened. If the belt on the fan is squeaking, you can find belt dressing at auto supply stores that can be sprayed on the belt to make it quiet. Sometimes a simple belt adjustment is all it needs. Your preventive maintenance routine should include lubricating the motor. Many oil ports are located directly on the motor. They have a small flap that lifts for filling.

NOT ENOUGH HEAT OR UNEVEN HEATING

If there is not enough heat, increase the thermostat setting to see if the furnace comes on. If it still does not come on or generate enough heat, check the thermostat for dust or loose connections. The filter may be dirty or the blower may need to be cleaned. Also, check your registers to make sure that they are all in the open position. If the furnace cycles on and off repeatedly, the filter could be the problem again and so can the blower assembly.

If some rooms are cool and others are warm, the system may need to be balanced. A professional can balance a system so that all dampers and diffusers more evenly distribute warm air.

Preventive maintenance on a heating system is required for longevity, and routine maintenance can keep your system operating efficiently, without interruption, saving you from hefty bills.

What to Do When Your Thermostat Fails

SKILL LEVEL

3

TIME

2–3 h

Almost every home has one. They operate your central air conditioner, your furnace, and in many cases, one thermostat will operate both the furnace and the air conditioner. They are also on your boiler if you have a boiler. And they all have something in common: They keep us comfortable. There are some that are digital. There are some that use mercury and a spring, and they are responsible for turning the air conditioner and the furnace on and off as needed.

Thermostats control the temperature by sensing temperature changes in nearby air. The mercury type thermostat is also known as mechanical, and the electronic type thermostat is also known as a digital thermostat.

For the most part they last for a very long time, but they can get to a point where, after use and wear and tear, they begin to malfunction.

Thermostats impact the efficiency of an air conditioner and furnace. If a thermostat is not operating properly, the heating and cooling units will not function cost-effectively, and may repeatedly cycle on and off.

1. Check the circuit breaker panel for a breaker that may have tripped, or your fuse box for a blown fuse.
2. If the circuit breaker or fuse is okay, and you still don't have power, you will need to check the thermostat. Before checking the thermostat, turn the power off to the heating or cooling unit.
3. Check for a battery in the thermostat and change it as needed.
4. Use a soft-bristled brush to remove any dust that may be hindering the function of the thermostat.
5. Check the low-voltage wires for loose connections and tighten them if needed.

6. Check the wires going from the heating or cooling unit to the thermostat by touching the two wires (red and yellow wires) together. This should close the circuit and power the unit on. If the unit does not come on, the wires leading from the heating or cooling unit may be severed or shorting and will need to be changed, or the problem located and repaired.

If the wires are good, and the thermostat is still not functioning, replace it. Thermostats are not very expensive and can save your money by decreasing your heating bills and making your home that much more energy efficient.

Clean Your Thermostat

SKILL LEVEL

1

TIME

1 h

If an air conditioner or furnace repeatedly cycles on and off, it may mean that the thermostat needs to be cleaned. If it does not turn off, that also may mean it needs to be cleaned or replaced.

1. To clean a mechanical thermostat, remove the cover by gently unfastening it, pulling it off, or by unscrewing it from the base.
2. Use an air dust remover, the type used to clean a computer keyboard, and carefully blow away any dust particles that are in any hard-to-reach places.

Hector Hint

Be very careful when handling a mechanical thermostat. There is mercury in the glass tube and, if broken, this can be ingested through your skin and cause mercury poisoning.

3. When an air dust remover is not available, use a small soft-bristled brush, to lightly clear any cobwebs or dust particles.
4. Tear off a small piece of heavyweight paper and slide it under each lever, cleaning them by sliding the paper back and forth. This will remove any oxidization or dirt that has built up.

5. If you have a mechanical thermostat and the boiler turns off and on often, or not frequently enough, adjust the thermostat by moving the indicator from or toward the farthest setting.

Replace a Low-Voltage Thermostat

SKILL LEVEL

1

TIME

1 h

A thermostat serves a very important purpose in your home. Without one it would be difficult to turn the heating or cooling on and off or to be able to adjust the temperature. Mechanical thermostats are the easiest to operate and install. The internal operation of a mechanical thermostat is much simpler than the internal operation and function of a digital thermostat. it does not use a battery or a constant supply of power to function. It regulates the temperature in the room by using a heat anticipator that detects when heating or cooling is needed. It also has a manual fan switch.

Installing a programmable digital thermostat requires encoding it for the temperature desired, day of the week, and twenty-four-hour operation. Many programmable thermostats require the use of a battery to maintain these functions. Battery-operated thermostats were developed to replace mechanical ones and most battery-operated digital thermostats require only two wires, while some programmable ones need three.

Most thermostats do not require AC current, and function on low voltage. A transformer steps down the electricity from 110 volts AC to 12 or 24 volts, which safeguards the delicate internal parts of the thermostat and makes them safer for a homeowner to repair, replace, and operate.

1. Cut the power going to the heating or cooling unit. Either shut the circuit breaker or remove the fuse in the fuse box.
2. Remove the cover of the existing thermostat. Be careful not to pull the entire thermostat off the wall when removing the cover.
3. Disconnect the wires one by one and use a piece of electrical tape to cover each exposed wire.
4. Unscrew the thermostat from the wall, pull each wire out from the back plate, and remove it.

5. Install the new thermostat by marking the screw locations for the base plate, checking to make sure it is level. Using an awl or a nail, make the holes for the anchors and gently tap them in.
6. Next, pull the wires through the back of the base plate to the front.
7. Secure the base plate to the wall and, checking the instructions, connect the wires to the appropriate terminals.
8. Insert the battery and install the cover onto the base plate.
9. Follow the instructions to program the thermostat.

Hector Hint

Check around the thermostat to see if you need to separate the base from the paint on the wall. If the unit needs to be separated, insert a utility knife blade between the thermostat and the wall. Taking the time to do this will save you from having to repair the wall if it tears the paper off the drywall.

Check the Accuracy of Your Thermostat

SKILL LEVEL

1

TIME

1 h

Thermostats are delicate instruments that detect rooms' air temperature. Air leaks in a wall can sometimes cause a breeze to enter through the holes where the thermostat wires enter, causing the thermostat to show the wrong temperature. Improperly sealed and drafty homes can also prevent a thermostat from getting an accurate reading and further wasting energy. An obstruction inside the thermostat can also prevent a true reading. To check the accuracy of your thermostat:

1. Place a room thermometer as close as possible to the thermostat on the wall. A glass tube thermostat is preferred for this test.
2. If there are open windows or doors, close them and let the air in the room stabilize for at least thirty minutes.
3. Check to see if the temperature on the thermostat is in line with the room thermometer. A difference of one or two degrees is normal. If the temperature difference is more than two degrees, placing another thermometer in the room can help to rule out the incorrect temperature. If you determine that the thermostat is incorrect, replace it.

Hot Water Heaters

Hot water heaters, like boilers and furnaces are usually set in the darkest, dingiest, and dirtiest part of our homes. They are ignored and forgotten about until the first day we don't have any hot water. If we don't maintain a hot water heater, we may have to purchase a new one before we should.

The most common types of hot water heaters used in homes are electric and gas. Electric hot water heaters heat with electric heating elements. When water reaches the desired temperature, the elements shut off. Gas hot water heaters have burners located at the bottom of the unit, which heat the water. These have a gas pilot light that stays lit; when the water drops below the desired temperature, the gas valve opens and the burners fire.

OTHER SYSTEMS

There are systems that utilize a boiler to heat the water. The problem with these systems is that if the boiler is not working, there will not be any hot water until the boiler is repaired or replaced.

Tankless hot water heaters heat water as it is used.

Clean the Inside of Your Hot Water Heater Tank

SKILL LEVEL

2

TIME

2–3 h

Hot water heaters should last ten to twenty years on average. Occasionally flushing out your hot water heater will extend its life, clear much of the deposited sediment that accumulates at the bottom of the tank, and lessen the chance of bacteria and rust formation.

1. If you have an electric hot water heater, turn off its circuit breaker. With a gas hot water heater, turn off the gas and pilot.
2. Attach a long hose to the drain valve at the bottom of the hot water heater and open the hose bib, letting the water run outdoors until it runs clear.
3. Close the hose bib and disconnect the hose.

4. Turn on the circuit breaker. Allow approximately 20–30 minutes for the water to heat up before using any hot water.

Clean, Organize, and Get Your Mechanicals Together

SKILL LEVEL

2

TIME

2–3 h

Operating systems in a home will work more efficiently and will last much longer when dust and dirt are kept out of their components. A few simple things are all it takes to clean up what is the dirtiest room in the house (the basement) and to keep the systems in your home functioning at peak performance.

1. Vacuum the top of your hot water heater and remove any cobwebs.
2. Wipe down the hot water heater and boiler.
3. Wipe down all the pipes and valves.
4. Organize the manuals, schematics, and warranties for easy access.
5. Vacuum or sweep out the utility room.
6. Tighten any screw terminals that may be loose. A simple loose wire connection can prevent an air conditioning or heating system from functioning.
7. If your heating or air conditioning system uses an air filter, monitor when it gets dirty and change it. A dirty filter can increase the possibility of mold growth and respiratory problems.
8. Hang a clipboard with the name of your plumber, service company, and all emergency telephone numbers nearby. You never know when an emergency might arise and you may need these numbers.

Some more important facts you should know and things you should do:

1. If the hot water heater does not heat the water to a temperature of 120 degrees, do not allow the water to be used. Bacteria can form, making it very dangerous to your health.
2. Make it a point to check the pressure valve on the water heater once every season. Tank relief valves release the pressure in the tank. Make it a point to lift and close the valve several times, making sure it functions properly.

3. The preferred setting for hot water is 120 degrees. Setting the temperature higher can cause scalding if skin is exposed for more than a half minute.

<table>
<tr><td>

Hector Hint

</td><td>

An anti-scald shower body is ideal when there are children and elderly people living in the house. This will prevent the possibility of someone being scalded accidentally. These can be purchased or ordered at your local home improvement store or plumbing supply and will need to be installed by a plumber.

</td></tr>
</table>

4. Check the top of the tank for rust and corrosion. If you find decomposition at the connection located at the top of the water heater, there could be a slow leak or corrosion caused by the chemical reaction of two different metal pipes.
5. *Keep all flammable liquids away from the hot water heater.* This has been the cause of many home fires. When the burner ignites, the fumes from flammable liquids can also be ignited.
6. Adjust the flames on the heater for maximum efficiency. A blue flame indicates that the burners are firing properly. An orange flame indicates that the shutters need to be adjusted on the burners. This adjustment requires a screwdriver and will only take a few minutes.

Are You Still Waiting for Water?

Some hot water heaters are so far away from the bathroom or kitchen that it takes a long time for the hot water to reach the faucet. This is because the water in the line needs to travel from the hot water heater to the spout and depending on the distance, can take more time than you would like.

This problem can be economically remedied by wrapping the hot water pipes with insulation. Most homes with basements have exposed horizontal pipes or access to them through a drop ceiling. Long runs can easily be wrapped with foam type insulation. Make sure to keep the seams under the pipes and not on the top. Most of these insulation strips have tape that easily peels back for installation.

Clear the Aerators

If you are experiencing reduced water flow through a faucet, it could be a clogged aerator. An aerator is located at the end of a faucet spout. They screw on and off and restrict sediment from flowing out of the faucet; some also restrict the amount of water being used. Where sediment is extremely bad, you can hear it grinding in the valve when turning the water on or off.

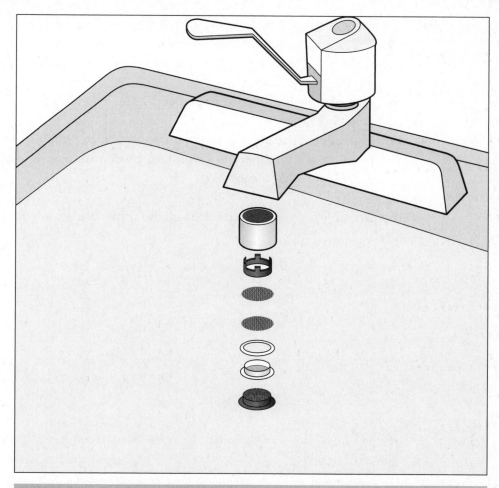

Aerators add air to the faucet's water flow, which cuts down on the amount of water used but not the water pressure.

1. Close or put the sink stop in place to prevent anything from falling into the waste line. If the sink does not have a stopper, stuff a rag into the drain.
2. Try to loosen the aerator by hand, turning it counterclockwise.
3. If the aerator is difficult to loosen by hand, use a rag to wrap around it and a wrench to loosen it. The rag will protect the finish from the pliers.
4. Once the aerator is removed, carefully dismantle the parts and place them down in the order that they are taken apart.
5. The parts that need to be rinsed are the water restrictor and the sediment screen. Sediment and lime deposits accumulate, restricting the flow of water.
6. Flush water through the screen and water restrictor to allow the lime and sediment to rinse off.
7. If the lime deposits and sediment are tough to remove, use a toothbrush to scrape them off. Poke through difficult places to clean with a straight pin or toothpick.

It is probably a good idea to tackle all the other faucets in your home, as well.

12 | 1 FT | 13 | 14 | 15 | 16 | 17 | 18

Fireplaces and Chimneys

I don't know about you, but I love my fireplace. Fireplaces are terrific for relaxing while reading a good book. They can enhance the ambiance in any home and, if correctly used and maintained, can cut down on your heating costs. With all the benefits of a fireplace, why wouldn't you stay on top of its maintenance?

Project Worksheet

MONETARY RETURN: $750–$1,000

PROJECT START DATE: _____

TASKS COMPLETED: _____
_____
_____
_____
_____

TOOLS NEEDED:

- ❑ Dust mask
- ❑ Flashlight
- ❑ Goggles
- ❑ Work gloves

Maintenance, Maintenance, Maintenance . . .

A fireplace can be dangerous if not maintained properly and regularly. Many fires are caused by creosote buildup in chimneys. You should have your chimney checked and cleaned yearly. *Don't wait until the last minute.* Chimney sweeps are hard to get in the fall. By this time of year they are booked up and very busy. Have your chimney cleaned now, before you find yourself looking at your fireplace wishing you could use it.

SAFE FIREPLACES

1. A hearth is a commonplace at the base of a fireplace. The hearth in front of the fireplace should extend a minimum of 16" into the room, and no less than 8" beyond the fireplace cavity on either side. Some hearths are raised and some are flush with the floor. Brick, bluestone, tile, granite, concrete, or other nonflammable material with a nominal thickness of 4" must be used.
2. A fireplace insert is a firebox inserted into an existing fireplace. These are great to use if your fireplace is no longer functional. These inserts are more efficient than your traditional fireplace and allow for wood, gas, or wood-pellet fuels. If this type of box is to be used, select one with a ¼" steel liner to reduce the potential for rust.
3. Free-standing fireplaces should be 3' from unprotected walls or other flammable materials, unless the unit is a zero-clearance unit, and it should be installed as per the manufacturer's instructions. Use wall protection to protect walls within the 3' proximity.
4. A fire-proof base to support a free-standing unit or an insulated fireproof material on the floor beneath the fireplace is required on all self-supported units.

Be sure prefabricated metal fireplaces, chimneys, and flues are approved by Underwriters Laboratories (UL) and installed as specified by the instructions. No pipe should be longer than 10' nor more than 75 percent of the vertical height of the chimney, whichever is less. If you choose a natural gas "log", follow instructions for installation and look for the American Gas Association label.

Maintain Your Fireplace

Fireplaces are not maintenance-free; they have to be cared for like any other part of your home. Although they look substantial and strong, they can deteriorate with time if not inspected and properly cared for.

1. Keep your fireplace in good condition by repairing any cracks or replacing any loose pieces in the flue lining. Over time, deterioration does occur and cracks in the masonry or flue liner can become a serious fire hazard, allowing smoke to enter your home.

Hector Hint

Have a professional mason check the interior of your masonry flue once every two years or so and make the needed repairs. If you can't find anyone, there are many fireplace companies that will inspect or be able to suggest someone who is qualified to inspect your fireplace and flue.

2. Depending on how often you use it, have a professional chimney sweep clean your flue annually.
3. Occasionally, dampers need to be cleaned, repaired, and sometimes replaced. These dampers are located just above the firebox between the firebox and the beginning of the flue. They are used to stop the warm air in your home from escaping, and regulate the amount of draft going up the chimney. Use a flashlight to see if it is off the pivots and moving freely. Dampers should be brushed occasionally and checked for rust.

Neglected chimneys fall into disrepair because of water freezing and expanding between the bricks, causing them to break apart and weaken. Chimney sweeps often have a solution to apply on the surface of stable masonry to protect this from happening.

SKILL LEVEL

3

TIME

2–3 h

AIR SUPPLY

A fireplace fire requires about five times as much air as most houses need for liberal ventilation. With today's tightly constructed houses incorporating weather-stripped doors, caulked windows, and self-closing exhaust vents, a fireplace can set up a reverse draft by drawing the poisonous carbon monoxide fumes from the hot water heater and furnace flues and discharging them into the living area.

In tight homes, the fireplace may also consume enough oxygen from the air in the house to cause problems for the occupants. To be safe, a positive source of outside air should be supplied to all fireplaces and wood- or coal-burning stoves to bring in enough fresh air for efficient burning. This can be accomplished by opening a window when the fireplace or stove is being used. To keep smoke from entering the room, turn off kitchen and bathroom exhaust fans and close the registers of forced-air heating systems which are near the fireplace.

For safe and sound operation:

1. Install a screen that completely covers the fireplace opening, to keep sparks from flying into the room.
2. Equip the house with smoke detectors. This is a standard building code requirement.
3. Have a type ABC fire extinguisher within reach.
4. Keep combustible materials such as carpets, furniture, paper, logs, and kindling at a minimum of 3' from the fireplace.
5. Arrange andirons so logs can't roll out.
6. Always check to see if the damper is open prior to kindling a fire.
7. Preheat the flue (warm the flue to establish a positive draft). This will prevent any smoke from backing into the room.
8. Be sure to dispose of excess ash in the fireplace. Don't let the ashes accumulate. Put ashes in a lidded metal container to prevent the possibility of a fire.

Between You and Your Fireplace— Fireplace Doors

SKILL LEVEL

3

TIME

2–3 h

Non-faced fiberglass insulation is commonly used to seal between fireplace doors and the firebox. Made from sand and recycled glass fibers, this type of insulation is naturally noncombustible and requires no additional fire-retardant chemical treatments.

Another type of insulation that can be used is called "therma-fiber" or "mineral wool." This form of fiberglass insulation is very dense. The fibers are also noncombustible, with melting temperatures that can exceed 1,800 degrees. It is used to prevent the spread of fire, mostly in commercial and industrial facilities.

If you need to purchase a fireplace door, fiberglass insulation strips are a part of the package. They are used along the top and two sides of the door frame. Double it up if you have gaps that are really wide. Be sure to neatly stuff the insulation in the channel between the face of the firebox and the door. You wouldn't want the insulation to stand out like a sore thumb, taking away from the beauty of the fireplace and the safety of your home. Don't worry about keeping the fiberglass fluffy, as you would with wall insulation— it's mainly there to seal the door frame, keep smoke from seeping out, and to protect the finish on the door frame from the heat.

Check the following items to prevent the possibility of a fire spreading outside the firebox:

1. Inadequate or absence of fire-proof insulation between the fireplace door and firebox
2. Unsecured or loose fireplace doors
3. A buildup of creosote in the chimney
4. An open or loose clean-out door hindering positive airflow
5. Flammable items too close to burning cinders in the firebox

When working with insulation make sure to wear:

- Long-sleeved shirt
- Long pants
- Work gloves
- Goggles
- Dust mask (with respirator)

The glass particles in the insulation can get into your pores and lungs, causing a rash or irritation. When you are finished, make sure you wash any exposed areas on your skin.

If you experiencing a problem with your fireplace, check the following items:

1. Make sure that the damper is fully open and there's nothing causing a blockage in the flue. If the damper is not fully opened or there is a clog, the fumes and exhaust can be backing up, causing a health risk and unsafe fire hazard in your home.
2. Open a window when you have a fire to allow for positive airflow. A fireplace, when lit, consumes quite a bit of oxygen in your home. Opening a window will allow fresh air to enter while increasing the draft in the chimney. This problem is prevalent in tightly built homes and is not an uncommon occurrence.
3. If an exhaust fan is on when the fireplace is lit, a depressurization can occur causing a backdraft effect. Opening a window between

the fireplace and the exhaust will ease the back pressure and allow the flue to flow freely.

4. Have a professional check the size of the flue. Improper sizing of a flue will not allow enough draft to freely pass through the chimney.

5. A backdraft can also be due to incorrect chimney height. Insufficient height on a chimney can hamper positive air pressure in your fireplace.

Here are some additional fireplace safety tips:

- Do not stack artificial logs in the fireplace as you would real logs.
- If you think the fireplace needs to be cleaned, don't use it.
- Fireplaces should not be used to burn garbage.
- Never use flammable liquids to start a fire.
- Keep small children away from fireplaces.
- Clean the chimney regularly.
- Never leave a fire unattended.
- Closing the damper too soon can cause a fire to reignite and spill out into the room.
- Anything flammable should be kept a minimum of 3' away.
- Keep an ABC-type fire extinguisher in the room.
- Make sure the fire is out before going to bed or leaving the house.

Flues and Chimneys

Just a few more things you should know.

1. If you need to replace the firebox, check that the flue is adequate in size. The flue should be equal to at least $\frac{1}{8}$ the area of the fireplace opening for chimneys that are 15' or higher, and at least $\frac{1}{8}$ the area of the fireplace opening for chimneys less than 15' in height.

2. Confirm that the contractor installs the flue at least 3' above the highest point where it passes through the roof and at least 2' higher than any portion of the building within 10'. If the roof is flat, the chimney should be at least 3' above the roof.

3. Metal flashing is necessary to protect areas where the flue goes through the roof. It is used to prevent water from entering between the flue and the roof. It should be checked annually and either replaced or repaired as necessary.

4. Pipes or flues that connect free-standing stoves and fireplaces to a chimney should be at least 24 gauge steel, double walled, UL listed, and installed accordingly.

5. Have a metal spark arrester placed on top of the chimney. These help to prevent any sparks that go up the chimney from landing on the roof, and catching the roof on fire.

6. A masonry fireplace and chimney should be supported on its own foundation wall and footing.

7. Installing a bird and animal guard on the chimney can prevent squirrels, birds, and raccoons from nesting and clogging the flue.

1 FT 13 14 15 16 17 18 19

Electrical Issues

The electrical system is probably the most complicated system in your home. Working on it yourself takes a certain amount of skill and experience. If you are someone with limited knowledge of a home electrical system, calling in a professional is a smart decision. If you have the expertise to perform electrical work, these tasks will help you to maintain and improve on your home's value.

Project Worksheet

MONETARY RETURN: $500–$750

PROJECT START DATE: _____

TASKS COMPLETED: _____
_____
_____
_____
_____

TOOLS NEEDED:

- ❏ Continuity tester or voltage alert detector
- ❏ Electrical tape
- ❏ Pliers
- ❏ Outlet tester
- ❏ Screwdriver
- ❏ Small torpedo level
- ❏ Step ladder
- ❏ Wire nuts

Check Your Breaker

Ugly electrical lines are best when they are "out of sight and out of mind." They can enter a home through an overhead feed or underground to an electrical meter and then to a circuit breaker panel or a fuse box. The circuit breaker panel or fuse box is the main distribution point for all the electrical circuits in your home. There are two hot wires and one neutral wire coming into a home. The purpose of the circuit breaker panel and fuse box is to prevent a fire from occurring and to protect people from electrocution. If a breaker trips or a fuse is blown, that is an indication that there is an overload or a short somewhere in the house. It can be an outlet, switch, an appliance, or something that is directly wired or plugged into a circuit.

If a circuit breaker is tripped, the toggle on the breaker can sometimes be seen halfway between on and off. At times, it can be difficult to tell if a circuit breaker has tripped. If it does trip, reset it by flipping it to the off position first, and then switch it to the on position. If you try to switch it to the on position first, it won't hold.

As added protection, the electrical code calls for Ground-Fault Circuit Interrupters (GFCI) in bathrooms, kitchens, garages, and on the exterior of a home. When located in a circuit breaker panel, they look like a circuit breaker except they have a red button that pops if there could be a problem. In other areas, they look like outlets and have two buttons between the plug slots with the word "reset" in red and the word "test" in black. If the reset button does not pop out when the "test" button is pressed there is a problem with the GFCI, the circuit, or an appliance that is connected to the circuit. These outlets are very delicate and trip easily for your protection. A GFCI will cut off power within a fraction of a second in order to protect homeowners from getting shocked or electrocuted. These should be tested periodically. On the exterior of a home, they should be housed in a plastic or metal rain cover.

At least every six months test your circuit breakers by switching them on and off a couple of times. This will make you aware if any of them has become welded in the on position. There have been occasions where a circuit breaker would not shut off, causing a fire to take place. If you are not sure how to work on electrical switches, outlets, or anything related to electricity, leave it for the professionals and hire an electrician. It's better to pay a few dollars to a professional than to risk getting hurt or causing damage to your home.

If a breaker needs replacement, never switch it for a higher amperage breaker. This can be very dangerous, allowing more current to flow through the wires than is suitable for the wire gauge.

Label the Circuit Breaker or Fuse Panel

It is a good idea to know which circuit breakers control the different outlets in your home:

1. Open your circuit breaker panel.
2. Flip the circuits one by one and record which parts of the house are controlled by which circuits.
3. Write the various parts of your house down on labels.
4. Apply the labels next to the corresponding breakers.

Change a Receptacle

Every house has them. What would we do without them? We wouldn't have food at our fingertips or entertainment at the push of a button. They make life easy for us and are suitably located throughout the home.

WHAT CAN HAPPEN TO THEM?

Occasionally they do go bad; they crack, short out, and need to be replaced. This is a fairly simple task, but whenever working with electricity, caution is definitely needed.

Outlets in newer homes have a grounding leg which is the round hole in the receptacle. This is for safety and to minimize the possibility of an electrical shock. Older homes have receptacles with two slots and no ground wire.

To change out a receptacle:

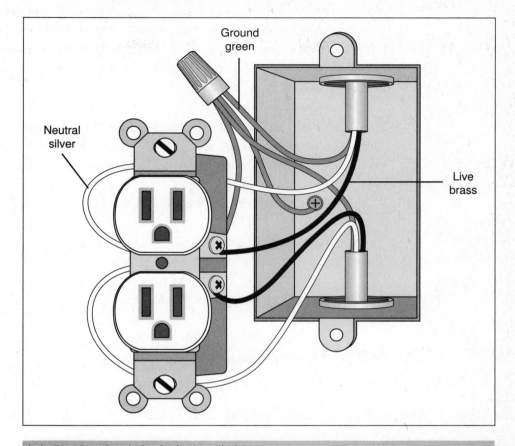

Labeling the wires helps in the installation process.

1. Cut off the power to the outlet at the circuit breaker panel or fuse box.
2. With the outlet tester, check to make sure the outlet has no electricity going to it.
3. Once you are sure that the power going to the outlet is off, you can continue.
4. Remove the cover plate and the screws holding the outlet in place.
5. Carefully pull the outlet out of the box.

6. Hold the new receptacle in the same position as the old one so that you can see how the wires line up for the new receptacle.

7. The receptacle should have terminals and slots. I prefer to use the slots because all you have to do is push the wire into the slots and the wire is grabbed and held in place. The terminals are used if there are two or more wires going to it.

8. Make sure you have no more than about ¼" of exposed wire. The rest of the wire should be insulated.

9. Once you have put the wires in the new receptacle in the exact same place as the old receptacle, you should cover any bare wires and terminals with electrical tape.

10. Carefully place the receptacle back into the box and secure it with mounting screws.

11. Put the cover plate back.

12. Go to the circuit breaker panel and flip the breaker back on or if you have a fuse box, put back the fuse.

13. Test the receptacle with the outlet tester.

Some outlets are operated by a switch. So make it a point before beginning to find out if a switch operates the outlet you are working on.

Replace a Bad Light Switch

SKILL LEVEL

3

TIME

1 h

A switch operates by starting and stopping the current flow. Replacing a switch is a fairly simple task to perform as long as you are replacing the existing switch with the same type. If you are planning to do something different, for instance, having two switches operate one fixture, call a licensed electrician unless you are sure how to do it.

TYPES OF SWITCHES
- **A standard switch** is called a single-pole switch and is used to turn a light, a fan, or a receptacle on or off. It does this by either allowing current to flow to the device or cutting the current to it.

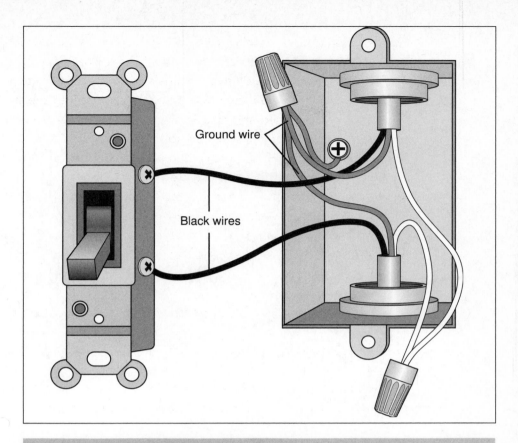

Ground wire

Black wires

A standard or single-pole switch

- **A three-way switch** turns a device on or off from two different convenient locations. The wiring of a three-way switch is a little more complicated than a regular switch. A regular single-pole switch cannot be used to operate a device from two or more places.
- **A dimmer switch** is used to increase or decrease the amount of current going to a lighting fixture. Chandeliers, recessed lights, and pendant type fixtures are the most common fixtures operated by a dimmer switch. Ambiance is the key reason for them. They are also used to adjust the speed of a fan by reducing or increasing the amount of current going to the fixture. Dimmer switches also turn a device on and off.

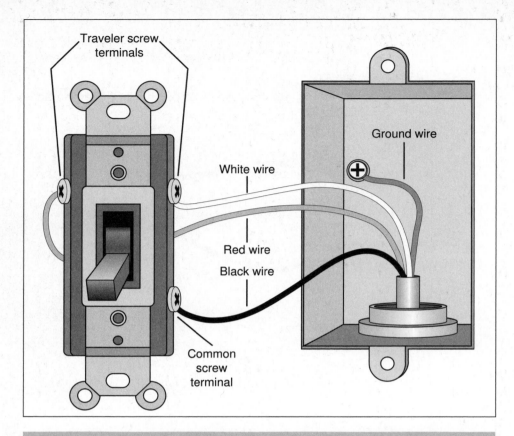

Traveler screw
terminals

White wire

Red wire

Black wire

Ground wire

Common
screw
terminal

A three-way switch

COMMON PROBLEMS WITH SWITCHES

- Sparking. This is a potential fire hazard.
- The toggle is worn out from use.
- Loose wire connections or no connection at all. This is also a potential fire hazard.

Here's how to replace a problematic light switch:

1. Cut off the power to the switch at the circuit breaker panel or fuse box.
2. Remove the cover plate to access the toggle switch.

3. Using a circuit tester test the switch to make sure the wires are not live by placing the testing probes on the wires going to the terminals.
4. Undo the mounting screws holding the switch in the box.
5. Check to see if there are any loose wires. If you find one, it is likely that that was the problem.
6. Holding the new switch in the same position, check to make sure the switch you are installing is the same type. Try not to hold the terminals of the existing one, just in case.
7. Remove one wire at a time and place it on the new switch.
8. Make sure the wires are securely fastened to the terminals. The switch toggle has holes in the back where you can insert the wires without having to use the terminals on the side.
9. Take the electrical tape and wrap it around the terminals. Two or three times should be enough.
10. Carefully put the switch back into the box and secure it with the mounting screws.
11. Put the cover plate back.
12. Go to the circuit breaker panel and flip the breaker back on or if you have a fuse box panel, screw the fuse back in.
13. Flip the switch on.

Match Your Outlet and Switch Cover Plates

SKILL LEVEL

1

TIME

1 h

(per average sized room)

This is the easiest task you will probably encounter but sometimes the simplest job is more aesthetically pleasing than any other.

First impressions mean a lot and when someone walks into your home, it's fun to *wow* them if you can. That means taking care of details down to matching the colors of the cover plates and screws on your outlets and switches. Switch cover plates are seen more often than outlet cover plates because they are at eye level and found in every room.

1. Cut off the power to the switch or outlet at the circuit breaker panel or fuse box.
2. Remove the old cover plate.

3. Install the new matching cover plate, making sure to keep it straight and level.

4. Go to the circuit breaker panel and flip the breaker back on or if you have a fuse box panel, screw the fuse back in.

Once you match the cover plates and the screws you will notice consistency in the appearance of the room. A subtle change like this makes a big difference in the look of a room. Cover plates and screws that don't match draw attention away from a room's décor.

COMMON COVER PLATE PROBLEMS

- Many different colored cover plates—consistency is important. Having brass, white, and brown cover plates in the same room is not aesthetically pleasing to the eye.
- A brown switch or outlet with an ivory or white cover plate doesn't cut it either. They should match each other.
- Cracked or dented cover plates should be replaced.
- Plastic and metal cover plates should be replaced to match.
- Cover plates with different colored screws should be changed to match the color of the cover plate.

Ding Dong

Most of us have a doorbell located at the entrance door, and in some homes, on side doors and rear doors too. There is a sounding device that is triggered when the button is pushed and an electrical loop is completed. Unfortunately, at some point something will go wrong and you will need to fix it.

The doorbell circuit includes a transformer, which requires caution when handling. Make it a point to unplug it, shut off the circuit breaker, or remove the fuse to prevent an electrical shock from taking place. The purpose of the transformer is to convert 110 volts AC to lower voltage DC.

COMMON DOORBELL PROBLEMS

- The wires can get severed or become crossed, causing a short circuit.
- The screws can become loose, releasing the wires from the button, the sounding device, or the transformer.
- Oxidation, corrosion, and dirt can prevent an electrical current from being completed.
- Sounding devices and transformers can burn out.
- Buttons can break.

Troubleshoot Doorbell Problems

When wires intermittently touch, it is very difficult to locate the problem. Since they are only working some of the time, the problem needs to be tackled at the time it is occurring. These wires are referred to as swingers since they can, by chance, swing back and forth, making a connection and disconnecting again.

Try the process of elimination to find the problem.

1. Check to see if the fuse has blown, or, if you have a circuit breaker panel, check to see if the circuit breaker has tripped.
2. Unscrew the button and check that the wires are connected properly.
3. Make sure that the wires that go to the transformer are properly secured.
4. Verify that the screws on the wires leading to the sounding device are also tight.

Once you have checked all of those items, see if the doorbell works. If it is muffled, or difficult to hear, you may have to clean the sounding device (meaning the bell or the chime). There may be something preventing it from ringing or sounding. The hammer going to a bell could be bent or the cover could be obstructing it and will need to be fixed or adjusted. If it is a continuous chime, the wires might be touching, causing the current to flow and making it continually ring.

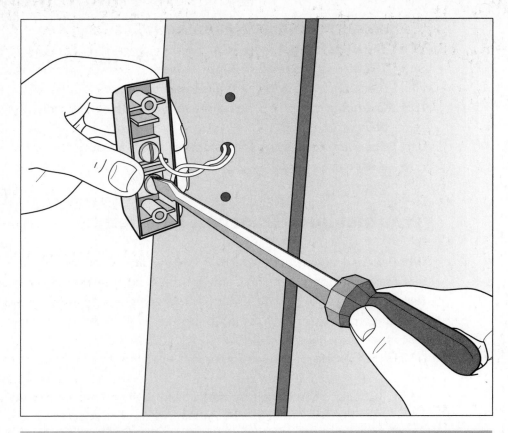

Unscrewing the doorbell will give you a better look at what could be wrong.

If it is still not working, unscrew the wires at the transformer and attach a volt/ohm meter to both wires (a volt/ohm meter and doorbell supplies can be purchased at your local electrical supply or home center). If the meter needle swings to the other side, this is an indication of a short circuit. If the needle does not move, have someone push the doorbell button and look to see if the needle swings to the other side. The needle swinging will confirm that the doorbell button works and that the problem may be in the transformer. Do not attempt to repair the transformer. Replace it.

Troubleshoot Smoke Detector Issues

Smoke detectors are vital for safety in a home. Smoke, not fire, is the major killer in a house fire. Many local building departments require a smoke detector on every floor, a smoke detector in every bedroom, and one within every ten feet of a hallway. Smoke detectors can be battery-powered, hardwired (a direct electrical connection), or both. The best smoke detector to have is one that is hardwired and has a battery backup. (If you have not done any electrical work before, this task is best done by a licensed electrician.) Having both is important. If for some reason, the electrical power is out, the smoke detector will still function. In some cases, battery-operated smoke detectors are sufficient, but it is suggested that the building code official be consulted to find out what the requirements are in your area.

A chirping sound is an indication that the battery is in need of replacement. Replacing a battery-operated smoke detector battery is a simple task.

1. Use a sturdy ladder to reach the smoke detector.
2. Hold the smoke detector and twist it counterclockwise to remove it from its base. In the back of the unit, there is a battery compartment. (If you try to put the smoke detector back in place without a battery, a flap holds the battery compartment door in the open position, preventing the smoke detector from closing. To close the compartment door a battery must be in place.)
3. Install the battery and replace the smoke detector in its base.

The smoke detector is now ready to protect you and your family.

CARBON MONOXIDE DETECTORS

Carbon monoxide is known as the "silent killer." Smoke and carbon monoxide detectors allow the occupants time to get to an area of safety. This is an important life-saving function in a home and is one home, fire, and building inspectors will try very hard not to overlook.

Home, fire, and building inspectors will check for carbon monoxide by using a digital carbon monoxide detector. They will also check for levels of combustible gas in a home.

Carbon-monoxide is odorless and does not have any particular color to it, making it impossible to see. The presence of this gas in high levels of concentration has led to many fatalities throughout the country. State legislation and city and town ordinances in many areas require homes to have carbon monoxide detectors within 10' of every bedroom. Check with your local building department since they generally will need to inspect your home before closing, making sure it meets fire code minimums.

It is very difficult to detect carbon monoxide gas. The symptoms are like that of the flu. Some of the symptoms are lethargy, nausea, dizziness, impairment to your vision, lack of coordination, muscle pain, and other nervous system damage.

Replace a Lighting Fixture

SKILL LEVEL

3

TIME

1 h

Replacing a standard light fixture is a simple task easily accomplished by the average homeowner. If a fixture is sentimental or a replacement can't be found that matches the décor, take it to a lamp or electrical repair shop. Fussing with wires that are old and fraying may not be worth the time and effort, and can turn out to be a fire hazard if not fixed by someone familiar with the process.

It can become more complicated when replacing a chandelier, recess light, or contemporary type fixture. Chandeliers for the most part are heavy and require solid mounting. Some chandeliers have motorized mounting bases so they can be lowered for cleaning and bulb replacement. Accessing recessed lights may seem complicated for a homeowner since they are housed in the ceiling and are not as easily accessible as standard fixtures. Some contemporary fixtures are very costly, having exposed wiring and special clips to hold them in place. Depending on the fixture, the lights and wire tracks are delicate and may require someone with special expertise to handle them. Replacing a standard light fixture is not as complicated as some people think.

1. Turn off the light switch and cut off the power to the switch at the circuit breaker panel or fuse box.
2. Using a stable ladder, get situated safely and comfortably. Having to look up to remove and replace the fixture may require you to be in an uncomfortable position.

3. Carefully remove the bulb globe if there is one.
4. Remove the screws holding the fixture base in place.
5. Without touching the copper on the wires, unscrew the wire nuts and put them in your pocket.
6. Being safe is better than being sorry, so use a circuit tester to see if there is power going to the fixture. Hold the tester probes to the black and white wires.
7. Once you are sure there isn't any power going to the fixture, disconnect the wires and set the fixture base down.
8. Begin the installation of the new fixture. Make sure to follow the directions included in the packaging.

Note: Bare copper wires found in the light box are grounding wires and may need to be connected to the new fixture.

Fix an Unbalanced Ceiling Fan

SKILL LEVEL

3

TIME

2–3 h

How many times have you heard that irritating click, click, click sound of the chain on the fan tapping against the light globe, or the fan shifting from side to side, looking as if it is ready to disengage and mulch a passerby? It's difficult to sit under a fan like that without fearing for your life.

To tighten the base:

1. Turn off the switch and cut off the power to the circuit at the circuit breaker panel or fuse box.
2. Using a screwdriver, remove the housing cover to the fan motor.
3. Try shifting the fan base to see if it is loose. If it is, tighten the screws holding it in place, replace the cover, and start the fan at slow speed to check for a wobble.

Hector Hint Ceiling fans are awkward and heavy and may require two people and the use of two ladders to remove them.

A wobbling fan can be caused by an imbalance in the blades, or the fan may not be secured to the mounting box.

If you are like most people, you threw out the fan blade weights that came with the ceiling fan. However, a little masking tape and some change ($) will do the job.

1. Spin the fan blades slowly by hand and observe whether one of the blades is off balance.
2. By the process of elimination, tape a coin to the top mid-center of one of the blades you suspect is causing the problem.
3. Turn the fan on slow. Check if it is wobbling. If it is still out of balance, continue checking the other blades. It may be necessary to adjust the size of the coin for better balance.
4. If you have located an unbalanced blade, using construction adhesive, glue the coin to the blade. Make sure to let the glue dry thoroughly before turning the fan on.

If all else has failed, it could be that one or more blades are warped, cracked, or defective in some other way.

1. Place a straight edge on the blade and look for a space that may indicate a deflection in the blade. Use a level or something else other than wood.
2. Check each blade for any possible cracks.
3. Inspect the brackets holding the blades to the motor. The fan could be out of balance if one of them is slightly bent.
4. Inspect the screws holding the blades in place. Make sure they are all in place, not loose or missing.

If the problem still exists, new blades or a new fan may be necessary. Fan blades can be obtained from the manufacturer.

CHAPTER
V

Keep It Safe and Clean

Striving to keep your home safe and clean goes beyond the desire to increase its value. You need to make sure your house is safe at all times for family and guests. It's important to see to everything from the structural integrity to the extermination of disease-spreading vermin. Many of the maintenance tasks found in this chapter should be completed a few times a year.

Project Worksheet

MONETARY RETURN: $1,000–$1,500

PROJECT START DATE: _____

TASKS COMPLETED: _____
_____
_____
_____
_____

TOOLS NEEDED:

- ❏ Drill
- ❏ Drill bits (assorted sizes)
- ❏ Dust mask
- ❏ Mixing pan for concrete
- ❏ Screwdriver
- ❏ Screw gun
- ❏ Shop vacuum
- ❏ Shovel
- ❏ Trowel

Keep a Handle on Things: Handrails and Safety

SKILL LEVEL

3

TIME

4–5 h

Handrails are an essential part of any home. We need them when going up and down our stairs. We need them when an elderly person visits or lives with us. We need them for our children, and so that we don't fall over the side of a porch or balcony. They are a lifeline for us. Handrails should be inspected periodically to make sure they are not loose, and the structure they are connected to is sound. There are wood rails, metal rails, cable rails, glass rails, and many more types, but they all need the same attention.

1. Begin by tightening any handrails that may be getting or are already loose. If they are loose now, they will only continue to get worse. This can turn into a dangerous situation if too much pressure is applied, especially if there is an elderly person that relies on their support to get around. Walk around the house and shake the rails to see which are loose and make sure they are secure and safe.

2. If a rail is loose and mounted to a wall, try tightening the screw that is holding the loose bracket. If that does not work and you think the bracket is not secured properly, relocate the bracket on the railing so that it is secured to a stud in the wall. Make sure to keep it at the same height.

3. A loose handrail and balusters system requires a little bit more work. To tighten loose balusters (the vertical pieces that are between the handrail and the steps), drill a hole diagonally from the baluster into the handrail and insert a screw, countersinking it. Make sure that it is short enough that it does not come out of the top of the handrail.

4. If the baluster is loose from the bottom and you have some play, apply wood glue where it can seep in, wipe off the excess, and let it set overnight.

5. Exterior rail: If the railing system is wrought iron and is not properly secured to the platform, weather and temperature permitting, clean out the hole where the posts enter the platform, and pour quick-drying cement around the posts and into the hole. Clean

up any excess immediately. This should not be done if the temperature outside is below freezing, as the cement will not properly cure.

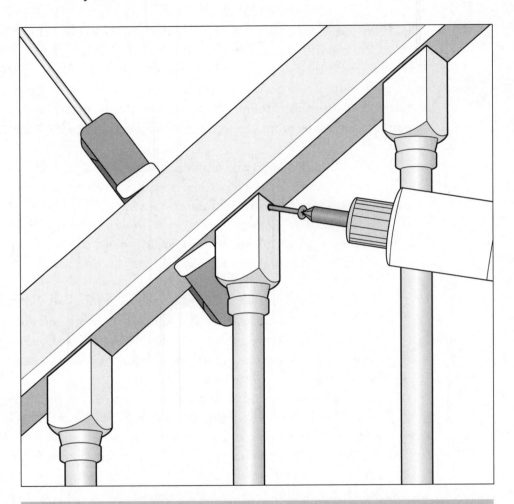

This should keep the baluster in place.

Whether a balcony rail or stair rail, we need to check, maintain, and repair handrails as required. To find replacement parts or someone to execute the work necessary, contact a local stair manufacturing company or your local lumber dealer.

Is There a Mouse in the House?

The last thing you want to see scurrying around your house are mice. They are known to carry disease and leave droppings. They will eat through electrical wires, causing appliances to short out and begin fires. If they die in a wall, they can leave a nauseating odor throughout your home that is difficult to eliminate.

These creatures need to stay warm in the winter and what better place to go than where there is heat, food, and water? The key to rodent control in your home is to prevent them from entering and scurrying around your home.

Here's how to keep them out from the *outside*:

1. Make sure all areas of possible entrance to your home are properly and tightly sealed. For example: door, window, and garage door seals.
2. Appropriately secure any places around the envelope of your home where pipes or wires penetrate the exterior foundation and perimeter walls.
3. Put a piece of wire mesh wherever there is a drain or any other pipe that may allow a mouse or other rodent to enter.
4. Keep your garage doors closed when you are not using them.

Here's how to keep them out from the *inside*:

1. Reduce and eliminate any possible food and water available for their consumption.
2. Store pet food, grass seed, and food items in thick plastic or metal containers.
3. Keep garbage cans tightly shut and replace them if they have holes or do not close properly.
4. Do not leave uneaten pet food lying around.
5. Leaving food around in bedrooms, family rooms, living rooms, etc., is inviting unwanted company.
6. Clean up any crumbs on counters and clean up dirty dishes in the sink as soon as possible.
7. Don't take food into rooms other than specified snack rooms, dining rooms, and kitchens.

8. If you have a media room, keep a constant check on what food may be under the seats or cushions.
9. Make sure everyone in your home cooperates.

PREFERRED AREAS OF LIVING

- Mice enjoy nesting in most any type of batt insulation.
- Check crawlspaces, cantelevers, and overhangs for disturbed or fallen insulation.
- Attics are one of their favorite places.
- Check for droppings, urine stains, and smells.
- Mice will also nest in furniture. So, rearranging furniture will disrupt their comfort and bring them out of hiding.
- Remove clutter like newspapers and other things you feel may give them a place of sanctuary.

Hector Hint

Wear a well-fitted dust mask and gloves when doing this task. Mice spread disease, and contact with their environment must be limited. Their existence in your home should not be taken for granted, especially if there are children around.

Getting rid of rodents is very important for many reasons:

- They can get into your food, contaminating it.
- Property damage is always an issue with rodents. They have very sharp teeth. Their teeth are so sharp they can eat through aluminum, lead, and some other metals, as well.
- Their droppings can carry disease that, in some cases, can be life-threatening.
- Remarkably, one female mouse can have 31,000 descendants in one year because they mature quickly and reproduce at alarming rates.
- It takes only 3 weeks for a young rat or mouse to start creating as much damage as their parents.
- Rodents can enter a building through a half-inch hole and it is thought that mice chewing through electrical wires cause 20 percent of all electrical fires.

Winter is when they seek shelter indoors and when you should be on the alert for their presence. Taking precautionary steps to capture them prior to their settling in is the best approach. Set traps early and remember where they are; it may pay to make a list of where you placed the traps.

Dealing with Termites

There are thousands of types of termites around the world. The most commonly found in and around a home are:

Subterranean Termites: These are the most common. They nest in the soil, building mud tunnels to travel back and forth, searching for food. Their mud tunnels are often found on outside foundation walls. Termites are much more noticeable in the springtime and can be found swarming by windows, especially when the sun is shining. This is the time they mate and form new colonies.

Damp-wood Termites: These nest in damp wood found in the soil and can also be found in homes along the beach.

MUD TUNNELS

Subterranean termite tunnels can range in width from ¼" to 1" and up to 50' or more in length. These tunnels protect them from low moisture and get them from the soil to their food supply. Instead of pushing the debris from their tunneling to the outside, they use it to build the mud tunnels along with fecal matter, soil, and sand. They turn this material into a plaster-like substance that shields them, especially when they're traveling up foundation walls into your house.

WHO DO YOU CALL? TERMITE BUSTERS!

If you find termites in your home, call a professional termite inspector to assess the situation. If it is determined that there are termites infiltrating your home, they will need to remediate the problem. A written guarantee that there are no longer termites in your home is important for your peace of mind and for when you want to sell your home.

Dust Control

SKILL LEVEL

1

TIME

2–3 h

It is good practice to reduce the amount of dust in a home when working on it. Although dust is inevitable when making certain repairs, any precautions to lessen the amount of pollutants in a home should be taken. It detrimentally affects the occupants and the workers, as well, not to mention all the dust that can accumulate on your furnishings, clothing, and carpets, leaving you with a huge cleanup afterwards. Even though the home may seem sufficiently protected, dust will find its way into the smallest of openings, especially demolition and drywall dust.

If you are having a contractor do work on your home, have them take preventative action to reduce the likelihood of dirt and dust entering the occupied section. Prior to beginning any project, the contractor should survey with the homeowner, the areas adjacent to the construction. A reasonable and acceptable course of action to protect the occupied section and adjacent areas should be devised and implemented, thus decreasing the amount of dust particles entering the other areas of your home.

Here are a few areas you should think about whether you are doing the work yourself or having a contractor do the work:

1. Seal the house off with plastic and tape. All door openings between the occupied section and area to be worked on should be securely sealed. Walls, ceiling, and floors should be taped with plastic and maintained, repaired, or changed out if damaged. Make it a point to secure adjacent areas. Use lightweight plastic sheeting. Using the lightweight plastic sheeting makes it easier to hang and makes it effortless for the masking tape to stick without all the weight from a heavier gauge plastic. If you really want to make a better barrier, on the construction side add a layer of heavier gauge plastic, as well.

2. Cover all recessed fixtures, also known as hi-hats, that will be affected by the work, so that dust does not seep through any voids. Make sure not to use them while they are covered. This can pro-

mote a fire hazard. The circuit breakers for these lights should be turned off or the switches taped in the off position.

3. Make sure the area where work is being conducted is swept at day's end with a sprinkling of water or sweeping compound to keep the dust down. If the contractor allows the debris to accumulate, it can be kicked around when workers are carrying equipment, tools, or materials, making it a hazardous environment for both the workers and you. Based on my past experience, maintaining a clean worksite is psychologically correlated to performing neat work.

4. If there is an existing air conditioning system in the work area, make it a point to turn off and seal any return and supply grills. If you don't take this precaution, the return air duct will draw in construction dust, clogging the filter, hampering the efficiency of the system, and spreading the dust throughout the rest of the house.

5. Make sure any windows adjacent to the work area are closed and that windows in the work area are open to allow particles to escape.

6. If it is very dusty, you may want to place fans in the windows with the air blowing toward the exterior not the interior of the area under construction.

7. Purchase good quality dust masks and have them available in case you or your family begin to feel the effects of the dust. Whether or not you are highly allergic, it is a good practice to wear a dust mask.

8. Use a shop vacuum to pick up the smaller debris instead of sweeping and creating clouds of dust. A dampened cloth material at the exhaust end will help to catch any dust that may escape the vacuum. This should be cleaned often and the filter changed and monitored as needed.

9. Make sure that all material brought into the house is dusted off first. You never know where it came from or what the storage environment was like.

10. Demolition debris should not be transported through the area of the house where work is not taking place. If demolition is taking place from the second floor or higher, install a chute from a window in the construction area and into the debris container.

11. Some older homes may contain hazardous materials, such as lead paint or asbestos. The lead was usually in the form of paint and the

asbestos was used to insulate pipes, water heaters, and furnaces. It was also used as a flooring material in the shape of 9" × 9" flooring tiles. These hazardous materials can become dangerous when disturbed and the particles become dispersed into the air. This easily happens during demolition or construction. If you suspect having any of these materials in your home, have a professional determine and remove the hazard prior to construction.

12. Make sure you and anyone that works on your home are on the same page regarding dust control and any possible flaws in the protection of the occupied section of your home.

During my career as a builder, I have renovated quite a few hospitals and nursing homes that uphold very rigid standards regarding dust control. It can be managed. A briefing and periodic evaluation with the contractor and workers will help to control the area under construction and reinforce the awareness and importance of the situation. Make it a point to meet and discuss safety issues at least once a week. A pre-construction meeting the day of or day before any work is to begin is a good beginning for the project. It helps to raise the comfort level of the homeowner and sets the pace for all involved.

Check and Monitor for Possible Signs of Toxins

Maintaining a nurturing environment and eliminating anything that can possibly expose you or your family to toxins in your home is a concern for many homeowners.

Every morning we tune in to the news to see what the weather will be like. What if we were to take the same time to evaluate the environment inside our homes? We spend much of our lives indoors, the majority of it in the home. And the people who spend most of their time in the home, children and the elderly, are at a higher risk of exposure to the environment inside the home.

People seem to be getting sick a lot easier than before and staying sick for an extended period of time. In the summer, windows are closed and locked and the air conditioning is turned on. In the colder months, we again seal our windows and homes so that heat does not escape, trapping irritants, pollutants and pollen and other allergens in the home.

Humidity, another environmental problem, helps mold spores develop. So it's possible to have mold in the kitchen, bathroom, basement, and attic. Finding water seepage often can be difficult, but using the process of elimination and some "due diligence," a remedy is almost always possible and your home and family will benefit.

Further affecting us is a more dangerous exterior pollutant that can enter certain homes through cracks and deficiencies in concrete slabs and foundations. This is commonly known as radon. Radon is a potentially dangerous gas that has been linked to cancer.

There is a common dynamic in people suffering from exposure to pollutants in a home. In most cases, the individual's symptoms begin to subside after being away from his or her home for several hours and recur after reentering it. This points out that the need for an environmentally safe home shouldn't be taken lightly. In my home, within the last few years I have noticed that my family has gotten sick more often, and in speaking with others, I am finding out that many families have the same experience.

These situations need to be monitored by the homeowner. An individual profile of each person in the household should be maintained. The outline should include:

- The amount of time spent in the home
- Age
- Known allergies
- Level of allergic reaction
- Change in reactions, if any, when away from the home

Make it as simple and easy as you can:

1. Hang a clipboard where it will be easy to access and not be forgotten. Indicate also if the home has been treated or altered in any way, including dates and specific locations of the work. If you think of any other questions that may help to determine the cause of problems, add them to the list.

2. Identify areas of concern by looking for mold in dark, damp locations.
3. Check for water stains, droppings, and charred areas in the attic and basement that may have not been eliminated by the previous owner. Use your sense of smell to detect chemical odors, like paint, smoke, dampness, tobacco, burned materials, and any odd odors in the fireplace.

The concern over energy conservation means that homes now are better sealed and insulated. While this is good for fuel and energy conservation, it allows for minimal movement of air and for dampness in the home to nurture mold spores.

Hector Hint

Invisible gases from your furnace and hot water heater can potentially be fatal, since they are not detectable without a functioning carbon monoxide detector. I suggest a minimum of two detectors. Place one by your furnace, and the other near your bedrooms.

Chemical pollutants can be found in:

- **Carpeting:** Chemical smells in new carpets and dust mites are typical problems.
- **Insulation:** Both loose and fiber insulation can emit particles that can be harmful to inhale and cause rashes.
- **Particle board:** Glue used in the fabrication of particle board, paneling, and plywood can emit toxic formaldehyde gases.
- **Asbestos:** Disturbed particles can be inhaled, causing a dangerous lung hazard.
- **Lead-based paints:** Lead dust is another very dangerous hazard. Lead dust is most common during construction or after the work is complete.
- **Cleaning products:** Anyone experiencing physical reactions like skin irritation or a lightheaded feeling should seek immediate medical care.
- **Clothes:** Smoke from tobacco, dry cleaning chemicals, and detergents are other irritants that can affect your environment.

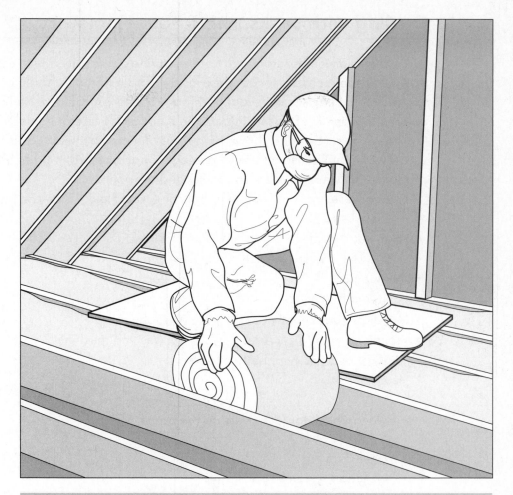

It is very important to wear protective gear whenever you work with insulation.

It's important to be aware and take action to rid your home of environmental hazards. Maintaining good air quality indoors is essential for fostering a nurturing atmosphere in your home. If a negative condition continues, or if you want to be certain of the condition in your home, have an environmental engineer assess the situation. It may be the best money you'll ever spend.

Dealing with Leaks Inside Your Home

When the cold weather stops you from venturing outside, it is much easier and warmer to redirect your focus to the inside of your home for some preventative maintenance. A leak in your bathroom or kitchen could cause hundreds or even thousands of dollars in damage if not taken care of immediately.

Always be on the alert for warning signs of a possible leak. Leaks not only waste water, but cause extensive damage if not stopped in time. Some by-products of a water leak are rot, mold, and erosion.

Check these areas for possible signs of a water leak inside the home:

- Hot water heater
- Hot water heating system
- Humidifier
- Water softener
- Medical equipment
- Toilet
- Sink faucets (kitchen, bath, and laundry tub)
- Bidet
- Shower
- Tub
- Icemaker
- Dishwasher
- Washing machine

Places to check for leaks outside the home:

- Hose bibs
- Irrigation systems
- Sprinkler systems
- Garden hoses
- Pools, hot tubs, and spas
- Water fountain

Hector Hint The best way to stop any damage from occurring is to catch it when it begins.

CHECK AND CHANGE WORN PARTS

Damaged parts are a major cause of leaks and wasted water in a bathroom or kitchen. Look over the following parts regularly, and repair or replace them if they are worn.

Quick Leak Fix

Obviously a small leak only leads to a bigger leak; however, if you want to avoid water damage in the time it takes to get a plumber to your house for a more permanent fix, here are three ways to handle small leaks:

1. Take a roll of electrician's tape and wrap it around the pipe, covering the leak and wrapping out about 5" from the source. This will prevent the water from undoing the adhesive.
2. Insert the tip of a sharp pencil into the hole and snap off the tip. As long as the water pressure in the pipe is not too great, this should keep the water from leaking.
3. Dry the area off as best you can and use a utility knife to spread epoxy across over the leak.
4. Shut the water off at the branch cut-off or at the water main.

GETTING RID OF THAT ROTTEN-EGG SMELL IN THE WATER

No matter how nice a home is, its value and the pleasure of living in it are severely diminished if the water is of poor quality. The problem can be corrected, however, and the water heater is the first place to look.

Water heaters have long metal rods in them called anode rods. These rods attract the corrosive elements in the hot water heater, extending the life of your heater tank. The cause of a rotten-egg smell in the water is anaerobic bacteria that react to the anode rods, producing hydrogen sulfide gas. This is not uncommon in well systems, and water softeners can sometimes compound the problem.

Getting rid of the smell is done by replacing the anode rods in the hot water tank. A licensed plumber should replace the anode rods in order to maintain the warranty.

Go Green

Going green means to take an active role in making the world a better place by helping to eliminate the spread of pollution and curbing over-consumption by reducing, reusing, and recycling. As a homeowner, you can go green by performing the various tasks in this chapter to make your house more eco-friendly.

Project Worksheet

MONETARY RETURN: $500–$750

PROJECT START DATE: _____

TASKS COMPLETED: _____
_____
_____
_____
_____

TOOLS NEEDED:

- ❑ Adjustable wrench
- ❑ Ladder
- ❑ Screwdriver
- ❑ Shop vacuum

What It Means to Go Green

Early in the 1990s, the United States Green Building Council developed Leadership in Energy and Environmental Design (LEED). To certify whether or not a building met the criteria necessary for certification, a rating system was developed. This began as a program for commercial buildings and eventually a program for residential homes was developed.

Although upfront costs for building green are more than standard building expenses, in the long term, they are eventually absorbed. Having a green home does not mean taking a single approach to a repair, conversion, or the building of a home. It means taking the shared parts of a home, overlapping green efforts, ultimately improving the efficiency, and furthering its sustainability.

Using a single recycled and sustainable product alone is not sufficient to label a home *green*. Creating a tight envelope around a home, efficient energy consumption, finding ways to limit the negative environmental impact of a home's surroundings, and wise utilization of available resources, together help make a home efficient and sustainable.

Keeping Things Tight

Insulation plays a key role in making sure the envelope of a home retains a comfortable environment unaffected by fluctuations in exterior temperatures. Insulation is used in the attic, perimeter walls, crawlspaces, and any other place that separates the interior of a home from the exterior. For years, insulation has been manufactured from fiberglass. The fibers in fiberglass insulation easily become airborne when disturbed. Fiberglass can irritate your skin and is unhealthy to inhale because it grates your bronchial passages and makes its way into your lungs. Recently the manufacturing of insulation has expanded, turning to recycled cotton for energy retention.

Roof shingle manufacturers also have made strides in finding ways to use sustainable materials. Roofing manufacturers have begun to use recycled plastic and rubber to produce new types of roofing shingles. Some of these products are better than conventional shingles in appearance and durability.

In keeping with this trend, siding companies have also taken on a "green building" approach for their products. Fiber-cement panels and siding have made a homerun in the "green" marketplace. There are many colors and textures to choose from, and with additional competition, these products may soon be more affordable for everyone.

For new or renovated homes, foam insulated blocks and foam concrete forms make for energy-friendly construction. With a forward-thinking approach, they incorporate insulating components and options for electrical wires and future build-outs.

Exterior walls need insulation in order to retain warmth in colder climates and to keep a home cooler during warmer months. There are several insulations used in "green building" favored for their use of recycled and sustainable products.

While having a well-sealed envelope for a home may be good for energy efficiency, contaminants inside a home, generated from furniture, adhesives, building materials, paints, cleaning products, and carpets, to name a few, can make the inside of a home unfriendly, to say the least. The introduction of fresh air to stabilize the gases emitted, or the replacement of existing products is a serious consideration.

Windows and doors are also a part of a home's envelope and contribute to conserving energy or wasting it. The use of double-pane thermal windows and low-E glass has played a big part in energy conservation for several decades, and recently have been challenged by the introduction of triple-pane thermal windows. Doors have also come a long way in thermal protection for a home, having tighter seals and better insulating factors.

Gas, oil, and electric are the main sources used to heat and cool a home. How efficiently fuel is used depends on the insulation surrounding the envelope of the home; the efficiency of the appliances, heating, and cooling unit(s); and how well the occupants conserve energy. Another element to take into account is the physical setting of a home, how it is affected by the landscape surrounding it, and how it is positioned in relation to the sun.

Water conservation is a major part of a "green" home. Preventing water waste indoors and outdoors requires thought and attentiveness. This can be accomplished through technology, design, and repair. Technology has helped to combine design and conservation. Design has incorporated conservation with beauty, and attention to repair is consistent with the effort to prevent waste.

Whether you repair or replace an item in your home depends on how old it is and the cost to repair it. In many cases, the cost to repair an appliance in a home can be almost as expensive as replacing it. Smaller items in your home, like a thermostat, can easily be changed by a homeowner and will pay for itself during the first heating or cooling season.

Without spending thousands of dollars on wind turbines, solar panels, and geothermal or hydro electric power, here are twenty simple things you can do to help conserve energy and cut back on heating and cooling costs.

Twenty Simple Ways to Go Green

Energy consumption is a real concern with the high cost of fuel. Homeowners worldwide are seeking ways to conserve energy by cutting back on high heating and cooling costs. Take the time to make a few of the following changes in your home and you can save a bundle on energy bills.

1. Adjust the cooling and heating thermostats to provide you with energy savings during the day and keep you comfortable when at home.
2. Replace the current thermostat(s) with a more efficient programmable thermostat.
3. Keep the water temperature on the hot water heater to a minimum of 120 degrees; any lower and you risk legionnaires' disease. Do not exceed 130 degrees; temperatures higher than that can cause scalding.
4. Check around windows, doors, baseboards, and penetrations for drafts. By sealing the envelope of a home, a homeowner can reduce his or her energy bill by as much as one-third.

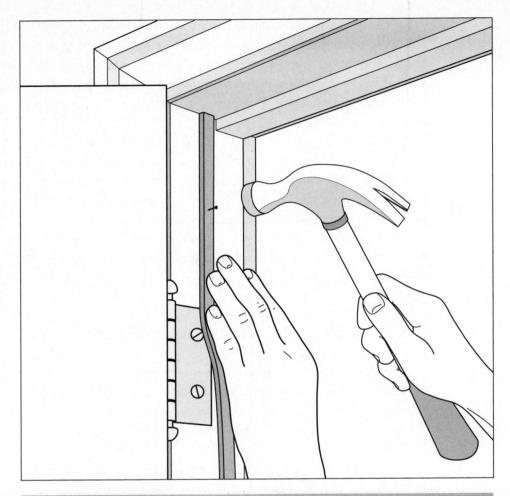

Weather-stripping around your doors will help seal in the heat.

5. Repair broken or cracked windowpanes.
6. Change the light bulbs in your home to compact fluorescent bulbs. These bulbs use 75 percent less energy and last ten times longer than incandescent bulbs.
7. Change air filters in the heating and cooling system monthly to ensure safe, efficient airflow throughout the home.

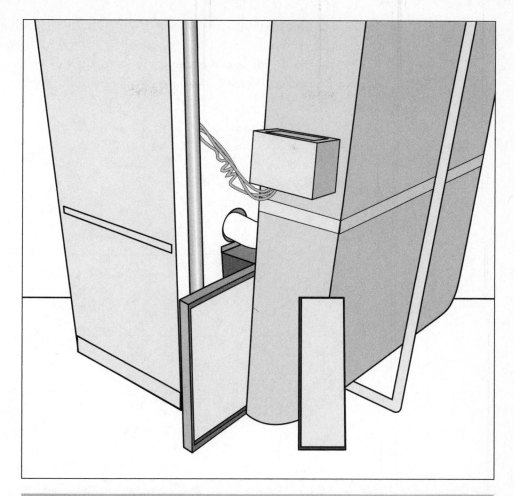

Changing the filter is a simple and easy way to make your furnace run more efficiently.

8. Keep lights turned off if no one is in a room.
9. Turn off the air conditioning or heating system on comfortable days. Open the windows to air out your home.
10. Have your system(s) checked annually before starting them up. Like a car, a tune-up for your heating and cooling system can keep it running efficiently.
11. Vacuum the blowers on your heating and cooling system to reduce friction and wear.

12. Tighten up the seal on penetrations going through the ceiling. Attic stairs and hatches are notorious for allowing energy to escape.
13. Check for air leaks where the foundation and siding meet.
14. Caulk areas around the perimeter that may be sources of air infiltration.

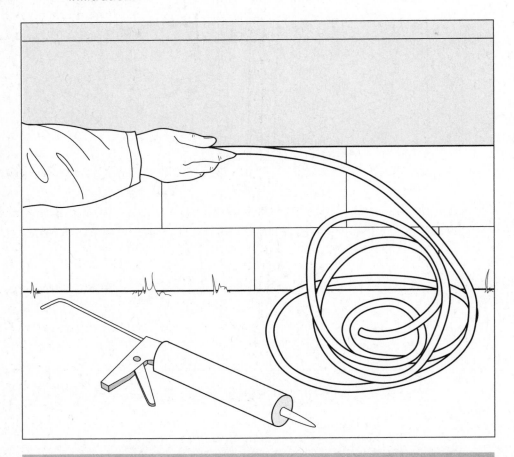

Caulking outside will also help to make your home more energy efficient.

15. Check the attic and crawlspaces for sufficient insulation and for any bare spots. Depending on the age of your home, what was sufficient years ago may not meet minimum energy standards today. Check with your local building official for the insulating requirements in your region.

16. When shopping for a replacement appliance, look for the "Energy Star" label. Newer appliances with the "Energy Star" label have to meet energy-efficiency minimums in order to qualify.
17. Insulate exposed hot water pipes to reduce heat loss.
18. Check and adjust the dampers on supply grills to maximize airflow. A partially closed register is not operating at full capacity.
19. Clean air conditioning and evaporator coils. This will keep your system from running longer and working harder.
20. Use shades, blinds, and curtains to adjust a room for light and energy consumption. Direct sunlight in a room can help to warm it and reduce your heating bill.

Don't Let Water Be a Drain on Your Wallet

SKILL LEVEL

2

TIME

4–5 h

With the cost of housing, the steady rise of gas, electric, water, and taxes, conservation is something you should get in step with. Here are some ways to save water in your home:

1. Make your own water-saver toilet. If you do not want to spend your money on a new water-saver toilet, this device will reduce the amount of water the toilet uses by up to 25 percent. Simply place a plastic bottle filled with water in the tank. Choose a bottle size that allows the toilet to function properly and that does not interfere with the flushing mechanism. Never use anything that may have fragments that break off and could possibly harm your plumbing. Be sure that at least 3 gallons of water remain in the tank for it to flush properly.
2. Do not use your toilet as a garbage can. Each time you flush, you can use up to five gallons of water. Using the toilet to flush something unnecessarily is a waste of water.
3. Try using low-flow, water-saving shower heads. These can reduce the amount of water flowing through your shower by up to 50 percent, but increase its velocity so that you rarely notice the difference. This also saves hot water and may help you to avoid buying a larger hot water heater.

4. Limit the time you spend in the shower. A five-minute shower can use up to fifty gallons of water. Instead of standing in the shower for fifteen or twenty minutes, make it quick and save a lot of money on energy and water.

Hector Hint

Low-flow devices are about the size of a nickel and have a small hole in the middle. They restrict the flow of water through a faucet or a showerhead. These devices are very easy and inexpensive to install, and are available at most hardware, plumbing, and home improvement stores.

5. Use faucet aerators. These can restrict the amount of water going through your faucet by up to 50 percent. They add air bubbles so the flow of water appears the same. These should be installed on all indoor faucets, not just the ones in your bathroom.

6. Check for toilet leaks. A toilet leak can waste hundreds of gallons of water each day. To see if your toilet tank leaks, put a few drops of food coloring in the tank. Do not flush. Wait a few minutes to see if the color shows up in the bowl. If color appears, check the flush arm mechanism in the tank to see if the chain attached to the arm is tangled. If the flush mechanism appears to be in proper condition, you may have to replace the flap valve at the bottom of the tank even though the valve may appear to be in good condition. If your tank is overflowing, adjust the water level control mechanism until the water level is at least one-half inch below the overflow level.

7. Turn off the faucet while you are shaving or brushing your teeth.

8. Repair leaky faucets. Worn-out washers and toilet tank valves account for up to 10 percent of all indoor residential water use. Leaky faucets can waste 15 to 20 gallons or more per day. This can equal 6,000 gallons of water per year. Repairing a leaky faucet is inexpensive and simple to do.

9. Using short-cycle options on your dishwasher and clothes washer are less water-efficient than running full loads.

10. Use a dishwasher to clean your dishes. This will save you more water than hand washing your dishes.

Save Water Outside Your Home

Watering our lawns and gardens, and washing our cars account for most of the water we use outside. You can reduce the amount of water you use for all of these activities by using a few simple techniques.

1. Purchase an on/off nozzle to wash your car and water your garden. Attach a pistol-type sprayer to the end of your garden hose. In addition to enabling you to adjust the rate of flow, this device keeps water from continuing to run out during those short periods when you put down the hose without turning it off.
2. Water your lawn only when necessary. Try watering your lawn every other day rather than daily. You can conserve several thousand gallons per week by doing this.
3. Put mulch around trees and shrubs. Mulch retains water for long periods of time, greatly reducing the amount of water lost through evaporation and decreasing the need for watering.
4. Utilize a drip irrigation system in your garden. This system supplies water only to plants where it is needed.
5. Use only plants that are well adapted to your environment and soil conditions. Inappropriate varieties will require greater amounts of fertilizer and water just to stay alive.
6. Collect water from your downspouts. Get a barrel or 50 gallon drum and put it where one of the downspouts from the gutter system on your home can fill into it. Using a small pump and hose, water your garden and flowerbeds with the water collected from your roof.

What we do today will help us tomorrow. Conserving water should not be taken lightly. It is a resource we share and need to appreciate.

Whole House Fans

A whole house fan is a large fan mounted to the ceiling, separating the living space from the attic. Its function is to remove warm air from the occupied area of your home, circulating the air in your home and forcing hot air out of the attic through the roof vents.

There are pros and cons to having a whole house fan. From a green perspective, a whole house fan uses less electricity than an air conditioner, saving you hundreds or even thousands of dollars a year, depending on the size and location of your home.

Personal preference plays a big part in whether or not to have one. Some people do not care much for air conditioning and would much rather have an attic fan drawing fresh air into their home through the windows and forcing the stuffy old air out through the attic. I myself like the option of having both. I don't care for humidity and appreciate the air-conditioning system removing warm clammy air from my home. On the other hand, I do like to open my windows on low humidity days and feel a nice breeze flow through my home.

Here is a list of pros and cons on having a whole house fan installed that I think should be considered:

PROS
- Removes stale air
- Uses less energy than air-conditioning
- Less complicated than air conditioning
- Lack of freon is safer for the environment
- Easier to repair
- Much cheaper than an air-conditioning system to install and operate
- Great on low humidity days
- Easy to replace motor
- Great during spring and fall
- Cools the house down quickly

CONS
- Noisy (older) units
- Blows insulation fibers onto stored items in attic

- Very dangerous if access to attic is attempted while fan is in operation
- Does not remove humidity
- Light structural framing needed for installation
- Allows for heat loss through the vents in the winter

Hector Hint

Here is a mistake that many people can easily make when identifying an attic or roof fan. An attic or roof fan is only used to remove hot air from the attic, whereas a whole house fan cools down the entire home.

I do not recommend using the whole house fan when all the windows in the home are closed. That is the only time I can see where it may be unhealthy. If all the windows in the home are closed, air can be pulled from the diverter on top of the hot water heater and boiler, causing carbon monoxide to be drawn into the home. Carbon monoxide gas can cause fatalities with little or no warning signs. If a whole house fan is used while the air conditioner is running it will pull the air-conditioned air from the occupied portion of the home. The whole house fan really poses no risk to your health if it is used to cool down the home and pull in fresh air from opened windows.

Hector Hint

When purchasing a whole house fan make sure to measure the size of your home in square feet and to take that information with you when you purchase the fan. This will help you to size the unit adequately for your home.

So whether it is keeping the air we breathe safe, watching how much water we use, or using recycled products, thinking "green" is important especially when it comes to protecting the environment for our families, our children, and their children.

Appendix A

How to Choose a Contractor

There will be times when you need to hire a contractor, but finding the right one isn't as easy as you may think. If you want your project to be successful, you need to be sure the contractor you choose is decent and qualified.

Rushing into an agreement without taking the necessary steps to ensure the contractor has the integrity, skills, and experience to work on your home is a disaster waiting to happen. Follow these simple steps to steer away from a potential home improvement nightmare.

1. Interview contractors that have already done work in your neighborhood. This makes it easier for you to see completed projects.
2. Ask the potential contractors how many projects like yours they have completed within the last year. Get a list of the addresses of the projects in your area and check if these projects are anything similar to what you want done on your home.
3. Ask the contractor for references. Get the names, addresses, and phone numbers of at least three clients who have projects in your area. Find out how long ago the projects were completed. Speak to the homeowners and find out how the contractor was to work with and if he or she was reasonably priced and ethical in business dealings. Question whether the project went according to schedule and if the workers were careful and courteous.
4. Contact your local Department of Consumer Affairs and Better Business Bureau to see if issues with your prospective contractor have been put on record. They can tell you if there are unresolved consumer complaints and/or any past or present litigation or mediation on file.

Hector Hint

Continue to be judicious even if the Consumer Affairs report comes back clean. Just because there are no complaints against a particular contractor doesn't necessarily mean there haven't been any previous consumer complaints in a different county. It may be that problems exist, but have not yet been reported, or that the contractor is doing business under several different names.

5. Check that the contractor is licensed and registered with the state. Many states now require that home improvement contractors, electricians, and plumbers be licensed. The licensing for a home improvement contractor can range from a simple registration to a detailed qualification process. If your state has licensing laws, ask to see the contractor's license and make sure it's current and note the registration numbers.

6. Make sure the contractor knows the proper steps that need to be taken to secure the necessary permits to do the work on your home. Most states and local governments require permits for small and large home improvement projects. A competent contractor will get all the required permits before starting any work. Be cautious if the contractor asks you to get the permit(s). This could mean that the contractor is not licensed, registered, or insured as required by your state or local government.

Hector Hint

Try to limit your down payment. Don't let the contractor get too ahead of you. Some state laws limit the amount of money a contractor can request as a down payment. Contact your state or local consumer agency to find out what the laws are in your area.

7. Home improvement contractors use subcontractors that are specialized and licensed in a particular field. Ask contractors for the names and telephone numbers of their subcontractors and vendors.

8. Make sure the subcontractors have workers' compensation and liability insurance coverage. Ask for copies of insurance certificates, and make sure they are current. Keep track of the expiration dates and make sure they do not expire before the job is completed. Doing business with contractors who do not carry the appropriate insurance can put your home at risk and make you liable for any injuries and damages that occur during the project.

9. Question the subcontractors and suppliers for any problems they may have in getting paid by the contractor. If they have had problems, this should be of concern to you, especially if the contractor

requests a deposit. On a large project the amount of the deposit could be substantial. That being the case, you want to make sure that your deposit is not used to pay back debt from a previous job. If contractors have outstanding debts, their subcontractors and suppliers can place what is called a mechanic's lien on your home. That means the subcontractors and suppliers could go to court to force you to satisfy their unpaid bills incurred from your project. Protect yourself by asking your contractor for waivers of lien whenever you make a payment.

Hector Hint	Make payments during the project contingent upon completion of a defined amount of work and make sure it is specified in the contract.

10. Make sure to have a completion date specified in the contract.
11. Ask the contractor how they plan on protecting the areas adjacent to where they will be working.

Asking questions up-front will help you avoid misunderstandings and let the contractors know what you expect from them when working on your home. Whenever possible, get any agreements, resolutions, and changes to the contract in writing.

Kicking Up
Curb Appeal

One of the most important things you can do, whether or not you've decided to sell your home, is to make sure it has plenty of curb appeal. The exterior of your home and property is the first thing people see, so it is important to make it as inviting and alluring as you can.

Seeing your home from the eyes of friends, neighbors, or your real estate agent is a great way to accomplish this goal. We sometimes have such a personal attachment to our home that it can be very difficult to see issues that may hinder its sale. Being objective and open to suggestion is the first hurdle to jump. Being aesthetically selective about what you choose is the second stumbling block. Staying within a well-defined budget is the third obstacle to get over.

Hector Hint	Take a few photos of the outside of your home from the angles that buyers will see when they drive past. Send copies of the photos to friends and family whom you trust and believe will give their honest opinion on what you could tweak to up the curb appeal of your home.

Remember that an outwardly attractive house will help to lure the buyers in and pique their interest in your home. Sure, the inside of your home is very important, but so are first impressions when prospective buyers drive by or view pictures.

Here are several simple things that can help you add to and improve the curb appeal of your home.

1. Cultivate the soil around your flowerbeds. Edge the lawn and make sure it is mowed and maintained. Doing this will enhance the look of your front yard.
2. Trim all your hedges, making the vertical and horizontal cuts as straight as possible. If you have rounded bushes be careful not to get carried away by cutting too much off. Rake up and discard any fallen trimmings.
3. Select several colorful plants that are specific for the season to put in your front yard. You can get some ideas by browsing home and garden magazines for photos of front yards that capture your attention.

4. Dress your trees by cutting off any dead tree limbs. Cut down any branches that obstruct the view of your home.
5. If your home is fenced in, make sure the gate opens and closes freely and any areas of disrepair are mended.
6. Scrape, patch, and paint areas on the fence or home that need some TLC. Painting the front door or trim around the windows can make a huge difference. Keep the colors standard. Using colors that are not simple and conservative can deter the average buyer from wanting to venture inside.
7. Clean the windows and replace any broken windowpanes and screens. As simple as this is, it makes a big difference when looking at your home.
8. If you have shutters, make sure they are not faded and that all the slats are intact. Check that the hinges are operational and the shutters are secure.
9. Repair broken porch railings and paint them, if needed. Remember, the person buying your home may have small children, and the potential customer's attention needs to be on looking at your home—not being worried about his or her children getting hurt by falling off the porch.
10. Power wash dirty siding and porch decks.
11. Check to make sure the exterior lights are working. Some prospective buyers may come by at night. Clean the glass enclosures and remove any cobwebs from the fixtures.
12. Keep the front and side yards free of machinery, tools, toys, or anything that may take away from the beauty of your home. Removing yard clutter will allow the person looking at your home to appreciate it without any visual distractions.

Improving your house's curb appeal could be what gets homebuyers interested in your property and you don't want to miss that opportunity.

Resources

American Architectural
Manufacturers Association
888-323-5664
www.aamanet.org

American Association of Poison
Control Centers
1-800-222-1222
www.aapcc.org

American Homeowners Foundation
1-800-489-7776
www.americanhomeowners.org

American Institute of Architects
1-800-242-3837
www.aia.org

American Society of Home Inspectors
1-800-743-2744
www.ashi.com

American Society for the Prevention
of Cruelty to Animals
1-888-426-4435 (Animal Poison Control
Center)
www.aspca.org

Association of Home
Appliance Manufacturers
1-202-872-5955
www.aham.org

Canada Mortgage and
Housing Corporation
1-613-748-2000
www.cmhc-schl.gc.ca

Ceramic Tile Institute of America, Inc.
1-310-574-7800
www.ctioa.org

Chimney Safety Institute of America
1-317-837-5362
www.csia.org

Electrical Safety Foundation International
1-703-841-3229
www.nesf.org

Federal Emergency Management Agency
1-800-480-2520 (publications)
www.fema.gov

Gas Appliance Manufacturers Association
1-703-525-7060
www.gamanet.org

Living with Wildlife (MSPCA)
1-617-522-7400
www.livingwithwildlife.org

National Association of Home Builders
1-800-368-5242
www.nahb.org

National Association of the Remodeling Industry
1-800-611-6274
www.nari.org

National Fire Protection Association
1-617-770-3000
www.nfpa.org

National Glass Association
1-866-342-5642
www.glass.org

National Lead Information Center
1-800-424-5323
www.epa.gov

National Park Service (Architecture and Heritage Conservation)
www.cr.nps.gov

National Safety Council
1-630-285-1121
www.nsc.org

National Wood Flooring Association
1-800-422-4556
www.woodfloors.org

Organization for Bat Conservation
1-800-276-7074
www.batconservation.org

Plumbing-Heating-Cooling Contractors Association
www.phccweb.org

Poison Prevention
1-301-504-7058
www.poisonprevention.org

U.S. Consumer Product Safety Commission
1-800-638-2772
www.cpsc.gov

U.S. Environmental Protection Agency
1-202-272-0167
www.epa.gov

U.S. Fire Administration
1-301-447-1000
www.usfa.fema.gov

Water Quality Association
1-630-505-0160
www.wqa.org

Window Covering Safety Council
1-800-506-4636
www.windowcoverings.org

Wood Floor Covering Association
1-800-624-6880
www.wfca.org

Index

A

Access panels, windows, 118-19
Air conditioner, 195-97
    central air conditioner maintenance, 196-97
    maintenance, 195-96
Arbor, 31-32
Argon glass windows, 112

B

Bathroom, 167-92
    accents, 181
    caulking and grouting, 187-88
    ceramic ties, 176-79
    drains, 183-85
    finishes, 180
    hot tubs, spas, and whirlpools, 190-92
    lighting, 174-75
    privacy, 172-73
    project worksheet, 168
    soap dish, replacing, 180-81
    shower curtain rod, crescent, 173-74
    shower door corrosion, 182-83
    shower door leak, 181-82
    showerhead leak, 186
    toilet bowl, plugged, 185, 186
    toilet, replacing, 175-76
    toilet, running, 189-90
    toothbrush holder, replacing, 180
    tub diverter, 186-87
    tub waste line, 185
    vanity, 169-72
Bathtub. *See* Tub

B (continued, right column)

Bi-fold doors, 95
Boiler furnaces, 198-99
Breakers, 225-28
    labeling, 226

C

Cabinets, kitchen, 159-63
    faucets, 163-65
    look, changing, 160-61
    painting, 160-61
    stripped hinge and door, repairing, 160
    under-cabinet light, installing, 161-63
Carbon monoxide detectors, 235-36
Carpet
    installation, 130-35
    padding, 131-32
    padding, replacing, 132-33
    patching, 133-34
    replacing, 132
    squeaky, fixing, 135
Casement windows, 114
Caulk
    bathroom, 187-88
    windows, 116-18
Ceiling fan, unbalanced, 237-38
Ceramic tile
    countertops, 155
    maintaining, removing, and replacing in
        bathroom, 176-79
Chimneys. *See* Fireplaces and chimneys
Concrete, 16-18
    checking slab, 86-87
    replacing concrete walkway, 17-18

Corian countertops, 155
Countertops, 153-59
    ceramic tile, 155
    Corian, 155
    edges, 154
    granite, 155
    installing new, 158-59
    marble, 154
    materials, 154-55
    measuring for new, 157-58
    plastic laminate, 154
    removing, 156-57
    seams, 153
    stainless steel, 155

D

Deck, 5-11
    flashing, 6-7
    railing maintenance, 8-10
    stair repair, 10-11
    structural maintenance, 5-7
    surface maintenance, 7-8
Doorbells, 232-34
    common problems, 233-34
Doorknobs, 102-3
Doors, 91-105
    bi-fold problems, 95
    hinges, silencing, 102
    knobs, 102-3
    locks, 98-100, 104
    pocket, 95-96
    problems, 93
    project worksheet, 92
    removing, 94
    sticky, 94
    storm, 97-98, 150
    strikes, 100-1
    types, 93
Double hung windows, 114
Double-pane glass windows, 111-12

Drainage, 68-71
    pitch, 69-71
    project worksheet, 64
    selecting an area, 68-69
Driveway, 43-45
    project worksheet, 42
    repairing cracks in asphalt, 43
    repairing holes, 44-45
Drywall, 142-48
    and bacteria, 143
    corners, restoring, 148
    cracked seams, repairing, 144
    cracks, pops and bows, 143
    cracks, repairing, 145
    fire safety, 143
    gouges, fixing, 145
    holes, fixing, 146-47
    nail pops, patching, 144
Dust control, 246-48

E

Electrical issues, 223-38
    breakers, 225-28
    ceiling fan, unbalanced, 237-38
    doorbell, 232-34
    lighting fixture replacement, 236-37
    light switch, replacing, 228-31
    outlet and switch cover plates, 231-32
    project worksheet, 224
    receptacle, changing, 226-28
    smoke detectors, 235-36
Electric furnaces, 202-3
Exterior, 3- 21
    cleaning, preparing for, 65
    cleaning, process, 66-67
    concrete, 16-18
    deck, 5-11
    pavers, 12-16
    pools, 18-21
    project worksheet, 4

F

Faucets, 163-65
    aerators, 211-12
    washer, changing, 164-65
Fireplaces and chimneys, 213-21
    air supply, 217
    fireplace doors, 218-20
    flues, 220-21
    maintenance, 215-17
    project worksheet, 214
    safety, 215-16
Flashing
    deck, 6-7
    roof, 60
Floors, 121-35
    carpet installation, 130-35
    hardwood, 123-26
    project worksheet, 122
    squeaks, removing, 127-30
Flues, 220-21
Forced-air furnaces, 198
Foundation
    checking concrete slab, 86-87
    pointing, 79-80
    sealing, 82
    sealing concrete foundation crack, 84-85
    sealing stone, brick, or block foundation, 83-84
Furnace, 193-204
    boilers, 198-99
    electric, 202-3
    filter, forced-air, replacing, 202
    flues, 202
    forced-air system, 198
    fuel, 197
    gas and oil furnace, 197
    hot-water system, 198
    noisy, 203
    not enough heat, 203-4
    not running, 199-201
    safety sensors, 201
    thermostats, 204-7
    types, 198-99
    zones, 198

G

Garage cleaning, 48-49
Garage door, 45-49
    maintenance, 46-47
    seal, 48
    safety features, 46
Gliding or sliding windows, 114
Going green, 255-67
    air-tight, 257-59
    project worksheet, 256
    saving water, 263-65
    steps to, 259-63
    whole house fans, 266-67
Granite countertops, 155
Gravel pathway, 32-33
Grout, bathroom, 187-88
Gutters and leaders, 71-75
    clearing, 73-74
    re-nailing gutters, 75
    repairing gutter seams, 74
    repairing holes in gutters, 74-75

H

Handrails, 241-42
Hardwood flooring, 123-26
    buffing, 125-26
    erasing scuffs and stains, 124
    polyurethane, 126-27
    quick transformation, 126-27
    types, 123-24
Heating and cooling, 193-212
    air conditioner, 195-97
    furnace, 197-204
    hot water heaters, 208-12
    project worksheet, 194

Hedge trimming, 36-38
    trimmer type and size, 37-38
Hinges, 102
Hopper and awning windows, 114
Hot tubs, 190-92
    maintenance, 192
Hot-water furnaces, 198
Hot water heaters, 208-12
    and aerators, 211-12
    cleaning inside of, 208-9
    cleaning mechanicals, 209-10
    waiting for water, 210

I

Interior
    blind windows, 112-13
    grille windows, 113

K

Kitchen, 151-65
    cabinets, 159-63
    countertops, 153-59
    project worksheet, 152
Krypton glass windows, 112

L

Landscaping, 23-39
    arbor, 31-32
    clearing, 34
    effects, 31-32
    gravel pathway, 32-33
    hedge trimming, 36-38
    lawn, 25-27, 34-36
    mulch, 30-31
    project worksheet, 24
    safety, 38-39
    sketch, 28-29
    yard design, 28-36
Lawn, 25-27
    edging, 34-35
    mowing, 27
    trimming, 35-36
    watering, 25-27
Leaks, 252-53
Lighting
    bathroom, 174-75
    fixture replacement, 236-37
Light, under-cabinet, installing, 161-63
Light switch
    common problems with, 230-31
    dimmer, 229
    replacing 228-31
    standard, 228
    three-way, 229
    types of, 228-29
Locks
    adjusting lockset, 98
    cleaning gummed lockset, 104
    lubricating, 98-99
    lubricating key cylinders, 99-100
Low-E glass windows, 112

M

Marble countertops, 154
Masonry, 79-82
    pointing, 79-80
    project worksheet, 78
    rebuilding, 81-82
Mice, 243-45
Mortar, 79-80
Mowing, 27
Mulch, 30-31

P

Painting, 139-42
    kitchen cabinets, 160-61
    preparation for, 139-40
    priming, 141-42
Pavers, 12-16
    alternative to, 16-18
    choosing, 12-13
    laying or replacing, 14-15

professionals for, 13
replacing or resetting individual stones, 15-16
value of, 12
Plaster, 148-50
    crack, repairing, 149
    removing wall, 150
Plastic laminate countertops, 154
Plumbing, bathroom, 183-87
Pocket doors, 95-96
Pointing, 79-81
    mixing mortar, 79-80
    tuck-pointing, 80
Pools, 18-21
    contamination of, 18
    filtering, 21
    keeping clean and fresh, 19-21
    opening, 20-21
Priming, 141-42
Project worksheets
    bathroom, 168
    cleaning and drainage, 64
    doors, locks, and hinges, 92
    driveway and garage, 42
    electrical issues, 224
    exterior upkeep, 4
    fireplace and chimneys, 214
    floors, 122
    going green, 256
    heating and cooling, 194
    kitchen, 152
    landscaping, 24
    masonry and foundation, 78
    roof, 52
    safety and cleanliness, 240
    walls, 138
    windows, 108

R

Railings, deck 8-10
Roof, 51-61
    cleaning, 53-54

flashing, patching, 60
leak, locating, 54-57
professionals, 61
project worksheet, 52
shingles, repairing, 59
shingles, replacing, 57-59
type, choosing, 53

S

Safety, 239-53
    handrails, 241-42
    landscaping, 38-39
    project worksheet, 240
    toxins, 248-51
Sash replacement, 113
Screens
    cleaning, 110
    replacing, 109-10
Shingles
    repairing, 59
    replacing, 57-59
Shower
    curtain rod, crescent, installing, 173-74
    door corrosion, removing, 182-83
    door leak, repairing, 181-82
Showerhead leak, fixing, 186
Smoke detectors, 235-36
    carbon monoxide detectors, 235-36
Soap dish, replacing, 180
Spas, 190-92
Sprinkler systems, 26
Stainless steel countertops, 155
Stairs
    deck, 10-11
    removing squeaks, 130
Storm doors, 97-98, 150
    adjusting, 97, 150
    replacing closer, 97-98

T

Termites, 245
Thermostats, 204-7
    accuracy, 207
    cleaning, 205-6
    failure, 204-5
    replacing low-voltage, 206-7
Tilt-wash windows, 112
Toilet
    replacing, 175-76
    running, fixing, 189-90
    unclogging, 185
    unclogging with auger, 186
Toothbrush holder, replacing, 180-81
Toxins, 248-51
Triple-pane glass windows, 112
Tub
    diverter, replacing, 186-87
    drain, clearing, 184-85
    waste line, clearing, 185

V

Vanity, bathroom, 169-72
    installing, 170-71
    removing, 169-70
    replacing with pedestal sink, 172

W

Walls, 137-50
    drywall, 142-48
    painting, 139-42
    plaster, patching, 148-50
    project worksheet, 138
Water pressure, 27
Whole house fans, 266-67
Whirlpool, 190-92
Windows, 107-19
    argon gas, 112
    casement, 114
    caulk, replacing, 116-18

    double hung, 114
    double-pane, 111-12
    gliding or sliding, 114
    hopper and awning, 114
    installation time, 114
    insulation with access panels, 118-19
    insulation without access panels, 119
    interior blinds, 112-13
    interior grilles, 113
    krypton gas, 112
    low-E glass, 112
    maintenance, 115
    options, 112-14
    project worksheet, 108
    replacement, 113
    replacing, 111-14
    sash replacement, 113
    screen, cleaning, 110
    screen, replacing, 109-10
    tilt-wash, 112
    triple-pane, 112
    types of energy-efficient panes, 111-12
    un-sticking, 116

ABOUT THE AUTHOR

Hector Seda has been in the construction industry for over thirty years, and is known as America's Home Improvement Coach.

Mr. Seda has been a subject-matter expert and regular guest on Your Morning, a Philadelphia talk show on Comcast CN8. His expert advice has been shared through Lowe's for Pros as well as many other print, radio, and television outlets across the United States. The author behind two syndicated columns on home improvement, "Ask Hector" and "America's Home Improvement Coach," Seda is an advocate for ethical construction and home improvement.

Mr. Seda is a member of the Society of Industry Leaders, a Standard and Poor's Company, and a consultant for Vista Research, a McGraw-Hill Company, which provides consultation on construction and real estate for institutional fund managers. He has also been a consultant for James Lee Witt Associates, an emergency and disaster consultation firm founded by Witt, former director of the Federal Emergency Management Agency (FEMA) during President Bill Clinton's administration. His work with that company focused on repairing damages to the University of Texas Medical Branch in Galveston, Texas caused by Hurricane Ike.

Mr. Seda currently resides in the coastal community of Gulf Shores, Alabama.